ATTENTION:
BAR CODE IS LOCATED
INSIDE OF BOOK

S0-BXB-124

MAGAZINE PUBLISHING
CAREER DIRECTORY
1986

A Career Directory Series Book

Career Publishing Corp.

New York

Copyright © 1985 by Career Publishing Corporation

9 8 7 6 5 4 3 2 1

Digit on right indicates the number of this printing.

The Career Directory Series

Magazine Publishing Career Directory 1986
ISBN No. 0-934829-01-2
ISSN No. 0882-827X

This book may be ordered by mail directly from the publisher.
(See back cover for detailed ordering information. Please include
$3.50 for postage and handling.)

Career Publishing Corp.
505 Fifth Avenue, Suite 1003,
New York, NY 10017

TABLE OF CONTENTS

5019198

A major resource work like this first **Magazine Publishing Career Directory** cannot be compiled, edited, designed and published without the input, help and contributions of many professionals. Collecting and codifying the data has been a herculean task. So, not surprisingly, we have many people to thank:

-- First and foremost, Bob Farley, Senior Vice President of the Magazine Publishers Association (MPA), the primary industry trade association (to which, you'll find, many of our authors refer). Bob was instrumental in the earliest stages, helping with advice, information and recommendations for contributing authors. Without his help, it would have been far more difficult to attract the top professionals who donated their time, experience and advice to this volume.

-- The many contributors who, while fulfilling their own significant job responsibilities, somehow found the time to write the articles which we believe are the core of this **Directory**. We commend them for the concern they've shown for you -- the aspiring young professionals some of them may eventually hire. And we think their practical advice and experience will make it easier for all of you to find the right jobs in magazine publishing.

Our most heartfelt thanks to: Peter Armour, Barrie Atkin, Adolph Auerbacher, Stephen Bernard, Burt Boersma, John Mack Carter, Art Cooper, Phyllis Crawley, Peter Diamandis, David Foster, John Harrison, Irving Herschbein, Sandra Kresch, Leslee Lenoff, Owen Lipstein, Tam Mossman, Harry Myers, Judy Nolte, Roy Payton, Barbara Raskin, Tony Rutigliano, Dale Schenkelberg, Eileen Hedy Schultz and Shin Tora -- and their staffs, who often helped with the research, dealt with our editors to make sure all the material arrived on time and handled the many administrative details endemic to such an undertaking.

-- Diane Moore, Executive Director of the Art Director's Club, who recommended the professionals represented in the Art & Design chapters and provided us with the information on the ADC's many student-related programs, which we've included in Appendix A.

-- The nearly 100 publishing companies that provided the detailed information on their operations, billings, employment and, most important, entry-level job opportunities. We thank each of them for helping us gather this information for you.

-- The many people at Career Publishing and our supplier companies who worked long hours compiling this data, editing articles, writing chapters, proofreading and doing all the other things necessary to complete a volume of this size and complexity. We thank all of them for their time, efforts and invaluable contributions: Abby Wittlan, Roberta Kopper, Harvey Kraft, Alan Levine, Tom Stein, Bill Killpatrick, Cy Chaiken, Michelle Gluckow, all the folks at Words at Work, Book Mart Press and the staff of the New York Public Library.

-- Last, but never least, my wife, Gretchen. Only she really knows how extensive, important and essential her help, advice, support and overall contribution to this project were.

Ron Fry, President
Career Publishing Corp.

How To Use Your Career Directory

Getting an entry-level job in a magazine publishing company is serious business. The magazine publishing industry is what employment counselors call a "glamour" business. Consequently, there is usually an ample supply of qualified candidates and a shortage of actual entry-level jobs. This Magazine Publishing Career Directory 1986, the first of a yearly series, has been specifically created to help you break out of the pack hunting for one of those few jobs.

The Magazine Publishing Career Directory 1986 is quite a bit more than those typical career guides that purport to tell you how to get a job in publishing. Because how to get a job is only one aspect of the complex learning process you will need to go through -- a process that includes learning about yourself, the magazine business in general and key companies and job specializations in particular.

It's a process of discovering what you want to do, where you want to work and then, and only then, how to break down the publisher's front door. This Directory is, therefore, a compendium of all the resources you'll need to make the series of decisions necessary to get that first job.

We've attempted to organize the Directory in such a way that reading it is a logical, step-by-step, educational progression. The Introduction by John Mack Carter, Editor-in-Chief of Good Housekeeping, and Section I (Chapters 1-4) offer an overview of the industry -- what it is, where it is, where it's going.

Sections II through VIII offer more detailed discussions of the major areas of job specialization -- Advertising Sales, Art &

Design, Circulation, Editorial, Production (Manufacturing & Distribution), Promotion and Public Relations. The seventeen chapters in these sections were written by top professionals from some of the major publishing companies and magazines in the United States -- executives like Harry Myers of Knapp Communications (publishers of Architectural Digest, Bon Appetit and Home magazines), Art Cooper (Gentlemen's Quarterly), Judy Nolte (American Baby) and Eileen Hedy Schultz (Good Housekeeping).

Section IX is for those of you who despair of working for others and are ready to start up your own magazines. We think you'll find the contrasting articles we've included helpful and interesting -- in Chapter 22, you'll learn about American Health, one of the '80s major success stories, from Owen Lipstein, the man who conceived it and raised $10,000,000 to start it. In Chapter 23, Tam Mossman offers a slightly different perspective -- the cash-poor entrepreneur just beginning the start-up process.

By now, you should be ready to figure out how to go about getting that first job. Section X (Chapters 24-27) includes a detailed job search process that will take you through evaluating yourself and potential employers (Chapters 24 & 25), preparing resumes and cover letters (Chapter 26), the interview process and sifting the job offers (Chapter 27).

Section XII (Chapters 28-32) is "Your 1986 Publishing Company Database." Chapter 28 lists nearly 100 major publishers, with detailed information on each, including actual job openings these companies expect to have in 1986. Chapter 29 is the most complete listing of available magazine internships and training programs ever published. And finally, Chapters 30-32 list some additional companies, broken down by publishing speciality, that you may wish to consider as potential employers (but for which we have more limited data).

Section IX consists of two appendices -- the trade organizations you may write for more information on this exciting industry and the publications you should be reading if you want to join it.

WHY EVERYBODY DOESN'T AGREE ON EVERYTHING

You'll discover as you read through our contributors' articles that they don't agree on everything; in fact, there are certain instances where they disagree on some very basic ideas, including their advice on how to break into their particular departments.

We think such occasional disagreement is only to be expected, given their varied career paths and experiences in the business. We also think it's important that you realize there isn't always one way in, one way to do a job or one way to think. We have attempted to insert "Editor's Notes" in the body of the articles to refer you to other sections and chapters where you may find a related, though contradictory, piece of advice.

4

In addition, while those writing chapters for a particular section frequently passed their articles back-and-forth to ensure that the entire section "held together," contributors were rarely privy to articles being written for other sections or, for that matter, to those chapters prepared by our own staff. You will find, therefore, that many articles give similar (and sometimes repetitious) advice about the job search, interviewing techniques, etc.

We have generally not edited out such duplications. First of all, someone interested in advertising sales may never even read the Art & Design section. Or someone just "thumbing through" the entire volume may miss an important piece of information if it's only in one chapter or section.

And second, although we believe we have offered an extensive and complete process for finding an entry-level job in our staff-written Section X ("How to Get the Publishing Job You Want"), it never hurts to repeat sound, sage advice.

S/HE, HIS OR HER, ETC.

We are not chauvinists; indeed, we are pro-feminist. Which is why we dislike the decisions forced upon us by considerations of editorial style and consistency. Finding gender-neutral terms that fit in with each writer's stylistic approach in a book with so many different writers is not easy. We personally find "s/he" to be strange, "his or her" frequently awkward.

We have therefore attempted to refer to a person's title, function, etc. (e.g., "the art director...") wherever possible in order to avoid gender identification. However, for the sake of consistency and brevity, when we had to use a pronoun, we have usually adopted the masculine form.

This does not mean that all people to whom we're referring are masculine. It simply is an editorial choice to keep the stylistic approaches consistent. We have occasionally allowed a contributor's "his or her" to stand, just in case someone doesn't read this Forward and wants to take us to task for our anti-feminist language.

A FINAL WORD

When we first began this project, students indicated an intense need for a guide to resources -- listings of the major publishing companies, who to talk to, potential openings, educational requirements, trade organizations to contact, periodicals to read. We hope you'll agree that we have succeeded in publishing the most comprehensive guide to the magazine business for new candidates entering the field.

Most important of all, we hope it helps you get exactly the job you want. Good luck!

Magazines: The New "Hot" Medium

By

John Mack Carter, Editor-in-Chief
Good Housekeeping

In an age fascinated with electronic media, the magazine industry is alive and doing quite well. And, if my thesis proves correct, we will be doing even better in the future. This bright future is assured by what has happened in the 18-month period from 1984 to mid-1985, during which a record number of American magazines changed hands. I figure the total paid for magazine acquisitions in this period was $1.5 billion.

This remarkable period of acquisitions began with the purchase of Gourmet magazine by Conde Nast, when they paid some $25 million for a magazine that was marginally profitable. Then came the sale of Institutional Investor magazine, which hardly anyone ever heard of, to Capital Cities Communications for $75 million. Then U.S. News & World Report was sold at auction and bought by Mortimer Zuckerman for $167 million.

Then things really got wild. Cuisine, a magazine that was losing money for CBS, was acquired by Conde Nast for almost $20 million...so they could fold it. Then, in the biggest magazine deal ever, Ziff-Davis sold a dozen consumer magazines to CBS for $362.5 million and another twelve business titles to Rupert Murdoch for $350 million. Gannett picked up Family Weekly for $40 million, and Conde Nast concluded its acquisition of The New Yorker for $160 million. Time Inc. went to the marketplace for the first time and paid an astounding $480 million for the Southern Progress Company.

ARE ALL THESE PUBLISHING COMPANIES CRAZY?

If one had been asked to estimate the value of these proper-
ties in early 1984, most media experts would have guessed the
selling price at half the actual amount. Have all the major publishers gone crazy? I don't think so. Then what is it that they
know that's worth our consideration today? In a television age,
how can the old-fashioned magazine medium be worth so much money?

There's a phenomenon occurring in America, one that will
occur in other nations around the world. Media habits are changing dramatically. Television indeed remains the number one media
force in the nation. But patterns of viewing have shifted. While
the total number of hours of household attention to TV has risen
slightly in the past year, up from 49:34 hours to 50:00 (per
week), the traditional family watching together has taken a major
turn downward. We've become a nation of two and three unit owners. Over 57% of our homes now possess two or more sets. Thus,
individual family members are each watching different programs,
using TV in different ways -- all occurring because our public is
approaching life itself and the media as individuals, not as a
family unit. As a consequence, the number of people watching a
prime-time TV property is dropping, even though our population
continues to increase.

WHY TELEVISION VIEWING IS FALLING

Now, the factors behind this are quite straightforward.
Although TV station owners and network people keep looking for
one salient excuse so that they can attack a single culprit,
there are many reasons why program viewing keeps failing:

1. The public is not satisfied with the content of the programs themselves; they are tired of too many shows sounding and
looking alike. Over a third of the programs featured on the
three major networks in the Fall of 1985 were new, and statistics
indicate that almost 80% of those will fail. That says a lot. The
result will be the continuing drop in average household prime-
time TV ratings.

2. Then cable TV, which now allows the average home to watch
12 or more channels, makes more choices a fact of life. If most
programs are alike, then one show, or even a single network, is
no longer the hot, unique property it used to be.

3. There's also the explosion of VCRs and personal computers. We have over 17 million homes -- 20% of all U.S. homes --
now equipped with VCRs. The American public, already unhappy
about programming, is now renting movies to watch on their units.
And, when they record programs for playback at their leisure,
they now tend to erase the commercials and view only program content itself. The advertisers end up with lost audience.

Thus, while the electronic giant still has many people

before the set, they are far more discriminating in what they watch, do not view as a family unit and utilize the TV screen to play back rented movies on their VCRs or as a monitor screen for their personal computers. TV is becoming more and more splintered and segmented; and with advertising costs continuing to rise, astute marketers are now asking questions about the total strength of the medium compared to its unqualified effectiveness in the past. If the trend continues, TV in 10 or 15 years could well end up like radio -- many channels to choose from, with each part of a family viewing his or her own choice of program.

The same has been occurring with newspapers. Where one or two large, center-city publications would once cover over 60% or more of a major U.S. marketing area, the American families' shift to the suburbs has necessitated a longer list of publications to achieve the same level of coverage. Thus, newspapers have become an extremely costly medium for reach.

WHY MAGAZINE ADVERTISING IS BECOMING MORE ATTRACTIVE

Well, where does this leave magazines? Over the years magazines have always catered to the individual tastes of a changing American public. In fact, magazine editorial has helped make these attitudinal and buying changes happen. So within a group of publications like the "Hearst Woman Power Plus" package, we edit a <u>Good Housekeeping</u> that covers a broad spectrum of American women deeply involved in home and family; a <u>Cosmopolitan</u> which speaks a slightly different language to the young and sophistica-ted; a <u>Redbook</u> that talks to the important Baby Boomer market of 25-44 year-old women who now balance a family and job together; a <u>Harper's Bazaar</u> which features fashion and fitness as its core editorial message; plus <u>Country Living</u>, which demonstrates to an affluent segment of our population new ways to decorate and entertain.

Combined, one ad in these five vehicles now reaches 37% of all the women in America 18-49 years of age, and a six-time sche-dule in each of the books covers over 57% of the marketplace and talks to each reader 5.1 times each.

Now, reaching these women is one thing, but talking to them in the proper environment is much more important. And that's where marketers in the United States are beginning to look with interest. During the years when TV totally ruled media decisions, a percentage point of audience delivery was the primary consider-ation. A number was a number and environment took a back seat. Now advertisers are recognizing that short, 30-second TV commer-cials, plus the new trend to even shorter 15-second lengths, just don't allow time to bring out a meaningful "reason-to-buy," the message that differentiates one brand from another.

Advertisers are beginning to understand that diversionary TV can only offer fast awareness, but print (particularly magazines) can present to a potential buyer why one brand is better than the other, and allow them time to study the selling proposition.

Advertisers are beginning to see that attractive, informational, but hard-selling copy in a favorable editorial environment, where people are thinking about cooking and fashion and decorating and entertainng, is the way to go today. We are now returning to the era of the media mix, where solid magazine copy can help add a deeper selling message to the awareness generated by TV.

* * *

Mr. Carter, in addition to his chores at Good Housekeeping, is also Director of New Magazine Development for the Hearst Corporation. He holds the unique distinction of being the only person in history to have edited all three of America's most influential women's magazines -- Good Housekeeping, Ladies' Home Journal and McCall's. He was also Editor of American Home and Assistant Editor of Better Homes & Gardens. The combined readership of these magazines is more than fifty million women. Mr. Carter's extensive editorial influence has been affecting the American publishing industry for almost a quarter century.

Mr. Carter also is widely known in the world of commerce and finance. Before joining Good Housekeeping in 1975, he was Chairman of the Board and Editor-in-Chief of the many publications of Downe Communications, Inc. He has served as a Vice President and Director of the McCall Corp. and he sits on the boards of a number of national charitable organizations as a ranking representative from the corporate world.

In 1977, he was named "Publisher of the Year" by Brandeis University. In October 1978 he was honored as a national "Headliner of the Year" by Women in Communications, Inc., which he joined in 1973 as one of its first male members.

I
The Publishing Industry:
An Overview

CHAPTER 1

The Changing Face Of The Industry

By

Sandra Kresch, Director of Strategic Planning
Time, Inc.

There has been much discussion lately about the demise of print media. Indeed, in the '60s and '70s, as television emerged as the primary means of communicating with consumers, magazines did languish. In fact, many people were predicting that print was dead.

While consumers spent more and more time watching television, advertisers became increasingly fascinated with this medium's ability to provide them with creative capabilities that they never had before. Sight, sound and motion -- characteristics of video not present in print -- allowed advertisers to demonstrate their products in a way heretofore impossible, and they moved into the medium in droves. Print advertising declined precipitously as a percent of total expenditures, and the amount of time spent reading consumer magazines followed the same trend.

In the last five years, another threat seemed to be emerging. Developing technologies, such as videotext, cable, computers and VCR's, seemed destined to compete effectively for ever-diminishing consumer leisure time. There was significant concern that electronic publishing would replace magazines in the not too distant future.

The proliferation of these other video alternatives seemed to pose a threat to the consumer magazine business. Not only were people watching television in the 1980's, they had an almost endless array of pay and basic cable channels available to them, as well as video tapes. As VCR's came down in price, their penetration of U.S. households increased at a rate far exceeding the marketers' most optimistic forecasts.

Leading publishing companies scrambled to create videotext systems, which would allow consumers access to any information

whenever they wanted it, all at the touch of a button. These publishers envisioned a future in which they no longer produced hard
copy newspapers and magazines, but rather transmitted encoded
data across great distances via satellite or telephone lines to
computer-like terminals inside consumers' homes. They predicted
an industry evolution that would see a small number of "information companies" replacing hundreds of "publishers."

Forecasters suggested that consumers would throw away their
books and magazines, trading them for elaborate television-based
information centers that could be used for everything from entertainment to shopping at home using a TV monitor, accessing an
endless array of data bases via links to libraries, connecting to
police stations for home security, and much more.

Changes in consumer behavior during the '70s and '80s also
suggested that print media would be in for a rocky time. Consumers became more materialistic and self-oriented than any time in
history. With jobs becoming scarcer in a low-growth economy, competition increased, and many people became far more focused than
in the past on getting ahead and finding financial stability. In
some cases, career path became an obsession and work hours became
longer and longer, reducing the amount of leisure time available.
As women entered the work force, they moved away from traditional
lifestyles and, in some cases, lacked the time to read or pursue
home-based activities that formerly fueled the sales of traditional women's magazines.

In addition, today's consumers are more active than any
generation in history. Rather than being politically active, as
was the '60's generation, today there is much more emphasis on
careers, active leisure, physical fitness and travel. Everyone is
busier, with more options for entertainment -- and the money to
spend on it -- than ever before in history. If time is limited,
there is greater competition for scarce leisure, and reason to
believe that traditional media would suffer.

The threat seemed more acute when one realizes that the next
several generations of potential readers will have been born and
raised in a "high tech environment." They will be computer literate and used to dealing with data processing and capabilities
unheard of in the past. Having been raised with video and computers, there has been considerable concern about whether they will
find magazines sufficiently interesting. Thus, for a time, the
question raised most frequently by the publishers was: "Will the
magazine industry survive?"

THE CURRENT STATE OF THE MAGAZINE BUSINESS

In fact, all of the technological and social change of the
last few decades has had very litttle effect on the magazine
industry in recent years. Print is healthy and vital -- and shows
every sign of continuing to be so in the future. In 1983, consumer magazines accounted for 80% of periodical industry revenues,
a total of $9.7 billion. Over the prior four years, periodicial
revenues increased by 74% -- well above the rate of increase of

14

the Gross National Product (GNP). Consumer magazines represented a significant portion of this growth. The number of titles continues to grow, with new magazines being launched year after year. Currently, there are thousands of consumer magazines on the market, with more being launched every day.

Despite increased competition for consumer expenditures, spending on media is increasing. While much of the growth has been attributable to expenditures on electronic media (cable and pay TV, VCR's, video games and home computers), consumer magazine spending totaled $6.2 billion in 1984.

Circulation growth

Magazine circulation is growing faster than the rate of the U.S. population, and circulation per adult has increased by more than five percent since 1979. Each U.S. adult reads approximately two magazine issues per week, although readership is heavier among upscale demographic segments.

New magazine entrants have been key to circulation growth. The industry is made vital by the continued development of new options for consumers in response to their changing needs. Not only did new magazine titles account for the major portion of circulation and revenue growth over the last five years, they accounted for a major portion of the growth in those circulation areas that have experienced the best performance. New magazines accounted for two-thirds of the circulation growth of a series of new categories -- Home Service, Sports, Science, Health and Maturity magazines -- that have developed in response to new demographic patterns or consumer interests.

Healthy advertising

Magazine advertising is also extremely healthy. While magazines represent a relatively small portion of total media dollars, their share has remained stable since 1979. The consumer magazine advertising industry is large and growing, with 1984 measured revenues of $5 billion, an increase of 15% ($650 million) over the previous year. Revenues have been increasing at an 11.6% compounded annual growth rate for the last five years -- a total increase of $2.1 billion since 1979. Thus, on both the circulation and advertising fronts, there is little to suggest that the magazine industry is looking at critical times ahead.

In fact, all of the current trends suggest continued and sustained vitality. Erosion of network television audiences is real. Advertisers are seeking alternative media with which to reach their best buying prospects. Increasingly, magazines offer the most effective way of doing so since cable has not developed large enough audiences for advertiser-supported programming to provide the reach required. And no other medium, with the possible exception of direct mail, provides as effective targeting as magazines.

15

More creative approaches

In addition, there seems to be a renaissance in the quality of creative approaches for use in print advertising. For the past two decades, the best art directors and copywriters focused on television as their primary medium for expression, using print under duress or as a supplement. Changing attitudes have resulted in increased interest in print as a primary medium, causing the quality of the creative product to push new limits.

With increased controversy over the advertising of alcoholic beverages, it appears likely that much of this advertising will move into print sometime in the future, fueling additional growth of magazine advertising revenues. In addition, many of the business-to-business categories such as computers and telecommunications seem likely to continue to grow, using magazines as the most effective medium for reaching their target audiences.

The emergence of the "Baby Boomers"

On the consumer front, there are signs of increasing magazine readership among "Baby Boomers," the largest segment of the population and the one likely to be most influential over the next few decades because of the sheer size of the group. There are more consumers in the 25 - 49 year-old age segment than ever before -- this has always been the primary readership group for consumer magazines.

Not only are there more consumers in the right age range for reading magazines, the Baby Boomers are more affluent, educated and interested in information than any generation in history. They are extremely goal-oriented, seeking information as a way of developing successful careers and enabling them to live the "good life." This generation of consumers wants to live life to the fullest, and are passionately focused on finding sources of information so they can "short-circuit" experience as a means of making their mark on the world.

The impact of women in the workforce

In addition, there is a whole new population available to the magazine industry as potential readers of a broader range of magazines. Women are entering the workforce in droves and, in the wake of this change, dramatically altering their media consumption habits. Whereas advertisers could formerly reach most women via daytime television, this is no longer possible. The most attractive audience for most consumer products -- the more affluent working woman -- is now less likely to watch any daytime television at all. This has resulted in increased competition for prime-time audiences, but the more significant outgrowth of this demographic trend is the increased desirability of consumer magazines as a way of reaching this attractive group of women.

More women are reading business magazines, news magazines and other categories than ever. As they increasingly need to be more aware of world events, trends in fashion and other such information -- and have more money available to spend on discretionary products -- both advertising in consumer magazines and their circulation are likely to grow.

HOW THE FUTURE IS SHAPING UP

While continued vitality in the magazine industry is predicted, it is likely that some significant changes in the structure of the business will take place over the next ten or twenty years. Some signs of this evolution are already apparent. Others are fairly predictable based on the industry's evolution to date.

The trend to more concentration...

The magazine industry has always been highly fragmented, with many companies participating, which creates a lot of career opportunities. This fragmentation is a function of the low barriers to entry in the magazines business. Capital requirements for start-ups are minimal, and entrepreneurs, rather than large companies, are the predominant developers of new publications. In fact, since 1965, two-thirds of the start-ups with circulations over 100,000 were by companies not previously in the industry.

In the past, all it has taken to get into the business is a vision for a new publication. Many have been started working out of people's homes with minimal financing and little relevant experience. While the larger, more sophisticated companies would seem to have a better chance at achieving great commercial success, the fact is that the most successful magazines have been those with a solid editorial concept and someone with the vision and zeal to support it. Being part of a large company is not critical for success. No amount of money behind a bad editorial concept can make a successful magazine. This suggests that there will be continued opportunities in the future for people in touch with the market and who have that great idea to launch a successful new magazine.

However, while there are a large number of new titles coming into the market each year, many of them the products of new entrepreneurs, major publishers <u>do</u> dominate the magazine industry and are likely to do so even more in the future. In 1984, the top five publishers accounted for 32% (or $3.1 billion) of total consumer magazine revenues. Time, Inc. was the leader, with $1.13 billion in revenues, followed by Triangle Publications (<u>TV Guide</u>) and Conde Nast (<u>House & Garden</u>, et al). The industry is even more concentrated in ad sales volume.

This trend toward concentration is likely to continue in the future, as competition within the industry increases and the costs of launching a large magazine escalate. While much of the industry growth over the past several years has come from small, special interest publications, large volume or high frequency magazines continue to be the most profitable. Thus, while opportunities exist to start magazines on a small scale, most of the revenue in the future is likely to be concentrated in a few large publishing companies. These latter companies will most likely offer the best career opportunities in the industry.

...And more specialization

Nevertheless, large, general interest magazines are increasingly being forced to fight for consumer attention and advertising dollars with emerging, specialized magazines that focus on individual topics. If consumers are looking for more specificity in the information available to them, in the next fifty years the industry may change significantly, resulting in an environment where a few, large, general interest magazines are supplemented by thousands of small ones focused on the needs of well-defined market segments. While there is a role in the future for both types of publications, each is very different from a business standpoint.

The emergence of small, specialized magazines is a signal that the structure of the industry is changing. Even the largest publishing companies will need to learn to manage small-scale publications or stables of highly-focused specialty magazines, each directed at a different market segment.

The Publisher of the future

The Chief Executive of a magazine publishing company in the future (or the Publisher of any individual magazine) is far more likely to be a business executive than an advertising salesperson, as was traditional in the past. He will need skills beyond an ability to maintain visibility in the advertising community and entertain clients. As consolidation in the industry increases, the companies either will be large and more complicated to run or very small, entrepreneurial operations unable to afford top specialists in all of the critical magazine disciplines. The keys to success will be strong business skills, an understanding of consumer needs and high-quality editorial skills.

The skills required are most likely to be a solid business education, with a background in finance and marketing. The ability to think innovatively, coupled with strong strategic skills, will be the key criteria for success.

In addition, the magazine industry will be more technology-based in all functional areas, so a familiarity with computers -- and comfort with technology -- will be helpful in adapting to the changes ahead.

As one looks to the future, there are likely to be some significant changes in all elements of magazine publishing, from the process of management to the way in which advertising is sold and, finally, in the areas of magazine production and distribution.

Surviving in a more competitive environment

As the magazine market becomes more competitive, success will require increasing sophistication in targeted marketing, not only to sell magazines to more narrowly defined groups of consumers, but also to understand the advertisers' need to reach such well-defined audiences. In addition, cost pressures are escalating in the industry, and future managers will need a better understanding of the economics of publishing, the flexibility to substantially change the publishing formula when necessary and the ability to focus effectively on cost management. As this trend continues, there will be a greater need for sophisticated financial controls to manage ever-increasing complexity in large companies, small titles where cost control is critical to profitablity, and in support of effective purchasing and lobbying to assure cost effectiveness in the production and distribution areas.

Long-range planning will become more important in a changing market environment, as will maintaining greater awareness of the needs of consumers who buy publications and form the audience for advertisers. The magazine executive of the future is far less likely to inherit a publication solidly entrenched in a stable environment than was the case ten years ago. Moreover, the potential changes in the magazine industry will require the managers of even the most successful publications to be ever-observant about changing consumer needs and market/competitive dynamics in order to assure that their publications remain on course.

Changes in advertising sales

As more media options emerge, there will be increased competition for advertising dollars, which are growing at a slower rate than they have in the past. This competititon will take place in an environment where the people spending the money will be more sophisticated than ever and more demanding of the media they buy.

The erosion of television audiences is providing an opportunity to sell magazines as the medium of choice in many product categories where that has not been possible for years. To do so effectively, advertising salespeople will have to understand the marketing needs of their customers and position their magazines as being more consistent with these objectives than television.

Increasingly, the most sophisticated marketers are targeting specific audiences for their products, and magazines are very well-suited to meet this objective. In the process of identifying target markets, the most innovative of advertisers are concentrating on better understanding consumers' needs and developing their products and positionings in response to this knowledge base. Target marketing has been around for a long time, with relatively little impact on the magazine business. However, in the next decade, it will become the primary force in marketing, as competition for consumer dollars becomes fiercer, the proliferation of products escaltes and the need to spend advertising dollars efficiently becomes the primary focus in media buying.

Changes in media buying

Not only are advertisers becoming more sophisticated, but the people who buy media for them are responding to this change in the way they approach the purchasing process. The availability of more information has made target marketing more possible than ever, and media buyers are becoming more information dependent and computer literate in order to do their jobs properly. Further, increased pressure for cost efficiency in media buying is forcing the people who plan schedules to justify their decisions better, a factor that has led to some significiant changes in the way advertising is bought and sold. This will become more the rule than the exception in the future.

Computers have made audience data on a broad range of magazines accessible at the touch of a button. Media buyers now have the ability to easily filter thousands of magazines and to choose those that most effectively meet their needs. It is becoming easier than ever to construct media schedules that achieve desired objectives at the lowest cost, and utlization of more or different magazines has been the result. In fact, technology has helped small, special interest magazines infiltrate schedules formerly using only large, traditional, general interest publications.

Given the need to be cost effective and have access to substantial information, magazine buys are likely to be based more on price and audience characteristics than on the qualitative factors that were important in the past. In the future, it will become easier to rationalize a decision and, more important, to provide data in support of the media buy. Purchases, therefore, are less likely to be based on personal relationships with major magazines' Publishers or advertising staff than on each publication's perceived effectiveness in meeting an advertiser's marketing objectives. The "need to justify the buy" also is likely to result in more desire for qualitative information about the audiences of individual publications, their lifestyles, purchasing patterns, and other data far more comprehensive than the demographic characteristics that form the basis of many media buys today.

Direct mail marketing is becoming a major force in advertising. It has the potential to compete effectively with magazines if advertising salespeople are not properly trained in meeting their clients' objectives for target marketing. Since most direct marketing techniques offer the ability to focus on very narrow segments of consumers, the ad salesperson of the future will have to position his product as offering the same (or more) kinds of capabilities if he is to be successful.

The future ad salesperson

As the media decision process changes and becomes more finely honed, the salesperson's role will change as well. The sales call will become much more focused on providing media buyers and potential clients with information about their products and markets. So the salesperson will need to understand the marketing philosophy of the target company, as well as the pros and cons of all of the media options. Much more effort will be required to help advertisers construct schedules that effectively meet their needs for increased targeting, a requirement that will force the salesperson to be facile with more options, including regional and demographic editions, magazine networks, and even individual parts of magazines (when the production process becomes suffi-

20

ciently advanced to allow advertisers to run in more narrowly defined editions).

In effect, the advertising salesperson will have to be an even more knowledgeable marketing professional, with expertise in segmentation, strategy and media options, in addition to being a personable companion. As competition gets fiercer, it is likely that the salesperson will have to do more cold calling and spend more time studying the market philosophy of his advertisers. He will require a better education and more familiarity with the basic marketing process, media buying, and the businesses of potential clients, resulting in more specialization and, perhaps, necessitating a background in the industries to which he will be selling.

Increasing opportunities in ad sales support

It also seems likely that there will be increasing opportunities in the area of ad sales support. As advertisers and their agencies demand more information (and more justification for their media buys) and technology allows easier manipulation of substantial amounts of data, analysts knowledgeable about research, media and consumer buying behavior will be in greater demand.

On the creative side of the support function, there will be significant changes as well. There will be a need for art directors and copywriters who are both experienced in print advertising and who have the creativity to take this medium and return it to the levels of quality that existed before the advent of television. Experience in print will be a significant advantage for people entering the advertising field, as will the graphics arts capabilities and layout skills that are unique to this medium.

The future of the circulation function

In Circulation, the future will be focused on developing ways to better target consumers through more effective use of data. As growth in circulation for mature magazines slows, innovation will be required to sustain the vitality of consumer demand. Over the last several years, there have been a number of innovations in the area of data base management, demographic targeting and market research that will allow circulators to be more effective in reaching desirable consumers in a cost effective fashion.

For mature publications, it is becoming increasingly important to understand the benefits they provide to consumers and how these vary by demographic and psychographic segments. In the future, there will be significant emphasis placed on studying consumer attitudes and behavior to enable circulation promotion and list selection for direct mail to be used at their optimal levels of efficiency.

While the market for certain publications appears to be saturated, with large bases of loyal consumers, the need to replace subscribers and sustain vitality at the newsstands will always be an issue. By better understanding consumer needs, pro-

21

motion to new market segments can be focused on those benefits that are most likely to build an effective case for subscribing, thereby expanding the potential universe into which magazines can be sold.

Greater utilization of consumer demographic information

As identification of prospects becomes more sophisticated and the ability to segment lists improves, it will be possible to use "unique selling propositions" for different target markets in order to increase the attractiveness of a particular publication. Doing this will require increased expertise in market research focused on segmentation and understanding consumer needs, coupled with sophisticated data base management capabilities. Given our ability to store huge amounts of data, over time it will be possible to learn so much about subscribers and people who do not subscribe that marketing efforts will be much more efficient.

PRIZM and other such research services that code neighborhoods based on demographic characteristics and lifestyle information have given circulators the ability to identify high potential customers and to target their circulation efforts without resorting to primary research. At this time, we can identify the specific demographic characteristics of particular zip codes or blocks and, by monitoring the performance of direct mail efforts targeted to different demographic groups, develop a profile of the best performing areas. In the future, lists will be able to be segmented to focus on specific characteristics desired and no mailings will be directed toward people who are not high potential customers. Computerized "merge/purge" capabilities will allow the list to identify current subscribers and, therefore, to avoid remailing these consumers. All of these techniques will enable Circulation to be supported at far lower cost, thereby offering the potential of dramatically increasing magazines' profitablity.

Building a more attractive subscriber base

A sophisticated understanding of the consumer population could also lead to identifying markets previously thought not to exist. A natural extension of this technology will be the ability to change the demographic characteristics of the magazine audience, which are so important for selling advertisers. As an example, if one can target the most desirable demographic areas through lists used for subscription solicitations, it is theoretically possible to mail only to those areas, thereby acquiring subscribers who meet the demographic profile most desired by advertisers. While it is difficult to determine whether directing circulation efforts at specific demographics targets, will, in fact, cause the total audience for that magazine to move in the desired demographic direction, there is reason to believe that it will. Thus in the future, it seems likely that Circulation will be able to select an attractive audience, solicit them more cost efficiently and generate a rate base for their magazines that is comprised primarily of readers most desired by advertisers.

Increased computer capacity and the technology to manipulate data allows for better use of existing subscriber information as well. In the future, it will become more possible and cost effective to track the success of specific circulation campaigns in order to identify those characteristics that are most effective in generating subscription sales. Similarly, it will be possible to monitor the renewal and payment history of subscribers and identify patterns that will be useful in structuring offers and predicting their success.

All magazines suffer some cycling in and out of their subscriber roles. The ability to track this will enable Circulation to put a value on different types of subscribers, which, in turn, can help determine how much money should be spent up front to solicit them. For example, if a particular group of subscribers can be identified as those that alternate between two directly competitive magazines, it might suggest to the Circulation Director of one magazine that special efforts are needed at renewal time to assure continued subscription to his publication rather than a shift to another alternative.

Along the same lines, it will become possible to predict which subscribers are likely to renew multiple times, thereby providing long-term revenue, as opposed to those who are likely to cancel earlier. If these differences can be isolated, different marketing techniques can be employed to increase the value of the potential long-term subscriber and to stabilize the behavior of the one that shifts in and out of the market.

More effective data base management

Sophisticated data base management techniques will allow us to do a variety of other things not possible in the past. As information is developed on each magazine subscriber, it will become possible to cross-reference individual magazine lists to determine which consumers are readers of multiple products or good prospects for new magazines. Data bases also will allow us to track the impact of price increases, giving us significantly better information about price elasticity that can be used in determining how the subscription price should be set and what will be the expected fall-off at newsstands if the price is raised to different levels. Not only will this help in pricing decisions, but it will also give us some basic economic information with which to manage decisions related to growth of circulation, selection of sources, and the balance among short-term subscriptions, long-term subscriptions and single-copy sales.

The applications of data base technology are endless in the Circulation area. A variety of manipulation techniques coupled with more sophisticated research will enable us to identify high potential customers in advance, at significantly lower costs than currently possible, and to establish new magazines with the demographic base most desired by advertisers.

We will also be able to add and subtract circulation in those areas that would be most helpful in increasing advertising revenues. For example, if a liquor advertiser is interested in greater circulation in the Southwest and the magazine is smaller than desired, over time it would be possible to target this area for subscription or newsstand efforts in order to change the balance of circulation. This would result in increased advertising expenditures and, of course, higher profitability.

Perhaps more interesting is the potential to use data bases as means to identify new magazine ideas. Theoretically, one could filter through information about heavy magazine readers and determine their common characteristics in terms of lifestyle, participation in sports, purchasing habits and a number of other factors that could help us to identify trends that could lead to new magazine concepts.

Expanding outlets for circulation promotion

On the promotion front, a number of changes in recent years have led to the potential for significant innovation in the methods by which we acquire subscribers. Direct mail and agent sales no longer are the most important sources of business. Whereas buying network television was extremely expensive, resulting in a cost per order too high to be viable for most magazines, the availablity of cable advertising space has made television a viable source for circulation. It is possible to achieve the benefits of direct response television at a cost effective level, which should result in more use of this medium for circulation development in the future.

Similarly, there will be increased use of direct telephone sales as it becomes more possible to identify households that have the characteristics that make them good prospects for subscription sales. Phoning these households may turn out to be more cost effective than direct mail solicitation, thereby opening a new source of circulation for magazines.

Future circulation skills

In the future, Circulation will focus more and more on modeling different sourcing scenarios in order to come up with the most efficient and effective approach to subscription acquisition and retention. Sophisticated computer skills and a solid knowledge of finance will be important. At the same time, in order to be successful in circulation, there is an increasing need for an understanding of consumer dynamics and a greater use of techniques heretofore associated with packaged goods marketing. As a result, it would be wise for people considering Circulation as a career to be trained well in statistics and marketing techniques, which would allow them to leap-frog over competitors who continued to focus on financial optimization in the circulation process.

Changes in magazine manufacturing and distribution

The Production side of the publishing industry -- now often referred to as Manufacturing and Distribution -- may well be the most exciting area of opportunity in the future. But it is also an area of great concern, because developments here could create

24

significant pressures on the profit margins of even major publishing houses.

Technology is likely to have more pronounced impact in this area than in any other in magazine publishing over the next few years. However, while technology will offer increased efficiency and, therefore, the potential for signficant cost cutting after a period of substantial capital spending, other manufacturing and distribution costs are likely to escalate, at least in the near future, nullifying some of these savings.

In some ways, the '70's was a very comfortable time for publishing companies. While manufacturing and distribution costs increased, they did so at a rate slower than the inflation level for other products and services. In a high inflation environment, publishing companies were able to pass through price increases to consumers substantially in excess of the increases in costs they were experiencing for paper, printing and postage. Indeed, an oversupply of paper during the period kept prices down, and there was no attempt to restructure postal rates. This was coupled with significant productivity savings in printing and distribution coming from a variety of sources.

Over the next several years, this situation will change. Costs are likely to escalate more than in the past decade, and in a low inflation environment (and one in which magazines are fairly priced relative to competing products), it is less likely that substantial price increases can be passed on to readers as a way of covering cost increases.

Paper supply is tighter now and, after suffering reduced profits because of a previous oversupply of paper, paper companies are understandably reluctant to add new plants to solve a potential undersupply situation. While it is likely that they will increase their manufacturing capacity to some degree during the next decade, it is uncertain whether or not there will be enough to assure publishers an appropriate supply of paper at the right price.

There also is likely to be increased pressure on the postal side. Significant deficits are becoming the norm with the Postal Service, and the new Postal Commissioner will be under pressure to restore it to profitability. This is likely to lead to a thorough review of price and service levels.

It is possible that the special treatment magazines currently receive, which assures delivery in a timely fashion, may be eliminated or that the price of this service will escalate. In any case, the postal rate will probably change, and any significant change cannot benefit the publishing industry. This is likely to lead to a search for alternative methods of distribution that will address the deficiencies or potential cost problems that may develop with the U.S. mail.

At the same time, other forces will impact on our ability to use alternatives like airlines and trucks. After deregulation, these industries began to compete for the first time, resulting in reduced margins and an inability to invest in new plant and equipment. Capacity already has decreased, and this trend is likely to continue in the future. Over time, this will probably increase distribution costs and reduce the number of available alternatives for getting magazines from one place to another.

The effects of the new technology

On the technology front, opportunities for innovation seem endless. Increased data processing and transmission capabilities will, over time, significiantly change the way in which magazines are produced. There will be opportunities for efficiencies in production, resulting in substantial cost savings.

However, in order to effectively use this technology, a magazine publisher will need to make heavy investments of time and capital. As systems become more complex and begin to seriously impact on the cost of production, those companies that are able to make the considerable up-front investment necessary to integrate the technology into their operations will enjoy a substantial advantage. In effect, this is likely to cause increased pressure on the small publishers who are unable to afford such automation, as the larger companies will be able to take advantage of the cost efficiencies and quality improvements that this technology offers.

The application of technology to publishing may dramatically increase the cost of entry into this business, in addition to widening the gap in profitablity between the larger and smaller firms. Over time, this could result in significiant structural changes in the industry, separate and apart from the very real benefits to be derived in the manufacturing and distribution process.

Where will technology have impact? The answer is in virtually every area of Manufacturing and Distribution. It is just becoming possible to transmit photographs and copy over long distances via satellite. This capacity will be increased as the years go by, making it possible to "close" later, thereby giving consumers more up-to-date information than ever before when their magazines hit the newsstands. In the last year, information on everything from hijackings to Wimbledon has been transmitted via satellite in a manner of minutes, from writers and photographers in Europe to printing facilities in the U.S., a significant reduction from the days required previously. Not only will consumers have access to "later-breaking" news, but also to better quality reproduction and more interesting photographs, as the time required between writing a story and getting the magazine printed is decreased.

Future production -- totally automated?

In the not too distant future, magazine production will be totally automated. Writers will input their stories into computers that will carry the copy through to final production with no need to reenter it. Art directors already have computerized layout capabilities, which allow them to do their job in significantly less time. Eventually, these will be linked into the production system, thereby eliminating the need for a variety of processes that have been required since magazines first began.

In the future, finished magazine pages will be transmitted by satellite, thereby eliminating transportation needs and, again, compressing the time between the creation of a story and its actual production. Computers will allow greater efficiencies and better control in the printing process, resulting in reduced paper waste and the ability to use less expensive grades of paper. Computerized roll splicers are starting to be used and will be improved in the future. Automatic scanners will dramatically decrease the labor intensity of dealing with ink in the printing process, as well as making more efficient use of it. It will be possible for ink density and the ink-to-water ratio to be maintained automatically. Filmless computer systems will reduce handling time and diminish the need for maintenance. Robots may be used for automatic press, storage and binding systems.

Also on the printing side, the speed of the presses is likely to increase. While this will necessitate other improvements and changes in the printing process, it will become a major factor in getting magazines out more quickly. The bindery process will evolve from a labor intensive to a capital intensive activity, as automatic handling in the binding, bundle loading and hopper areas of the printer reduce manpower needs and improve efficiency.

Production-enhanced marketing

In addition, improvement in addressing capabilities will allow more flexibility than in the past, providing printers with the ability to personalize magazines, thereby opening significant marketing opportunities. Selectronic binding will allow the selection of forms without having to stop the presses and, through this process, the ability to produce individualized magazines for individual types of consumers. The impact of this will be felt long-term in the ability to service advertisers more effectively. They will be able to target their ads to specific consumer groups -- the best prospects for their products. Production facilities will have the capacity to create far more editions cost effectively and, perhaps more importantly, be more responsive to the marketing needs of both advertisers and circulators.

SUMMARY

For an industry that has been around for as many years as magazines, it is exciting to see the great potential for future change. Technology, as well as changing consumer needs, will have significant impact. It appears likely that there will be more fragmentation of the industry, with more and more specialized magazines to address many different kinds of audiences on a broad range of subjects of interest. Specialization will be the key note, as consumers buy precisely what they want and advertisers increasingly have the ability to target their best prospects. The industry is likely to be healthy and exciting, offering many opportunities for attractive careers in the future.

* * *

     Ms. Kresch joined Time, Inc. in 1983 as Vice President, Mar-
keting -- Development and Information Services Division, Video
Group, and ascended to her current position in March, 1984. She
manages 17 people, has responsibility for a 6-person systems
development staff and is credited with, among numerous other corporate achievements, creating a new strategic planning and market
research capability for the $1.4 billion Magazine Group.

     She previously spent 13 years with Booz, Allen & Hamilton,
Inc., a well-known international management consulting firm.
Starting as a Project Director in their National Analysts Division in Chicago, she became a Vice President in 1975 and the
first female partner of the company. Transferring to BHA's New
York headquarters, she held a variety of executive positions and
was responsible for projects for a number of Fortune 500 and
other major national and international corporations.

     She began her career as a Research Associate for Simat, Hel-
liesen & Eichner, Inc., after graduating with her BS from the
University of Pennsylvania. She has completed extensive course
work at both the Wharton School of Business and the Stanford University Graduate School of Business and is active in many non-
profit organizations and professional associations.

CHAPTER 2

Are You A "Magazine" Person?

By

Barrie J. Atkin, Director of Corporate Planning
Rodale Press

Do you carry magazines with you everywhere -- to the gym, to bed, to the bathroom?

When you pass newsstands, do you stop and flip through the new magazines?

Do you enjoy being in touch with popular culture -- perhaps reporting on it or predicting what is likely to sell?

Do you work best under deadlines, but prefer them to be weekly or monthly rather than daily?

Do you get a thrill from seeing your name in print?

Would you be comfortable knowing that the article you worked so hard to create gets thrown out with the kitty litter?

Do you like working with interesting, creative, dynamic people, many of whom have big egos and strong opinions?

Not everyone in magazine publishing will answer "yes" to all of these questions. But if _you_ did, magazine publishing may be the career for you.

IT TAKES A SPECIAL KIND OF PERSON...

Like magazines themselves, magazine publishing is dynamic and lively. It attracts dynamic, lively people -- idea-oriented people who want to present fresh concepts, new insights and exciting information to the public. Magazine publishing is a communications business with a tangible product. For its creators, each new issue of a magazine provides immediate, tangible reinforcement and a chance to make changes and try new things.

Why do people choose magazine publishing as a career? Those in the business cite many reasons -- the excitement of working on an ever-changing product; the pleasure of being around talented and articulate people; the psychological satisfaction of being associated with an idea leader. Magazine publishing is an exciting, well-respected industry. Indeed, there's an aura of glamour surrounding the magazine industry.

As one Advertising Director commented, "When you go behind the scenes, it's really just as much 'schlep' work as any other business, but there's still a luster that you share in."

As my colleague John Mack Carter has pointed out, magazines are "hot." Over 40 magazines with more than 30 million circulation and nearly $2 billion in revenues have changed owners from early 1984 to mid-1985. During the same period, hundreds of new magazines started. Not all will survive, but the net effect is an increase in the number of new magazine titles.

In contrast, the number of new newspapers begun in the last two years is quite small. And some major ones have folded, as one-newspaper towns become increasingly the norm. Mergers and acquisitions have also reduced the number of newspaper and book companies.

A Circulation Manager summed up the difference between working on magazines and working on newspapers: "Magazines are usually national in scope, and people can relate to what you do. Newspapers are much more community-oriented. When I told people I worked on the local newspaper, they would tell me about the carrier throwing their paper into the rosebush; now that I work for a magazine, they tell me what they think of the product."

An Editor commented on why she chose magazines over books or newspapers: "Books develop at a glacial pace which is inherently less exciting than magazines; newspapers are a flash in the pan, with no time to develop ideas or go into background. In contrast, magazines are dynamic, exciting, current. The frequency gives editors a chance to think about an idea, let it ripen and evolve. And you still have the excitement of starting a whole new one the next month."

Yes, creating a new magazine each month can be challenging and exciting, but, as one editor admits, it can also be a bit scary: "A lot of editorial coverage is large doses of intuition mixed with an element of whimsy. You never know how people will respond to your choice of cover, illustrations or articles. But living a little bit on the edge isn't bad."

On the business side, magazines often attract people who "always wanted to be writers" but who, for one reason or another, changed career direction. This gives magazines a special dimension -- employees with a strong appreciation and enjoyment of the product.

"Magazine publishing is a crazy business," one salesperson told me. "There's room for brilliant ideas and enormously stupid mistakes."

...TO JOIN THE SPECIAL AND UNIQUE WORLD OF PUBLISHING

Ask anyone in magazine publishing -- magazines are special and unique. What other product affects so many peoples' lives,

informs,   influences and entertains....and can be carried around
with you wherever you go? What other product do people order a
year or more in advance,   not even knowing what is going to be
covered?   What other product includes customers' opinions (even
negative ones) about the product -- often right up front?

An Associate Publisher commented,   "Magazine publishing is
Liberal Arts to the 'nth degree.' Magazines demand an ability to
take broad wisdom and apply it to your product."

Magazine publishing is an unusual business with respect to
competition. In many industries, competitors go to great lengths
to keep information about price, new products, customers and market share confidential. But in magazine publishing, magazines
often place advertisements in trade publications to trumpet this
type of information. Moreover, publishers hire auditing organizations to verify their circulation figures and make this information available to their advertisers.

Why? Because that's the information that will help persuade
those advertisers to buy space in the magazine.

Most   products have only one revenue stream   -- the buyer.
But with magazines, income comes from three sources. There's the
$1.95 customer -- the newsstand buyer who can see exactly what he
or she is purchasing. Second, there's the $11.95 customer -- the
subscriber,   who has a pretty good idea of what's being ordered,
but is still purchasing with some degree of anticipation and
trust.   And then there's the $11,950 customer -- the advertiser,
who is buying a page of space, the most intangible product of
all, with the hope of sending a message to all of those $1.95 and
$11.95 customers.

As vehicles for advertisers, magazines offer a window to
what's happening in dozens of industries. One salesman told me he
felt like an industry voyeur -- since he often knew the marketing strategies of his clients long before they became apparent to the public. A good salesperson knows the advertisers'
marketing goals and presents the magazine as an effective medium
to help those advertisers achieve their objectives.

THE BIG APPLE -- WHERE IT'S STILL HAPPENING

The necessary connection to the advertising industry -- and
to Madison Avenue -- makes New York City the magazine publishing
capital of the U.S. Of course, there are successful magazine companies -- such as Rodale Press -- that are headquartered elsewhere. But, like Rodale, they typically have an ad sales staff
based in New York.

The Big Apple serves as host to industry-related associations,   seminars and events, and helps determine the style and
pace of the magazine business. The close proximity of so many
publishing houses creates lots of opportunity for the sharing of
ideas. Publishing is a social business. People often work hard,
but they play hard, too, often with other people from the publishing business.

The proximity of publishing houses also creates the opportunity for ongoing "comparison shopping" by staff members. Mobil-

ity in publishing -- especially among salespeople -- is wide-
spread. Salespeople see job changes as a way to stay fresh, a way
to sell a new product and perhaps an opportunity for salary
increases. Editors, too, tend to move around.

DON'T ASSUME YOU'RE GOING TO GET RICH

While magazine publishing offers both tangible and intangible rewards, few people go into publishing simply to make money.

In general, magazine publishing is not known as a high paying field. This is partly due to supply and demand. The perceived glamour of magazines attracts far more applicants than the
industry can possibly absorb. So salaries, especially in editorial, tend to be lower than in other fields. As a result, magazine
publishing often attracts people who are strongly motivated by
factors other than money.

Of course, some people do very well financially -- owners,
key executives, top salespeople. And magazine publishers do crop
up in the _Forbes_ list of the 400 wealthiest people in America
(including Publisher Malcolm Forbes himself).

DISCOVERING THE FIELD

It has been said that magazine publishing is an "accidental
career." After all, how many guidance counselors ever steered
students into magazine publishing? In fact, I suspect very few
people grow up planning to work in magazines. More likely they
intend to be writers or artists or work in sales, marketing or
finance, and find that magazines have a range of opportunities
for all those interests.

As a result, people enter magazine publishing in a variety
of less traditional ways. Some people are introduced to publishing through relatives or friends in the business. Many enter from
related industries such as book and newspaper publishing, direct
marketing, advertising or production.

INTERNSHIPS & COLLEGE PUBLICATIONS -- "TESTING" YOUR INTEREST

Luckily, with magazine publishing, you don't have to wait
until you're looking for a job to find out if this field is for
you. There are lots of opportunities to "test out" your interest
and talent on a trial basis. College yearbooks, newspapers and
magazines often offer real-life experiences and skills. Potential
employers are impressed by students who have worked on school
publications, routinely met production or editorial deadlines and
still managed to generate good academic records.

In reviewing resumes, I look for experience with college or
community publications. For editorial applicants, published writing samples tell me far more about their potential magazine
writing talent than the best term papers ever could. And for

business applicants, experience in a related field may offer clues to a student's level of interest and commitment.

Internships also offer wonderful opportunities to test a career interest, gain experience and make important personal contacts. Perhaps best known are the editorial internships offered through the American Society of Magazine Editors and the business internships available through the Magazine Publishers Association. Some publishers, such as Time, Inc. and Rodale Press, run their own intern programs. Many others hire interns on an occasional basis.

While internships are usually in the summer, many publications are quite eager to hire interns during the school year. Such internships may be harder to find, but are generally less hotly contested than summer jobs.

Internships also give valuable insight into the culture of a company. Special interest publications, such as <u>Bicycling</u> and <u>Rodale's</u> <u>Organic</u> <u>Gardening</u>, will often attract people with a passion for the subject matter (although this is less true of trade magazines, general interest magazines and lifestyle magazines. <u>Playboy</u>, for example, does not have a lot of employees living a "playboy" lifestyle. And <u>Time</u> and <u>Newsweek</u> have very different corporate structures and cultures despite publishing a similar product.)

Best of all, internships often lead to future job offers. Companies are hiring a known entity who already knows something about how the company works.

But if you should decide that magazine publishing is <u>not</u> for you, magazines can still be a part of your life. All it takes is $1.95 at the newsstand. As for having your name in print, you can still have it -- even if it's only on a computerized mailing label on the cover!

* * *

Ms. Atkin first joined Rodale Press in the summer of 1981 through the Magazine Publishers Association MBA Intern Program. After graduation from business school, she returned to Rodale full-time as Assistant to the President and Director of International Licensing. In her present position, to which she was promoted in early 1985, she is also responsible for managing the company's in-house intern program.

She received her MBA with honors from the Harvard Business School, where she was Publisher of the <u>Harbus</u> <u>News</u>. Prior to business school, she was a manager with the Massachusetts Department of Public Health and a consultant to small businesses, including a number of community newspapers. She received her BA from Brown University.

CHAPTER 3

Magazines: The Magnificent Profession

By

Peter G. Diamandis, President
CBS Magazines

We develop our own explanations of why we work. In the beginning, it's usually to make a living. Hunger and poverty are not pretty sights, and most people learn quickly to avoid them. Marriage brings on responsibilities; eventually there are other mouths to feed. The first ten years of your career you will be preoccupied with holding body and soul together, paying the rent and trying to scrape together enough for an occasional movie.

After a while, if you're moderately happy and successful in what you do, you will begin to develop reasons for working other than money. Money alone is not enough to make you happy -- the sooner you realize this, the better. You will develop your own explanation of why you work. There are many, and they are acquired in various ways for any number of reasons. Challenge, excitement, risk, creativity, fun -- alone or in confluence -- may fit the bill, but the bottom line is accomplishment.

When I look back on my career, for example, I don't remember the raises, I remember the accomplishments. I recall the successes and failures of my work -- not how much money I made. Money is a minor punctuation mark in your life. The major punctuation marks are marriage, having your first child, college graduation, getting your first job, seeing your first article in print, selling your first ad (not necessarily in that order).

Perhaps you're <u>looking</u> for punctuation marks in your life. Well, maybe we're <u>all</u> looking for punctuation marks. Getting ready to take one of the first major steps in your life, you may be feeling like the old Greek who was forced by his rather rude hosts to sit at dinner under a very sharp sword, hung from the ceiling by a very thin hair. In your case, resolving this Damoclean situation may come from discovering in yourself what you want to accomplish. Then you can go ahead and try.

WHY I'M IN MAGAZINE PUBLISHING

I've done many things in my life -- been a perfume salesman, taxicab driver, naval officer, President of the company. I've been able to take a look at American business from a number of angles. At one point, I discovered what I wanted. I decided that of all the things I'd done, publishing -- specifically magazine publishing -- was where I was going to spend the rest of my life. I picked it for several reasons.

The first -- and clearly the most important -- is the people in the business. Magazine publishing is a very sophisticated business. It attracts very intelligent, sophisticated people. You find people who are "quick studies," witty and acerbic -- people who are fun to be around. I decided that those were the kinds of people I wanted to be around.

It's a sophisticated business, a reflection of what our world is about, and a highly creative one. It's a business where there are bright and exciting people working alongside you. It's also a business where all of these parts add up to a lot of fun.

And it's a glamorous business, in the sense that you find the "trappings of success" to a large degree. You go to the better towns in this business. Without castigating any one in particular, there are many towns in America filled with warehouses. In the magazine business, you don't go to these places. For some reason, that's not where the magazine industry lives. The magazine industry is photographers, artists, editors, writers, and everyone who wants to work at making magazines.

IT'S NOT AN EASY INDUSTRY TO ENTER

The very things that make this an attractive business make it a difficult one for young people to enter. An awful lot of educated people -- particularly women -- want to get into the magazine business. For every open job, there are ten candidates. In the beginning, the salaries are not grandiose. Many people get discouraged.

But I don't mean to discourage anyone. Once you get in, the advancement is rapid. If you're really good, people are not concerned with your gender or level of experience. If you know writing, even if you happen to be 28 years old, you could be the Editor-in-Chief of a magazine. If you can really sell, even if you have very few years of experience, you could be the Advertising Director of a magazine. In this business, people are very quick to recognize ability.

Once you are in, the money will come. It is much more important, when you are beginning, to be good at what you do. And you will get in if you have the zeal, the need to get in. Then, if you have the tenacity, you can rise like a rocket. It's not at all like working in a bank or retail store, where you can expect to spend 20 years in the place before you make Vice President.

From the standpoint of a "fast-tracker," the magazine business is ideal -- you're not held back by age or experience levels.

WHAT I LOOK FOR IN AN ENTRY-LEVEL CANDIDATE

Initially, I look for three qualities in a person: energy, judgement and creativity. Energy is self-evident. Judgement is a combination of experience and chemistry -- something in one's brain and body that is well balanced. And creativity, a much-misused word. People think we have a "Creative Department," meaning art directors and writers. Actually, all the departments should be creative departments. Certainly, a salesman who comes up with a brilliant idea for a client -- who goes in and does a wonderful, kinetic presentation -- is a creative human being. He's using his mouth as a form of creative communication.

It sounds corny, but having considered thousands of candidates, I find that those who have these traits to the fullest extent, and who have an ethical quality about them as well, are the people who eventually succeed. By ethical quality, I mean good character. Having seen success and failure from a very intimate perspective, I know that it sometimes takes a few knocks to really develop someone's ethical sense. It's very similar to the way an athlete feels after he's given it his absolute best and lost. He's not disappointed for long, because the effort is self-fulfilling. He's not afraid to fail. It's that kind of person who somehow develops stamina -- the staying power to make a difference in the world. Call it integrity.

When I find all of these qualities in one human being, I know I've found a gem. It takes getting to know someone beyond first impressions. That's why I've stopped hiring people after only one interview -- sometimes it takes four or five to get to know a person.

I find many people in the magazine business with these qualities. There are a high percentage of people here who feel good about themselves. They're attracted to magazine publishing because it truly is a creative business, and they bring energy, good judgement and integrity to their positions. It makes my job exciting.

TAPPING MANY TALENTS

I often liken myself to an orchestra leader, uniting and harmonizing all the different parts of the symphony. It's a lot of fun.

In another sense, I often feel like the Wizard of Oz, sitting here at my desk, trying to pull all the right levers to make the magazines the best they can be -- trying to get the business right. Because, in the end, a magazine is nothing more than the product of someone's imagination. We get a pile of white paper every month, and we can do with it whatever we want.

In the course of my career, looking at the magazine business very carefully, I've grown quite a bit and learned a lot. With regard to those qualities I find essential to be successful, I don't think I always had all of them. I had the energy, but I don't think the creativity or judgement were always there. I'd like to think that I've developed them a little through observation. I saw there was a right way and a wrong way to do things. Sometimes the right way was tough. But, in the magazine industry, it is most important to get the business <u>right</u>.

CONTINUALLY STRIVING FOR EXCELLENCE

Too many people forget that at the core of the magazine business are still great headlines, great cover lines, great photography, great illustration, great positioning, wonderful writing, and, after all that is done, great promotion and great salesmanship. That's what <u>we</u> choose to do with that pile of paper -- make something really good. And you <u>can't</u> make a silk purse out of a sow's ear, though some have tried. You have to get the front-end right.

One of the things I encourage, therefore, is pursuit of excellence in <u>all</u> areas. And not only excellence, but surprise as well -- taking chances, doing unusual things inside a magazine to get the reader excited. Then, once you're through the creative process, you accelerate the success you've already put on paper. That's the side of the business I started in -- advertising sales, promotion, circulation. It's the part of the business that hits the accelerator once things are going right. But if you don't get the front-end right -- the pictures, the copy, the headlines -- you can't accelerate. You'll find yourself trying to sell air, and you won't be able to do it for long!

AND ALWAYS WORKING TOGETHER

So, a magazine must have great leadership. Everyone must understand what a magazine represents. If the Editor is going one way and the Publisher another, you're finished. There must be a partnership -- a marriage -- between the Editor and the Publisher. They need to find a common ground in order to get the business right.

First, they must agree on where a magazine fills a need. Then they must create its "face" -- that's where promotion comes in. Promotion may only be a sign over an Editor's or Publisher's desk that says: "This Is What We Are!"

Then <u>everyone</u> must understand what that magazine represents. The minute everyone understands the positioning of the magazine, life becomes easier. At that point comes some risk-taking. Magazines constantly need maintenance and updating, which means taking risks with what you've already established as the magazine's identity. It's like being on a surfboard, with the world around us as the wave. The magazine must constantly be on the crest of that wave if it is going to be successful, and it has to maneuver down its face without being crushed or simply left behind.

37

All of this adds up to a lot of fun for me and all the people who work on our magazines. We can look at our business and be proud that we produce works of quality. There are no kick-backs, no payoffs. We build something cleanly, maybe even help people along the way.

If I were looking for the root meaning of life, I don't think I would consider it making a living or just "getting through" it all. It may possibly be to alter and improve the situation in which we find ourselves. For me, magazines create something positive, and, therefore, I feel that I'm creating something positive.

UNDERSTANDING THE CHANGES IN YOUR "AUDIENCE"

Back in the 1960's, Marshall McLuhan was predicting the demise of the printed word because of the power of television and film to rivet attention through more direct communication. He called them the "hot media." McLuhan's "the medium is the message" is really a gross overstatement, but there is a kernel of truth in it. It's not that reading has been eclipsed by broadcast, but that reading habits have changed. We're only recently understanding how and why.

There was a time when people would "take" a magazine. That was the expression. They would take a magazine and spend the weekend with it, curl up with it in a chair and pore over it in long, five hour sessions. People don't read like that anymore.

Today, people "spot-read." The public's "eye" has changed and magazine formats have been consistently redone to reflect changing tastes. The average length of an article is 2,500 words. Years ago, it was 5,000. Older magazines did not feature the contiguous articles we use today. Now we run four or five continuous pages, no jump lines, spot-art, spot-reads. When I ran New York Magazine, the best-read section -- Best Bets -- used a design calculated to attract the American eye. You'd read a paragraph of copy, look at spot-art, pick it up and read two "Best Bets" and put it down. For some reason -- probably the impact of television and its instant gratification -- that kind of design is what attracts the American eye.

In Europe, people read differently. Television is not very important -- there are usually only two or three stations and they do not carry much programming. So people read magazines. In Germany, an issue of Geo may have twelve contiguous color spreads of photography and fourteen of copy. When they tried to clone Geo in the U.S., it failed, even though 95% of the people tested in Germany and 89% of those in France believed they were getting an educational value from the magazine. In the U.S., only 4% thought so. The fact is, nobody read that magazine in this country. The American eye is trained to read one and two columns of type, preferably less, so magazines are beginning to use half-columns of type interspliced with art and lots of "white space."

If you are a magazine Publisher or Editor, you've got to know about these changes -- that's what I call "being on the crest of the wave." And that's why it's a fascinating business. It's very eclectic and you learn a lot about many different things.

SOME PREDICTIONS THAT <u>WON'T</u> OCCUR

If the change in readership is one of the trends the magazine business is undergoing, there are others that have been predicted and that, from my perspective, will not occur.

Sandra Kresch talked about the once-threatening "computerization" of magazines, both in the office and in the home. Experts foresaw a time when "electronic magazines" would either be read off home computer screens, or print-out an individual copy at the push of a buttom. In point of fact, I don't think readers will ever choose to be glued to a computer screen for hours at a time if they can possibly find any other way of getting the information they want. Also, the costs of producing such magazines -- and the whole new industry that would surround them -- would simply be too great to be economically practical.

We learned about such cost problems in the cable television business which, five years ago, was being called the likely successor to many kind of magazines. It's still easier and cheaper to make a magazine. The fact is, today the magazine business is more efficient, leaner, and, financially speaking, years ahead of the broadcast industry.

We are ahead in the way we have trimmed our companies (staff, expenses, etc.) and confronted our many problems over the last two decades. This leanness has come from necessity, of course, but we are going to see -- and Capital Cities' purchase of ABC is a case in point -- the necessity for the broadcast industry to undergo the same kind of traumatic and severe self-accountability as we have in the magazine business.

The magazine business is now extremely well-run, stronger, in fact, than we've ever been. We've learned how to compete, and we've slimmed ourselves down to be most efficient. We're up against a lot of tough media, all of us competing for the same share of mind and the same advertising dollars. We're going after it. It is going to be decades before our media competition is where we are now in efficiency.

A CAREER WITH A GROWING FUTURE

For all of these reasons, and more, I would encourage anyone just starting out to strongly and carefully consider a career in magazine publishing. The future of this industry is brighter than it has been in some time: We're now a well-honed business in high gear; still an effective and economical way for thousands of people to express themselves and share ideas; and, purely from the standpoint of the human need to participate, nothing is going to replace it. There are, perhaps, some unforeseen changes coming around the bend, but people have been predicting rolling sidewalks and taxicab helicopters since the 1930's. The sidewalks still don't move and we all still risk our lives trying to cross the street during rush hour!

Magazines have something no other medium -- broadcast, outdoor, direct mail, etc. -- has. It's difficult to quantify what it is, but perhaps it's best defined as the dignity of the printed word. Reading is a participatory experience, not a passive event. When you read, you unite all of the faculties of the mind. You open up to the printed word; advertisers learned this and include printed messages in their television commercials to improve communication. Reading is an immersion, a warm and comforting bath. It sustains itself and engages the mind.

In addition, there is an unquenchable reservoir of subjects for the magazine industry to drink from. The world is a moveable feast today and our industry a willing gourmet. One reader wants ballet, another skiing, a third, high finance -- they're all out there in specialized magazines.

There are many opportunities in this business -- to make a living, find a niche, learn, grow and be good at what you choose to do. It's exciting to be on the inside of this business, creating, reporting and illustrating the feast, allowing readers to pick what they want. If you have the energy, judgement and creativity, come and join us. You're in for a real treat.

* * *

Peter G. Diamandis was named President of CBS Magazines in September, 1983. During an illustrious 25-year career in the communications field, he has worked in both publishing and advertising. He joined CBS in 1982 as Vice President & Group Publisher of CBS's Women's Magazine Group and Publisher of Women's Day.

Previously, he was Executive Vice President of Gruner & Jahr, Inc., where he had earlier served as Publisher of Geo. Prior to Geo, he was the Founding Publisher of Self, Conde Nast's first new magazine in 40 years, and the most successful new American women's magazine launched in the past three decades. Mr. Diamandis has also held the Publisher's title at Mademoiselle, New York and New West magazines. In 1962, he started his own advertising agency, which he took public and, subsequently, sold. He also served as President of MLA Advertising.

In 1980, Mr. Diamandis was selected as the Marketing Man of the Year by the American Marketing Association. He is on the Board of Directors of the Magazine Publishers Association and the Publishers Information Bureau, as well as various other fraternal and civic associations.

A graduate of Bucknell University, and a member of its Alumni Advisory Board, Mr. Diamandis is a former naval officer. He resides with his wife, Joan, and 6 children, in Rowayton, CT.

CHAPTER 4

Considering Your Career Options

By

Adolph Auerbacher, VP/Group Publishing Director
Meredith Corporation

No degree of success or amount of experience qualifies someone to tell you why you should choose a career in magazine publishing. That decision should be yours, based on your own perception of whether your talents lend themselves to a rewarding career in this business.

At this point, you may be considering a career in magazines based on your existing skills or interests. Perhaps you are a gifted writer or artist. Maybe you are interested in advertising, photography or promotion. Or you may just enjoy reading magazines, and feel that your enthusiasm would help you accomplish great things in the magazine publishing business.

Of course, the ultimate reward for a person in any area of magazine publishing is that of having a tangible, finished product. Whether you're a writer, advertising salesperson, photographer or one of the many other professionals who put together a magazine, your work culminates in a published package.

A UNIQUE FORM OF COMMUNICATION

Unlike television or radio, magazines can be enjoyed at a reader's own pace. They can be stashed in a briefcase, taken to bed, displayed on a coffee table or read immediately. Once an image is printed in a magazine, it remains available until the reader decides to dispose of it.

This level of semi-permanence is also the distinguishing factor between magazines and newspapers. Most daily or weekly newspapers are designed to be read and disposed of in a day. Magazines are designed to be more lasting, although the information is just as accessible as that in newspapers.

As a result, magazines are unique information packages and have graphically detailed personalities. With the help of modern production techniques and the availability of sophisticated graphics, magazines have their own styles, their own characters. Type, photos, art and design are the tools which fine-tune a magazine and make it an individual statement. No other medium can effectively utilize these elements to create a lasting package that has such a great impact on its audience.

These packages are designed to appeal to <u>people</u>, so magazine publishers must keep in touch with world happenings, especially those that have immediate impact on their readers. Of necessity, people in our business also keep up with trends which would be of interest to their target audiences.

Keeping a magazine human and friendly is a greater challenge that you might imagine, especially in today's high-tech publishing world. But the solution to this dilemma is one which makes magazine publishing even more enjoyable. We are in a <u>people</u> business, so we meet new people all the time in order to keep up with our readers. It is impossible to create a magazine that appeals to any audience unless the producers of the magazine know about the people they are dealing with.

...WITH SPECIAL DEMANDS

At many magazines, especially those with national audiences, staff members must do a lot of traveling to keep up with the people their magazines affect. Writers, researchers, executives, advertising salespeople and public relations representatives are usually well-traveled. Their jobs demand it.

Business travel can be hectic and a tax on your patience and stamina. Still, young people in publishing tell me that travel adds an important dimension to their work. I agree. It stretches your ability to adapt to new and unexpected situations. It broadens your horizons -- geographically, socially and intellectually. In short, travel makes you and your work more interesting.

Successful magazines require a broad range of talented staff members. Some positions are more visible than others, but each facet -- editorial, art, advertising, research, circulation, subscription fulfillment, production and delivery, etc. -- is essential. As you explore a career in magazines, find out what each of these areas contributes to the overall product, no matter what your own area of interest may be.

This may sound like a tall order for a person who is just starting to prepare for a future in magazine publishing. But there are things you can do right now, in addition to your education, to familiarize yourself with the industry and enhance your knowledge of publishing.

PREPARING FOR YOUR FIRST PUBLISHING JOB

People unfamiliar with the magazine business often assume that nearly everyone in publishing calls New York home. So you might be surprised to learn that magazines are published all over the United States. In fact, some of America's most popular magazines are based in places as diverse as Long Beach, California, Des Moines, Iowa, and Washington, D.C.

Wherever the magazines which interest you are published, the best way to prepare for a job in magazine publishing is to find someone who works for a magazine and talk to them. Focus on the area that interests you most. Develop specific questions for that person. Then arrange a meeting. You might be surprised at how willing these professionals are to share their wealth of knowledge with the future movers and shakers of their business!

Whether you set up an appointment to gather information or have a job interview, you will be wise to follow these rules:

1) Realize that a professional's time is very valuable. Find out everything you can before your meeting. You'll ask better questions, receive better answers and make a better impression.

2) Read several issues of the magazine you will be discussing prior to your visit. This shows your commitment and your appreciation for the professional's product.

3) Let your experience show, whether it's related to publishing or not. Have you worked in a parking garage, sold birthday cakes, painted houses, stocked grocery shelves, delivered flowers? In an entry-level job, you're being hired more for your character traits than your skills. Honesty, initiative, punctuality, flexibility, self-confidence, ability to take criticism, creativity, loyalty -- all of these traits and others like them demonstrate your potential.

4) Follow up each interview with a brief letter of thanks, whether you get a job, advice or information. Thank you notes are an accepted business courtesy.

5) Keep the people who give you their time apprised of your place and your progress -- even after you land a job. Your increasing experience coupled with their changing employment opportunities may ultimately result in a match-up.

Once you make the first contact, you should feel free to follow up with more questions as they occur to you. Maintain this relationship throughout your preparation for a magazine career. When you begin searching for your first job, you'll have more than education and introductory experience. You'll have a friend in the business.

Another rich source of information exists in publishing trade publications. These "magazines about making magazines" are a great way to stay up-to-date about happenings in the industry. You can also find articles about your specific areas of interest.

Another valuable resource is the Guide to Business Careers in Magazine Publishing, published by the Magazine Publishers Association. It was written expressly to help people find entry-level jobs in our field. The Guide describes the kinds of entry-level jobs generally available and qualifications for them. You may receive a free copy of the Guide by writing the MPA (575 Lexington Avenue, New York, NY 10022).

It's also a good idea to look in the subject index at your library and pick out a few publishing magazines to browse through. Decide which ones contain the information most pertinent to your areas of interest and read several back issues. If possible, subscribe to one or two of these magazines. It is imperative that you know what goes on in this business before you try to be a part of it.

Keep in mind that you are preparing for a <u>career</u>. While you are learning the ins and outs of your areas of interest, you should also be getting an idea of what your first job will be like. Your school's placement office should be able to help you here.

Find out which graduates from your college have landed jobs in magazine publishing and get descriptions of their jobs. Find out which companies hire the most graduates in your field of interest and, if possible, how much they are being paid. This will help you to plan your job search and give you some idea of what to expect when you get that first job.

THE INDIRECT APPROACH -- SOMETIMES IT'S NECESSARY

Don't be surprised if many graduates are starting out in jobs which are not directly related to their fields of interest. Advancement in the publishing business, as in most others, is earned with achievement. Trained workers are needed in every facet of the magazine publishing industry. Your starting place, no matter which department it is in, will be one more means of getting your footing before trying to excel in your desired career. Starting out in some other area of magazine publishing will be no problem for a person who has kept up-to-date on the various developments in the business.

Broadening the realm of your knowledge to include many aspects of magazine publishing will be helpful, but you may need to take that one step further. As magazines get more and more specialized, the need increases for people who have a strong second area of expertise.

Some of your job experiences or hobbies might not seem to be related to publishing. But your background might make you the perfect candidate for a job at magazines devoted to automotives, grocery chains, guitars or computers. In this age of trade magazines and special interest publications, expertise in a specific area could lead to a job.

In short, your first job upon graduation may not be the job of your dreams. But if you keep up with developments in the industry, if you get as much experience as possible through internships and part-time positions, if you supplement your formal education with valuable contacts in the field, your first job might <u>lead</u> to the job of your dreams.

You should choose a career in magazine publishing because you love the business. The people who excel in this industry are the people who enjoy the day-to-day tasks as much as they like receiving their paychecks. With the proper resources and contacts, anyone who truly wishes to pursue a career in magazine publishing should be able to find a niche in our ever-growing business.

* * *

In his current position, Mr. Auerbacher is responsible for the overall management of <u>Country Home</u> and <u>Wood</u> magazines, Meredith Publishing Services (custom publishers) and the 17 magazine titles produced by <u>Better Homes & Gardens</u> Special Interest Publications.

He joined Meredith in 1963 as Mail Order Manager for <u>Better Homes & Gardens</u> magazine. He was named Publisher of <u>BH&G</u>'s Special Interest Publications in 1973. Two years later he was promoted to Associate Group Publishing Director, accepting additional responsibilities for <u>Metropolitan Home</u> (then <u>Apartment Life</u>) magazine and <u>Better Homes & Gardens</u> Tour Services. Most recently, he was also Publisher of <u>Country Home</u> and <u>Wood</u> magazines.

Before joining Meredith, Mr. Auerbacher was an advertising sales representative with <u>Saturday Review</u>. Prior to that, he was on the ad sales staff of the <u>New York Herald Tribune</u> for ten years, leaving as Assistant Classified Advertising Manager.

A native of New York City, he graduated from Syracuse Univ. with a degree in Business Administration. He currently resides in Chappaqua, New York.

Mr. Auerbacher is active in a number of industry associations and is the current Chairman of the Education Committee of the Magazine Publishers Association.

II
Advertising Sales

CHAPTER 5

Portrait Of The Ideal Ad Salesperson

By

Harry Myers, Senior VP/Magazine Group Publisher
Knapp Communications

Magazine advertising space sales. What in the world is that?

Well, it's simple. But not easy.

It's not neurosurgery. Neither is it one, long, glamorous luncheon.

It can be wonderfully satisfying work because your customers (or, as it seems increasingly common to say, "clients") are quite frequently people of integrity with whom, of course, you have much in common.

But often simultaneously with the great satisfactions come rather heavy doses of frustration.

Basically, when you sell "ad space," you're asking an advertiser or his agency to invest anywhere from a few hundred to several million dollars in the publication you represent. Because it's going to be very difficult for him to measure the effectiveness of that investment, no matter how small or large, your success is heavily contingent on how deeply that customer believes in you and your magazine. Creating that belief among the two to two dozen people who will make the investment decision at each company is your job. Simple. But not easy.

In the chapters that follow, Burt Boersma, a good friend from Meredith Corporation, will consider the day-to-day activities of an ad salesperson (frequently called account managers, these days) working on the consumer side of this business. John Harrison deals with similar concerns on the trade side. And another old friend, Roy Payton, talks about the unique existence of an independent sales representative.

Given all this other editorial detailing functions and responsibilities and duties, I'd like to consider here what you should be like to be successful in this career choice. What set of personal attributes add up to great conquests? What training should you have that will assure your getting hired and achieving excellence? Where do you turn to find out if this sort of endeavor is something you want to do and can see yourself doing well?

CHARACTERISTICS OF THE BEST

Well, Burt would be quick to agree that selling advertising space in magazines amounts to a continuing series of positive impressions on all those who participate in the decision. He and I learned that much -- and a whole lot more -- from the late Karyl Van, one of the true giants of our industry.

Karyl spent most of his years with the Meredith Corp. as Advertising Director of Better Homes & Gardens, then became President of Parents Magazine. While at Parents, he collaborated with John Hahn, who is still there, to write the definitive work on this topic, Guidelines in Selling Magazine Advertising. Unfortunately, this comprehensive book is out of print. But if you really want to know about this business, I hope your library has a copy.

Beyond that, there are some characteristics the best sellers of advertising always seem to have:

*Discipline
*Energy
*Resilience
*Honesty
*Enthusiasm
*Business Savvy
*Competitive Spirit

These seven attributes are, to me, absolutely essential. In addition, some combination of the following characteristics tend to prove most helpful:

*Thick-skinned, determined, tenacious.
*Thoughtful, caring, sensitive.
*Creative talker, writer, listener, researcher.
*Reliable, organized, punctual.
*Memorable, daring, opportunistic.
*Affable, confident, optimistic.
*Telephone prone, shoe-leather user, travel
 endurer.
*Patient and impatient.

And you should love magazines. Or, at the very least, the subject matter your magazine deals with.

HOW TO PREPARE

Now, if some of these attributes seem to contradict others, that's simply because selling advertising space is inherently contradictory. Your customers or clients at every level, and in every business, will tend to have contradictory characteristics. You will have to "read" those contradictions and tailor your selling efforts accordingly. Using the same techniques on each person is not only boring, but usually thoroughly unsuccessful as well.

Furthermore, it scarcely makes a difference what your educational background may be. Some of the very best magazine space sellers have little or no college background. But they're mighty savvy. And some of those with brilliant educational records have failed, mainly because they're able to figure out all the "reasons" not to make a call or a sale.

Some solid business training in advertising and marketing is, however, becoming increasingly necessary, particularly as one seeks to advance in magazine management.

As for getting into advertising sales, that is a trick. And not one that's always easy to accomplish. Mostly it's using those talents we've already discussed -- the ones essential for success in this business -- to sell yourself. It surely helps if you've had some specific selling experience, maybe on your school paper, maybe on your local paper during summer vacations. Best of all is to know or find someone in the business who can point you -- armed, of course, with a first-rate resume and all the confidence you can muster -- in the direction of several other people in the business. The simplest entry point is probably on the staff of a small periodical whose demands for hustle and hard work exceed those for specific experience.

But there are any number of successes in our business who got in cold just by inundating publishers with bright letters that demonstrated desire, smarts and persistence. Most frequently, these people started in the Promotion, Research or Merchandising Departments, those areas which support specific field sales efforts. And (should I really say it?) there are any number of highly successful sellers of space who started as secretaries.

In all, it's very simple. But not easy. If you succeed, however, you're sure to like the life, find it rewarding -- both monetarily and intellectually -- and stimulating.

* * *

Mr. Myers joined Knapp Communications in 1982 as Publisher of Geo. He rose to his present position, overseeing Knapp's current titles (Architectural Digest, Bon Appetit and Home) in 1983. Prior to that, he spent 20 years at Meredith Corp., where he held a variety of promotion and sales jobs, working primarily on Successful Farmer, Better Homes and Gardens and Apartment Life (which he successfully repositioned as <u>Metropolitan Home</u>). He also started and oversaw the development of Meredith Publishing Services, a successful custom publishing organization still in existence. Mr. Myers majored in English & Economics at the Univ. of Colorado and later attended the Univ. of Missouri School of Journalism.

CHAPTER 6

Ad Sales:
A Rewarding Career Opportunity

By

Burt Boersma, VP/Publishing Director
Meredith Corporation

Having been involved in advertising sales -- one way or another -- for 35 years, I can honestly say that I have no regrets, no second thoughts about choosing this career path. It has been challenging, rewarding and one helluva lot of fun! What more can one expect from a job?

There have been disappointments, of course. No salesperson worth emulating has managed to survive without a few setbacks. This goes with the territory. But overcoming adversity, turning negatives into positives, is one of life's greatest feelings of satisfaction and accomplishment. Indeed, if you are looking for an opportunity to challenge your mind, to hustle and be rewarded for it, advertising sales may be the right answer.

Every trade and consumer magazine needs salespeople because no magazine can exist very long today without advertising. For most magazines this is the primary source of income...more significant than the revenue derived from circulation. This means that good salespeople are very visible within the organization -- visible <u>because they are so important in making the magazine a success.</u>

ADVERTISING IS SOLD, NOT BOUGHT

There is an adage in the business that most advertising space is sold, not bought. This simply means that very few magazines sell <u>themselves</u> to prospective buyers. The reason for this is that there are so many good magazines available, and differences between magazines in a given field are often subtle or rather minute. The effective salesperson must know what these differences are and learn how to interpret them properly, so he can persuade buyers that <u>his</u> magazine is the right and proper choice. Therein lies the challenge.

Advertising sales must often be made on several different levels at both the client company and agency. Recommendations to buy (or not to buy) generally originate in the Media Departments of advertising agencies that work for specific clients on a fee or commission basis. The standard agency commission is 15% of media billings. The agency earns this commission or fee by serving as the marketing partner for the client -- recommending strategies, positioning the product or service vis-a-vis competition, writing copy, creating art, producing mechanicals and placing ads. Many people are involved in this somewhat complicated process. And many of them often have a say in where these ads ultimately run.

From an advertising salesperson's point of view, work usually begins in the agency Media Department. These are the people whose business it is to know everything there is to know about magazines -- their strengths and their weaknesses. This is an impossible assignment. No one can <u>possibly</u> know everything about every publication. That's why there is a real need for advertising salespeople. They perform a service for the agency, as well as a vital function for the magazine.

But Media Departments are not the entire answer. Creative people -- artists and writers who are often called Creative Directors -- may influence media decisions. So do the Account Management people -- Account Executives, Supervisors and Directors are the ones who maintain the most direct contact with clients. They are the advertiser's representatives within the agency -- the primary liaison between agency and client and, as such, may have a great deal of influence on the selection of magazines for an advertising campaign or schedule.

This suggests, of course, that the effective salesperson must call on all three departments within the agency -- Media, Creative and Account Services. The frequency and depth of these contacts will depend on the nature of the client, the size of the agency and probably the number of assigned accounts the salesperson is handling. I have always operated on the theory that the more people that are in a position to influence the media choice, the harder I have to work to assure that everyone agrees that <u>my</u> magazine is the logical one for their product's advertising.

But selling the agency is only half the job. The client (advertiser) must also be sold. After all, it's the client's product and the client's money that is being spent.

There are a number of job functions within the client structure that may influence the selection of media. The degree to which this influence is exerted depends on the industry, company size and the people themselves. Large packaged goods companies often operate on a <u>brand</u> <u>manager</u> <u>system</u>, in which case the <u>brand</u> <u>manager</u> is usually your most important client contact.

In other companies, the principle contact may be the <u>advertising</u> <u>manager</u> or <u>media</u> <u>manager</u>. Others with input may include the <u>sales</u> <u>manager</u> and <u>marketing</u> <u>manager</u>. It's up to the salesperson to find out who the key players are at each company and agency assigned to him, in order to maximize his time and effort and, in the process, <u>sell</u> <u>the most advertising.</u>

You must realize that time management is a very important part of this job. No one can do this for you. And in every sales operation I know of, there is a direct correlation between the number of calls and the number of sales (assuming, of course, that you are calling on the right people -- those with the power to make the decision).

The people you meet in this business are first-rate. They are intelligent, personable, hard-working and creative. Because that's what it takes to succeed. I could not begin to count the number of people I have met in 35 years in this business. But I can only think of two people that I did not genuinely like. And today many of my best friends are people in advertising whom I've met in the course of business.

WHAT IT TAKES TO SUCCEED IN AD SALES

Assuming that I've succeeded in stimulating your interest, let me tell you what you need and make a few suggestions about how you might go about getting into this business.

An MBA is not required, but it may help you progress more rapidly than the person without it. A bachelor's degree in Business, Journalism or Liberal Arts will prepare you well enough for an entry-level position. Experience on a school newspaper or yearbook is a definite plus. Any part-time sales experience is an important asset -- especially if you have some documented record of success.

I talk with a lot of college graduates about advertising and publishing. Many are attracted by the so-called "glamour" aspect of the business. It <u>is</u> a glamorous business, but this part of it has been vastly overrated by television and the movies. Few realize the highly competitive nature of ad sales -- the time spent after business hours travelling, writing sales presentations, rehearsing the "sales pitch," entertaining clients. But then, I know of no business where the willingness to work hard pays off better than it does in advertising sales.

What kind of person succeeds in this business? Someone who is natural, polite, friendly, articulate, curious, confident and energetic. Someone who can think fast on his feet, who can muster more reasons to buy than the prospect has reasons not to buy. Indeed, if you fill this bill you have a great future ahead of you -- in magazine publishing or whatever you choose to do.

Do a little homework. Try to decide whether you are better suited to the trade or consumer side of this business. As we'll discuss later in this chapter and those that follow, they are quite different. If you are a technically-oriented person or have an intense interest in a particular field like computers or electronics, you might find more satisfaction working for a publication that deals exclusively with your field of interest. There are hundreds of trade publications, appealing to every conceivable industry, function and professional occupation. And it is often easier for a novice to break into the trade field, where the **immediate** financial rewards are frequently greater (though this may change "down the road").

McGraw-Hill is one of the few companies in this industry that has a structured sales training program. I believe they have 6-8 trainees on their payroll every year. Other large, multiple-magazine publishers hire occasional sales trainees as the need (or opportunity) arises. Meredith is one of these, and this plan has worked fairly well for us over the years.

My advice to anyone who is interested in pursuing advertising sales as a career is to choose your prospective employer carefully -- and then do what it takes to get a foot in the door. Go to a large newsstand and study the various titles on display there. Buy the magazines you find especially interesting and study them. The mastheads will give you the name and address of each Publisher and Advertising Director. Prepare a resume of accomplishments (don't be bashful) and write a sales letter asking for an appointment. You'll be amazed at how effective a good sales letter can be in establishing an interview.

Remember, any entry-level job is "experience." Experience that is translatable to advertising sales. For instance, an entry-level job in the Circulation Department can be valuable experience for the advertising salesperson, who certainly needs to understand how subscription sales are made and fulfilled, how the newsstand distribution system works, etc. This knowledge will help to sell advertising when the opportunity arrives. The same can be said for an entry-level position in Production or Editorial. The effective salesperson needs to know how a magazine is manufactured and how an Editorial Department works and thinks. You can never have too much knowledge about the publishing business. It is all relevant and useful in the sale of advertising.

I spent three years as a Meredith advertising trainee working in the Production, Circulation, Editorial and Advertising Departments before I was turned loose as a salesman. Those were perhaps the most important years of my career, because it was then that I learned the basics of the business. As I look back on that experience, I feel that the time I spent in the Advertising Department as a **sales analyst** and **promotion copywriter** (still potential entry-level positions) was the most valuable in terms of direct application to my career in advertising sales. After all, the job of the copywriter is to sell the magazine via the written word and graphics to the advertising community. Promotion pieces and presentations produced by the copywriter are tools with which the salesperson sells. This is probably closer to the sales bulls-eye than any other non-selling function. Promotion is salesmanship in print.

Another key entry-level position is that of a **merchandising account executive**. This position does not exist everywhere, and the title may vary from place to place, but essentially the job is designed to help the manufacturer promote his advertising to his own channels of distribution. This often involves personal contact with dealers, distributors, wholesalers, franchisees, etc. It's an excellent way to learn the value of advertising, because you start at the place of purchase or point of sale and work backwards.

RAISING A FAMILY OF SALESPEOPLE

I have two sons involved in the sale of advertising space, one on the trade side, one in consumer magazine sales. Both are happy in their jobs because both are earning a good living doing something they truly enjoy. Their career paths four and eight years after graduation from college may offer some clues as to how to get into this stimulating business.

Gregg started in the Promotion Department of a technical trade magazine in Boston. Because it was a relatively small company, he had an opportunity to do a lot of things and learn a great deal in a short time. When opportunity knocked, he was ready. And it happened within a year. It meant a change of employers and a relocation. But it was the right decision -- Gregg is now selling advertising for High-Tech Marketing from its home base in Westport, Connecticut. His rather large territory is the Eastern United States, but his major accounts are concentrated in New York and New England. He travels to trade shows in Chicago, Las Vegas and Los Angeles, which provides an interesting change of scenery from time to time and adds variety to the job.

My older son, Todd, took off on a different tack. He banged on the doors of Tennis magazine for six months, and I believe his sincerity and polite persistence won them over. He started in their Sports Marketing Division, where he ran advertiser-sponsored tennis tournaments and developed merchandising programs for advertisers. Then he was promoted to sell advertising. Apparently, he was quite good at this, because a competitor hired him as Advertising Director at a very handsome salary at the ripe old age of 27. Now, two years later, he is the Advertising Director for Natural History magazine, where he is responsible for promotion and research as well as advertising sales nation-wide. His office is in New York, but his "territory" is the entire country and he travels a great deal. He's single and this aspect of the job appeals to him.

TRADE VS. CONSUMER SALES

What are the basic differences between trade and consumer magazine sales? Trade sales are often more client-oriented and, I believe, less complicated. The magazines are more obvious. Turn a few pages, read an article or two and you'll have a pretty good idea who the trade magazine is edited for. This may be a prejudiced point of view from one who has spent his whole career in consumer magazine sales, but I feel it's fairly accurate. The sale of consumer magazines requires a great deal more sophistication in the use of syndicated research, demographics and readership data. There is a myriad of material that must be understood before it is used. Often it must be understood just so it can be refuted, as the sale of magazine space can be (as I've said before) a very competitive business. However, I don't mean this in a negative sense. <u>The competition is the challenge! And the challenge is stimulation</u>. Rewards are measurable in terms of increased commissions.

It may seem rather obvious, but I should point out that "pages" are the measurement of success. The "evidence" is printed every month (or every week). And it's there for all to behold. Your competitors, your peers, your bosses. It is irrefutable evidence of your success. If you like to be measured -- and measured accurately -- this is the place for you!

One of the very significant side benefits of consumer advertising sales is the opportunity to learn a lot about many kinds of businesses. In selling a home service magazine like <u>Metropolitan Home</u> or <u>Better Homes and Gardens</u>, for instance, you call on manufacturers of furniture, appliances, automobiles, building products, food products and many others. Because you need to know something about their business in order to sell them advertising, you ask questions, study their markets and visit retail stores ...and you learn. You become a marketing generalist.

In my opinion, the psychic rewards are well worth the effort and the financial opportunities are certainly above average. The starting salary for most advertising sales trainees is in the $18,000 - $20,000 range. A salesperson with three to five years experience can expect to earn between $30,000 and $40,000. Experienced salespeople, with a proven track record, can make over $50,000 at a relatively young age. Advertising is a young person's business. And the opportunities for women are every bit as good as they are for men. Some say they're even better.

I may speak of ad sales as the end of the rainbow, but of course it isn't. While many have made a satisfying career out of selling advertising, others have climbed the ladder in publishing mangement. The typical progression on the consumer side often moves in this fashion: from <u>advertising sales representative</u> or <u>account manager</u> to <u>branch office manager</u> (usually retaining specific account assignments), to <u>regional manager</u> or <u>advertising sales manager</u> and then <u>Advertising Director</u>. Successful Advertising Directors often become <u>Publishers</u>. Some go beyond that and become <u>Group Publishers</u> or <u>Publishing Directors</u>, <u>General Managers</u> and <u>Presidents</u>. No two companies have the same titles or structure. Some Publishers have only advertising responsibilities. Others oversee circulation and/or production. Some are responsible for all business functions. A few have editorial responsibilities.

But regardless of their specific job descriptions, they all

seem to have two things in common: They enjoy what they're doing,
and they are not starving. This makes it a worthwhile pursuit.

* * *

In addition to his responsibilities as Vice President and
Publishing Director for Meredith, Mr. Boersma is also President
of Sail Publications, Inc., a wholly owned subsidiary of Meredith
Corp. In his current position, he is responsible for magazine
acquisitions, the management of <u>Metropolitan Home</u> magazine, SAIL
magazine and is liaison for <u>Better Homes and Gardens</u> magazine,
Australia.

He joined Meredith in 1950 as a sales analyst and, during
the next eleven years, held positions as copy chief, sales representative and manager of the <u>Better Homes and Gardens</u> advertising
sales office in Chicago.

He left Meredith in 1961 to join <u>Reader's Digest</u>. He became
manager of their Philadelphia office in 1964, associate New York
manager in 1969 and New York manager in 1971. In 1974, he was
named Vice President and Advertising Director, a position he held
until rejoining Meredith in 1977 as Director of Magazine Development. He was promoted to his current positions in 1982.

Mr. Boersma is a 1950 graduate of the Univ. of Minnesota,
where he earned a BA in journalism. He is a resident of Westport,
CT, and works out of Meredith's New York office.

CHAPTER 7

Selling Ad Space In Trade Publications

By

John Harrison, Associate Publisher/Advertising Director
The American Journal of Nursing

Many students are familiar with consumer publications like TV Guide, Seventeen, Time and Newsweek. Few, I would guess, are as familiar with the very specialized world of trade publishing.

A trade magazine reaches a group of people in a specific industry or occupation with editorial information that pertains to their jobs. The magazines my company publishes, for example, are exclusively for nurses. Trade magazines are concerned with providing their professional readers with the necessary facts and figures they need to know about their specific industry, its companies and people, new products, trends, etc. For the most part, therefore, all of the editorial content is, in some way, related to helping the readers do their jobs better. While consumer magazines may be of a specific type (travel, self-help, fashion, etc.) and/or attempt to reach a certain audience (women 18-45, men 21-45, etc.), they have a much broader range of topics they can cover. They're not nearly as confined within editorial boundaries as the typical trade magazine. The differences in the circulation - who reads the magazine - and the editorial - what they are given to read - lead to some key differences in the way each magazine is sold.

TRADE VS. CONSUMER MAGAZINE SELLING

When you are selling a trade magazine, you get involved with the industry it serves. You get to know the trends, characteristics and people that make up that industry. You attend its trade shows, seminars and conventions.

Sales calls will be made at multiple levels at both companies and their advertising agencies. You will often act as a "market consultant" for the people you call on. After all, you are (or should be) an industry expert and are thus in a position to give your clients industry-related information that will help them do their jobs more effectively. Media buyers at large, diverse agencies will especially look to you for such particular information. Since they generally work on a number of accounts in completely different industries, they need the help of the many trade advertising sales representatives to stay abreast of the various industries in which their client companies operate.

The advertising sales representative (whom I'm going to refer to from now on as either a "salesperson" or "space rep") for a consumer publication will also call on various companies in his sales territory, but will generally spend the most time with their advertising agencies, especially the media buyers. The consumer salesperson sells the quality of his publication, a sell that is related, in one way or another, to numbers. Media buyers want to know total circulation of the magazine, the average household income of the readers, their median age and a lot more. All numbers. These numbers are then often plugged into a computer. The publications with the "best numbers" are then put on the "Buy List."

Numbers are important in the trade market, too, but industry circulation coverage, editorial quality and industry leadership are more important factors.

Both trade and consumer space reps entertain clients over a breakfast, lunch, dinner, cocktail or ice cream soda. But I think consumer publications generally place a heavier emphasis on entertaining. A trade space rep doesn't always need to entertain; often, he can get a buyer very interested in his publication just by announcing that he has some new and interesting industry data which will be of great interest to the client.

Generally, the big glamorous luncheons, dinners, parties and trips are given by the consumer publications. If you like to entertain, you'll like most consumer publishing companies. If you enjoy an occasional lunch or dinner, but prefer to become involved in the nuts-and-bolts of a single industry, the trade route might be right for you.

THE ROLE OF THE ADVERTISING SALES REPRESENTATIVE

The trade space rep has two sales jobs ahead of him. First, he has to convince his sales prospects that trade advertising, in general, should be a key part of their marketing plans. Second, he has to convince them that the particular publication he represents will effectively reach that company's own list of prospective buyers. In other words, the space rep must convince the buyer/decision maker of **the benefits the buyer would accrue as a result of advertising in that particular magazine**. Reaching that goal -- convincing the buyer to advertise -- is generally achieved as a result of formal presentations and appropriate follow up via letters and phone calls.

The position can be mentally, emotionally and monetarily very rewarding. It requires organization, preparation and a knowledge of the selling process. Below are listed the typical functions of an advertising sales representative. (While I am writing strictly from a background in trade magazine publishing, I think you'll find the consumer space rep needs to accomplish the same tasks):

1. Develop and maintain a list of active accounts and prospects.
2. Plan, create and develop presentations.
3. Make formal presentations to clients.
4. Study and understand the market the publication reaches.
5. Know fully all reasons why your magazine is read and subscribed to.
6. Be fully acquainted with all statistical information regarding the market, your magazine and the competition.
7. Understand the position of your magazine vis-a-vis the competition.
8. Make appointments, answer questions, deal with problems and, in general, assist your accounts.
9. Develop follow-up letters and reports to your clients.
10. Attend industry functions such as trade shows, seminars and conventions.
11. Understand the psychology of selling.
12. Know how to sell and how to close a sale.

WHAT TYPE OF TRAINING CAN YOU EXPECT?

Formal classroom training is not common among trade publishers. Most often, the training is a combination of informal seminars and "on-the-job" training -- learning from your sales manager. The kind and extent of the training available will often vary according to the size of the publishing organization:

1. Large Organizations (25+ publications)

They will sometimes have a formal or semi-formal program. In this program, you will learn (from both an instructor and other experienced sales reps) how to sell ad space. Classroom instruction may be coupled with role-playing sessions and visits to accounts with accomplished representatives.

Some of the larger publishers in our business will start a trainee with a combination of a formal training program and telemarketing. This gives the trainee an education in ad sales, as well as an immediate opportunity to use the techniques and skills on a telephone sales call. More publishers are finding telemarketing to be a very effective and efficient adjunct to their outside ad sales teams.

2. Medium-Sized Organizations (10-25 publications)

Such firms have fewer resources generally and hire fewer new salespeople, so the need for formalized programs is not as great.

Consequently, formal classroom training programs are an exception. Yet these firms will typically have their top sales managers and salespeople lead training sessions for both existing salespeople and trainees. Again, placing trainees in the telemarketing program is often a good starting point for the trainee and a positive step for the company.

3. Small Organizations (less than 10 publications)

Generally, they don't have any kind of formalized programs. Training is often left up to the Publisher and/or sales manager of each publication. Occasional training sessions may be held for the entire sales staff.

No matter what the size of the organization, a great deal of your initial training will come from the Publisher and sales manager of the publication you're selling. If they truly know publishing, and how to sell space, the knowledge you gain from them will prove invaluable. It can put you on the "road to success."

Excellent training is also available outside the trade magazine industry. Many major newspapers and the Reuben H. Donnelley Organization (a major seller of advertising space in the Yellow Pages) have excellent training programs. Some of the major consumer magazine publishers offer structured training programs.

THE ADVERTISING SALES CAREER PATH

As we've discussed, you begin as a trainee. Depending on the organization you join, this could mean purely "on-the-job" training or some classroom training as well.

Once you are adequately trained, you will be given a sales territory or list of accounts to cover. You are now a full-time advertising sales representative (a "space salesperson") and selling these accounts "space" in your publication is your job. Your territory may be geographical (7 mid-Atlantic states, New England, the mid-West, etc.) or categorical (all liquor or tire or automobile manufacturers). The latter set-up is generally more common on newspapers and consumer magazines. Most trade books use geographical territories.

If you are successful as a salesperson, you may be considered a candidate for advertising sales management. Below are some of the factors that the top management of the company will take into account regarding your potential promotion:

1. Your sales record
2. Your knowledge of the market, magazine and the competition
3. Creativity -- Have you developed "sales winner" ideas useful to the rest of the staff?
4. The ability to get along with your accounts & the rest of your magazine's staff
5. Intelligence and common sense
6. Appearance

7. Work habits
8. Desire

The following would be a typical progression for a talented advertising salesperson who scored well on the above list and continued to progress:

Regional Advertising Manager:

Would maintain a sales territory and have the responsibility for the training, coaching and development of one or more salespeople within the region. Would have input into the direction of the magazine's circulation and promotion pieces.

National Sales Manager (or Ad Sales Mgr., Advertising Director):

May or may not maintain a sales territory, depending on the philosophy, needs and resources of the publishing company.

Would be very involved in the training, coaching and development of the entire advertising sales staff. This would be top priority. Strong input into the salaries of the staff, direction of circulation, market research and development of the promotional materials. Also would give input into what editorial material would prove of interest to readers but also help attract new advertisers.

Would develop whatever marketing services the publication offers advertisers and would generally be the one who approved the use of subscriber names for mailing list purposes.

Associate Publisher:

Generally does all of the same functions as the National Sales Manager, but has shown an ability to get involved with the industry. This title is often conferred in recognition of the professionalism and overall excellence of the individual (rather than to differentiate specific job functions). Has been tapped as the successor (if he lives up to expectations) of the present Publisher.

Publisher:

Generally does not maintain a sales territory, but may within certain organizations. His chief role is to understand the industry, its direction and define how his publication can best serve that industry.

The Publisher directs the circulation of the publication, insuring that the magazine is going after all groups that would find the publication of interest. He coordinates upcoming editorial features and makes sure the advertising staff understands how best to sell them to increase ad space.

Directs all research and has the final say on all promotional pieces. Creates the magazine's overall budget and approves salaries for all staff members working on the publication.

Insures that the direction the Advertising Sales Manager has taken is correct. Is the "third party" utilized when there is a problem between a staff member and his immediate supervisor. Serves as an industry figure -- gets very involved in the workings of the industry and will often serve on a variety of committees or even as an elected official of various industry trade associations. Entertains top management of companies and agencies and often speaks at major industry functions.

Group Publisher:

Generally in charge of one publication with input into the operation of the others within his group. There are a number of firms, however, where the Group Publisher does not direct any single publication but is solely responsible for overseeing the complete operations of all the publications of his group.

The Group Publisher must thoroughly understand the market of each publication and how each of them serves that market. He makes sure that each of the Publishers who report to him are "on target" with the publication's direction, budget and supervision of the staff.

Vice President Sales:

This person is very involved with the bottom line (the profit and loss) of each of the company's publications. The Vice President makes sure that each publication has the right mixture of staff to allow it to run effectively, yet efficiently.

He reviews the progression of each publication and is the corporate troubleshooter -- looking for trouble spots, prepared to fix them. Assists in the revival of troubled publications and makes sure all learn of the "hows and whys" of the successful publications.

Is responsible for the national sales meetings and oversees individual publication meetings. Also, generally has the last word on all sales staff hiring and firings.

President:

Directs and guides the entire company. All Division heads (Vice Presidents) -- advertising, editorial, promotion, production, research, etc. -- report to him. It is the President's responsibility to make sure that the firm is profitable and smoothly run.

The above, of course, is a generalized outline of a successful career path in trade publishing. Companies differ and, as a result, the paths and duties mentioned above can vary greatly. How long do such progressions take? That's virtually impossible to answer, as the period of time spent in any one position can vary enormously according to your own talents and abilities, the industry, others on the staff and the needs and philosophy of the company you work for.

PREPARING FOR A CAREER IN SPACE SALES

Ideally, someone looking to break into space sales should have a college degree. The preferred majors would be Marketing, Advertising, Management or Publishing. There are a few colleges that now offer a major in Advertising Space Sales specifically. An MBA may be helpful, but is not necessary,. Experience, knowledge and general intelligence are the most important factors in getting a first job and advancing in space sales as a career. Working in the Advertising Sales Department of your college newspaper or yearbook is probably most helpful.

Many publishers are looking for experienced salespeople. They don't want to do a lot of training and would rather pay a little more money in order to get someone who is already trained and a proven success. So getting experience somewhere else is often a way to "get in the back door." We've already mentioned the training programs available at many newspapers and other "space sales" companies like Donnelley. Another good tactic is to first get a job buying media at an advertising agency and then moving over to one of the magazines with whom you've worked.

Once you have a year or more experience at such a firm, you can begin investigating openings in trade publishing.

Openings can be found in the classified section of any major city newspaper, Advertising Age, Adweek and, of course, in later chapters of this Career Directory.

You should also become familiar with Standard Rate and Data (SRDS). Their various volumes list virtually every magazine publisher in the U.S., both trade and consumer, and include listings of key management personnel at each publication. These books can be an excellent resource in your investigation of potential employers and publications as well as general markets you may wish to consider. They can be found in most major public and university libraries.

WHAT I LOOK FOR WHEN I HIRE SALESPEOPLE

Presuming someone with no specific experience in ad sales comes to me looking for a job, there are some basic factors I consider when I interview them. If the candidate is right out of school and has, therefore, little or no actual job experience, I evaluate:

1. Education
2. Pattern of success - Is his academic record superior? Is he involved in athletics or other extra-curricular activities?
3. Leadership - Does his life show leadership qualities, a willingness to both give and get involved? Has he held office in student government, a club or fraternity?
4. Desire to achieve and succeed
5. A high level of energy
6. Willingness to travel and work long hours, if necessary
7. Appearance, comeliness and presence

If the candidate is not a recent graduate, but is attempting to get into the field on the basis of some related (or even unrelated) work experience, I would tend to evaluate the same seven categories, but add:

1. Record of success with past employer(s)
2. Enjoyment of selling
3. Ability to handle rejection
4. Management potential

SOME PERSONAL EXPERIENCES AND THOUGHTS

My career in advertising space sales began with a major New York newspaper, one with a good training program.

I didn't particularly care for newspaper ad sales and considered leaving the profession, but decided to give ad sales itself another try. I landed a job with a small trade publishing company. My training came mainly from the Publisher, who also acted as the national sales manager. It was here that I discovered how fulfilling and rewarding the ad sales profession could be.

From this base, I took a job selling advertising with a much larger trade publishing firm.. I chose this particular company because of the tremendous growth they had shown during the previous fifteen years. My desire was to get into publishing management and I figured a company with a strong growth pattern offered me the best opportunity.

I was right. I got a job selling with this company, worked very hard demonstrating my abilities and two years later was named Sales Manager of one of their publications. After getting more deeply involved with the industry, I was named Co-Publisher (along with the Editor-in-Chief) of that magazine. I was later promoted again to Sales Training Manager for the company's ad sales staff, including all the reps and sales managers.

In May, 1983, I joined the American Journal of Nursing Company as the Director of Ad Sales and Associate Publisher of its seven publications. I find my current job to be very stimulating, fulfilling and rewarding. Each day is different and brings new problems, questions, frustrations, opportunities, joys and rewards. A career in trade advertising space sales, at whatever level, will bring you each of these elements in varying degrees.

Sales for a trade publisher can be very mentally and monetarily rewarding. Along with these rewards go years of learning, training, hard work and frustration.

Happily, I've noticed lately that many more people of both sexes seem to be interested in pursuing careers in trade sales. When I began my career, there were few women in space sales. Now there are many in the industry at both the sales and managerial levels. **There are definitely increasing opportunities for women who want to get into this business.**

Of course, there are also many more publications around than when I began my own career. The competition for jobs and advancement is, therefore, very stiff. But because of the consistent tremendous growth of the trade publishing industry, there will always be jobs for bright, talented and ambitious people.

* * *

In his current position, Mr. Harrison is responsible for developing the sales and marketing strategies for seven publications. This includes overall supervision of the sales, promotion and training functions for all of the publications' staffs.

Mr. Harrison spent seven years at Gralla Publications, rising from advertising sales representative to Associate Marketing Director for the company and Co-Publisher of Health Care Systems. He spent four years at Geyer-McAllister Publications and received his original sales training at the New York Daily News.

He is a graduate of Nichols College and is completing his MBA at Adelphi University.

CHAPTER 8

The Life And Times
Of Independent Sales Reps

By

Roy Payton, President
Payton & Associates

Most academic institutions do not offer a curriculum in salesmanship. They do not teach the techniques of selling or even offer an overview of the jobs available to men and women who want careers in sales. So, I'll attempt to show you an area in sales where you may be able to make a lot of money and, at the same time, enjoy your job.

Selling is important and <u>everybody</u> does it. Every four years, the most powerful man in the world -- the President of the United States -- has to go across the country explaining the importance of his ideas and the effectiveness of his Administration to the American people. He is selling. He is asking you to renew his contract for another four years because he believes (and is trying to convince <u>you</u>) that keeping him in office will bring you the most benefits.

Salesmen are the first ones to bring innovations into the business community. Presidents of large corporations have lots of case histories about their failures to invest in extraordinary products or services, because no one could sell the concept to upper management and make them include it in their corporate planning.

Selling is what advertising is all about. There are lots of skills to learn, things to do and tools you may use, but I think all of them have been covered in detail in preceding chapters. So instead of talking more about ad sales in general, I'd like to talk very specifically about the difference between selling advertising for a single company or magazine -- where you're an employee -- and becoming an independent sales representative -- where you might sell many different publications for a variety of different publishers and, in my opinion most important, be your own boss.

If advertisers could afford to personally sell every sales prospect themselves, they would highball their marketing train onto that track. They can't, so they have to come up with creative approaches that are really attempts to replace personal selling. They determine who these prospects are, create the advertising to reach them and then turn over the sales effort to a team. That's the battlefield of the space rep, who helps to educate the advertiser about the particular characteristics of his publication, one that he believes can effectively reach that target audience.

In other words, if you wish to enter the advertising profession, you must want to be a salesperson.

It's not so bad. You may make a lot of money. You may represent influential publications. You may even (and it happens) have the thrill of seeing one of your concepts influence the habits of millions of Americans. But, first and foremost, you are still a salesperson and have to accept that "title."

If words such as "hustling", "pushing", "door-knocking" or "hammering" -- slang words endemic to the sales profession -- are acceptable to your sensibilities, you'll find some of the nicest people you could ever meet willing to teach you advertising space sales.

IN-HOUSE SALESPEOPLE VS. INDEPENDENT REPS

Somebody has to sell advertising for "Magazine A." And its Publisher has a choice. He can hire salespeople to work for him as full-time employees or he can contract with outside sales firms to be responsible for his sales. He can even use a combination of the two, some employees and a few independent reps.

On what basis does a Publisher decide to hire an outside rep firm, rather than employees? There are three good reasons.

First, he may need an advertising salesperson with a very specialized knowledge of particular accounts. Such a salesperson may be an authority on direct response or mail order advertising, for example. Since the Publisher wants his own staff to be "generalists," he has to go outside the company to find the specialists.

Second, a geographical area may have a limited number of advertisers that cannot support all the expenses of a branch office. So hiring an independent rep or rep firm may be the only way to stay under budget and still cover that territory.

Third, the total revenue generated by the magazine might not be great enough to support the expenses of a professional sales division at all, in which case independent reps do all the selling. This is frequently the case with brand new (and often under-captilalized) publications.

An independent sales rep generally needs to work for a number of publications, because he only gets paid for the space he

<u>sells</u>. He can often afford to take on even a very small publica-
tion with a limited number of advertising prospects, combining
income from that magazine with revenues from the others he represents. The single title publisher doesn't <u>have</u> any other source
of income.

Corporate salespeople are usually paid a salary, though some
bonus or commission arrangements may be included for sales incentives. If you work directly for a magazine, all of your expenses
will be paid by the publishing company.

If you are an independent rep, your compensation will depend
upon the publication and the assignments. Generally there is a
commission arrangement based upon the revenue potential of the
magazine. Terms may or may not include guarantees and/or retainers.

While a corporate salesperson will for the most part work
only for one magazine, the independent may -- and will probably
have to -- have several publications.

You'll find independent rep firms listed in <u>SRDS</u>. They are
as varied in the services they offer as the many books they
represent. (I know they're magazines, but we generally refer to
them as <u>books</u>.) Some specialize only in trade books, others have
combinations of consumer and trade books. Some work within
regions, while others have international offices.

WHAT AN INDEPENDENT REP DOES

Unless you have a relative that owns a huge publishing operation using independent reps and who thinks that you are the
finest salesperson in five generations of the family...do not
attempt to open your own independent firm.

Independent reps are already successful salespeople

Independent reps are usually very successful sales people
with impressive experience in the publishing business. They are
so confident of their abilities that they've laid their sales
skills on the line to create that most American of all endeavors:
their own business.

An independent rep has to be able to compete -- while repre-
senting any number of magazines -- against salespeople who have
only one book to sell. Since the operation is usually modest in
comparison to the size and assets of many publishing companies,
he is seeking the <u>immediate</u> sale. He doesn't have a choice -- he
has to cover his sales (especially travel) expenses. He often
can't afford to look for the "long range sale," an effort a large
publishing company may be able to underwrite for its sales staff.

That's why most independent representatives will not represent "new" magazines without retainers. They can't afford to
invest in new ventures that may not succeed and which, even if

they do, will have the cash-flow problems associated with any new business.

Identifying with the magazine

In the eyes of the advertiser and his agency, the independent rep is indeed the salesman or woman for the magazine. Particulars are defined in the legal agreement with the company, but the rep will usually be supplied with the magazine's stationery, calling cards, reporting forms and promotional pieces. But, and it's the big but, he has to assume all of the direct selling costs himself.

Corporate sales staffs have easy access to, and frequent discussions with, the key people in many other departments -- circulation, promotion, editorial, etc. The independent rep generally works with one or two people at each publication.

If there is one truly characteristic difference between any corporate salesperson and any independent rep, it's probably regarding career paths. The corporate salesman is working to get promoted, eventually, he hopes, to Publisher, getting higher salaries along the way. The independent **owns his own business** -- he's attempting to gain maximum profits from each of the magazines he represents.

Day-to-day operations

While there are marked differences in organization between the two sales forces, they both follow about the same operating procedures. Many of the day-to-day functions have been covered extensively in previous chapters, but let me add my own two cents anyway.

No sales job anywhere is 9-to-5. You often have to devise creative approaches and the "ideas" don't disappear from your thoughts when the sun sinks in the Western skies. And, because you're responsible for so much money -- thousands, even millions of dollars in a single publication -- you have to carefully prepare for future sales calls in between your current ones. (An independent, though, has a number of "masters", so his preparation work is often more detailed because he has to call upon _more_ advertisers in completely _unrelated_ fields with _different_ marketing objectives.)

While we try to set up "quotas" as to the number of sales calls we'll make each week, it never seems to work any better than asking a traffic cop to meet a weekly ticket-writing quota. It's simply not easy to get all the advertiser and agency people you need to see -- especially the key agency media people -- to adhere to your cleverly worked-out schedule. While they are interested in your ideas and probably require your current information, their time is limited. They make plans...buy for the plans...supervise the implementation of the plans. And, somehow, still interview advertising sales people.

I attempt to make personal calls when I have to -- those significant meetings where I want to present data that can't (or

shouldn't) be presented in a letter or over the phone. I find
that limiting my calls to those times when I have some new information to offer, rather than just stopping by to "chat," makes
buyers look forward to seeing me.

I try to set aside two days of every week for calling to
make appointments...correspondence...research. If you want to see
anybody important in any major cities, you must have an
appointment. Setting up all these necessary appointments is quite
time-consuming, but a major and necessary chore any salesman
better get used to. You'll learn fast that the most important
expediter in American business is the secretary. She can become
your greatest ally in helping you conserve time. (Or your worst
enemy, effectively shielding her boss from your plaintive cries).

Since independent reps, for the most part, can't utilize a
magazine's Sales Manager or Advertising Director to answer
immediate questions, we try to organize our operations in such a
way so that at least _we_ are always available to answer advertiser
inquiries, no matter where we are. To get the most out of our
trips, all of us work towards "cluster" calling -- trying to see
as many people at each agency or company whenever we are at that
location. We might not get back there for weeks or even months.

Here is another point. Few people can make a recommendation.
A lot of people can kill it. In scheduling our sales time, we try
to reach the decision makers when they are in the planning process. And you can't ignore the others who, while not supposedly
decision-makers, can influence the schedule -- negatively. I use
a lot of methods -- like offering them free subscriptions to my
publications -- to leave a positive impression in their minds.

Reporting, reporting and more reporting

Few Publishers are completely satisfied with their reporting
systems but every "contact", whether in person or by telephone,
should be reported. You will learn to record objections or appro-
vals and note the immediate and long-term actions you need to
take as a result of the call. Your reports should be brief, current and specific. If you are making intelligent calls, the
reports will be easy to write.

Depending on the frequency of publishing -- weekly, monthly,
etc. -- you'll be periodically required to forecast ad space you
expect to sell for each publication. This helps the Publisher
determine the amount of paper that has to be purchased, the
amount of editorial to be written and many other things. Fore-
casting systems differ, but you will usually need to record each
firm's probable and possible ad insertions, issue-by-issue,
magazine-by-magazine.

SELLING A MAGAZINE'S EDITORIAL CONTENT

Any magazine, new or old, has to have a strong editorial
platform to exist. No one reads a magazine unless they are interested in the contents. No advertiser has any interest in appear-

ing in a publication that isn't read by the subscribers. In fact, a successful publication continuously evolves its editorial package, always attempting to reflect the changing tastes and needs of its subscribers (audience). Farm publications have changed, for example, because farming practices have changed. Men's magazines are now changing -- both in terms of editorial content and the audience that wants to read (or look at) them. "Underground" publications have become "respectable."

The editorial content of your magazines is most important to your sales. You'll read each issue from cover to cover and in this manner began to learn how the reader reacts to each book's particular editorial mission. You will do the same thing for every publication serving the same marketplaces as your magazines.

Good salesmen or saleswomen in this business become authorities concerning the editorial content of the books they represent and can discuss everything from the latest hair styles to plastic pipes and interest rate predictions.

SELLING CIRCULATION

But, regardless of what an editor may think of the "need" for a magazine...the magazine must produce revenue to exist.

Publishing revenues are derived from two sources: circulation and advertising. Today, the costs of printing and distributing a magazine are so high that circulation revenues alone are not great enough to insure the life of the book. Therefore, advertising revenue is the single most important financial factor in publishing.

A number of trade publications discovered some years ago that the cost of acquiring circulation in a specific professional area was so great that it was more profitable to circulate the magazines free of charge. Your doctor, for example, does not pay for most of his professsional magazines. In these cases, advertising revenue is the only revenue generated by the magazine.

Advertisers want guarantees that the Publisher delivered the number of copies that he promised to deliver, regardless of how he obtained the subscribers (or, for that matter, whether they're even paying for the magazine).

Most consumer magazines, which are generally paid for by their subscribers (or via newsstand sales) are audited by the Audit Bureau of Circulations. Twice a year, the Bureau issues an ABC Statement for each consumer magazine, detailing the geographical area where the subscribers and newsstand buyers are located, how much they paid for the publication by term of subscription, etc.

Trade publications use a Business Publications Audit (BPA), which counts both paid and non-paid circulation and breaks out the magazine's readers by job title and function.

In other cases, a Publisher may elect to offer his own sworn statement as to how many issues he has distributed and sold. This is often used for those annuals published once a year and sold primarily on newsstands.

An effective advertising salesperson will learn to "read" audit statements and to share the facts with his accounts. For instance, some magazines will guarantee the sale of a certain number of copies of each issue, but the audit statement will disclose that they failed to meet this "rate base". This is a very serious problem, as it may entail offering rebates to the advertisers. It's only one such problem any good salesperson has to know about and be ready to handle.

HOW TO GET STARTED

By now, you should have a good, basic insight into advertising sales. And you still want to sell space? Ok, so how can you "come aboard?"

You should have some knowledge of the advertising profession. You don't want to become lost in the "jargon" during an interview.

Your courses are important in that they reflect your interests and, therefore, may point you in the direction of a particular kind of book. Science graduates, for example, are always needed on technical and professional publications.

Liberal Arts degrees are indicative of a splendid "generalist" viewpoint, as well as a degree of excellence in communication. You might be perfect for some of the more general audience consumer books.

Any work experience -- part-time or full-time -- and any work involving the public is important, as it will verify your ability to work well with people.

Be prepared to write dozens of cover letters, each one directed to a particular publication, telling them how your skills will make them money. This is, remember, the print business. Make sure your sentences are properly composed and that the words and names are spelled correctly. You may want to write to two or three people at the same publication. You may want to take a non-sales job until an opening appears in sales. Always, _always_, _always_ ask for a personal interview.

Although there are insensitive (and generally ineffective) people within publishing who will not answer such letters, the majority will reply. I would recommend that you personally call every one who replies and thank them for their consideration and ask if they know of another opportunity. If the person is unavailable, talk to the secretary who, trust me, can be most helpful.

Working for a publishing company vs. an independent rep firm

In order to determine whether or not you want to work for an independent firm or directly for a publishing company, the consideration is where you want to be in three or four years. Do you want to stay in a small operation immersed in one function or are you looking towards the moment when you will be publisher of a magazine? Are you goal-oriented towards supervising an array of projects or more comfortable concentrating on one objective?

Although you may not stay within the same job for more than two or three years, you must consider the possibility that this entry-level job might indeed become your life-long profession.

Most corporate sales people move about from publication to publication, while independent reps remain independent reps, frequently tied to a particular part of the country. But, of course, independent reps may represent a large variety of magazines over the years, so it's not easy getting bored with the subject matter of the magazines you rep.

While independent reps can earn very impressive dollars, they can't -- unlike the corporate sales people -- guarantee any level of income year after year. Heck, they don't get paid at all until they actually sell the space!

WHAT I LOOK FOR IN A REP

What type of person would I hire for an entry-level position? First, I look for enthusiasm, both as a basic personality trait, but also for the subject(s) the magazine tends to cover. The theory is that if the enthusiasm is strong enough, it will overcome the rejection that every salesperson encounters. Second, experience of some kind with the "public". Third, an ability to communicate. And, fourth, a basic understanding of the profession.

While the employment situation in ad sales is always competitive, the doors are always open for new people to enter the profession. Your job hunt is similar to selling space -- you have to find the spot that matches your interests, "hustle" appointments and "hammer" home your abilities to make a great deal of money for the publisher. Any interview requires "selling yourself" to the company. The requirements are a little stiffer when you're trying to sell yourself into a sales job!

But then, the rewards can be, too.

* * *

After more than twenty years of sales and sales management experience on a number of magazines, including Better Homes and Gardens, Cuisine, Family Weekly and House Beautiful, among others, and a short stint as the Account Supervisor for Datsun at Parker Advertising, Mr. Payton founded his own independent sales firm. He currently represents a number of consumer and trade titles and frequently wonders how he manages to do it all himself. He is a graduate of the University of Missouri School of Journalism and learned about selling space (along with two of our other Advertising Sales experts, Harry Myers and Burt Boersma) at Meredith Corporation.

III
Art & Design

CHAPTER 9

The Glamorous World Of Graphic Design

By

Eileen Hedy Schultz, Creative Director/Advertising & Sales Promotion
Good Housekeeping

The career of a Graphic Designer is complex and yet quite simple in structure, but it need never be dull. Every day is a new challenge and for any creative person, it's a glorious profession to enter.

I use this title of Graphic Designer rather than Art Director, Creative Director or whatever, because it's a less limiting career path. If you become a good graphic designer, you can go in any direction that you wish, working for art studios, agencies, publishers, or in more specialized areas such as book design, record album cover design, poster design, annual report design, corporate design, promotion, etc.

Talent in graphic design is, of course, desirable, but your yearning to succeed, your perseverance and your willingness to work incredibly hard -- certainly in your early years and perhaps all your working life -- are even more important. The pace, I've found, is really up to you.

Luck -- being at the right place at the right time -- has a lot to do with it. And self-confidence is probably a trait common to most successful Art Directors.

GET THE RIGHT EDUCATIONAL PREPARATION

I've been in "education" for as long as I can remember. That means that I've learned my craft the hard way, working "up through the ranks," paying my dues. It didn't come easily, but I have learned from years of experience (looking for jobs, hiring people for jobs, talking with others in the profession) what seem to be the accepted requirements for entering this field and what you need to know when you face that first job as a graphic designer.   I'll try to impart that information to you as best I can in this chapter.

There aren't any actual rules governing your educational preparation, but I do suggest that you get the most solid education that you can in the arts. Meaning: Experiment in and with everything, and learn as much as you can to prepare yourself for everyday work. This includes a knowledge of typography, hand lettering, production, mechanicals, magic marker rendering, the basics of photography, etc., as well as overall design skills.

<u>No, a college degree is not necessary</u>. College may well be the happiest time in your lives -- making new friends, having new experiences -- and it undoubtedly opens your mind to many new ideas you might never otherwise experience. You may need it if you wish to go into education one day, but if you have earned your fame, even then it won't be necessary. So it really isn't mandatory in our profession.

What <u>is</u> necessary is that you be able to perform on the job -- not only conceptually, but with "hands on" studio skills. The best way to convince a potential employer that you will be able to perform up to professional standards is to put together a portfolio of your artwork that's as good as you can make it. It's all you have to prove yourself in the beginning. You should also have an intelligent resume that will tell prospective employers what they really want to know.

THE KIND OF RESUME I LIKE TO SEE

Your resume should be set up on one page so an employer can see your qualifications at a glance. It should be concise; avoid long, flowery phrases such as "It is my goal to have a position that will be challenging, career-oriented and consistent with my training." What does that mean? No one has the time to decipher it.

What you <u>should</u> say is: "Career Objective: Graphic Designer." (<u>Not</u> mechanical artist or paste-up, unless that's all you want to do. Even if you think your skills don't add up to the lofty title, you might get lucky and get a break as a designer anyway, so why lessen your chances by limiting your objective right from the start?)

Many of us still do our own mechanicals, so you should know how. And you'll be expected to do them on the job somewhere, sometime, but I do advise you to stay away from limiting yourself on your resume, especially at the beginning of your career. Why? Because you'll possibly be stuck in a job one day and not have any idea what else is out there. Instead, my advice is to keep moving in the industry until you've learned what you can -- unless, of course, you're quite happy where you are. Then by all means stay and work your way up (assuming that you have an opportunity to do so).

After "Career Objective" comes "Education." List your art school and any special, art-related studies. List your high school only if it was art-related, (e.g. The High School of Art and Design).

The next listing should be "Employment" -- in the art field only. If you have had no art-related jobs, then list whatever freelance work you've done. Anything in art at all? List the firm and the specific work you did there.

Next, list "Honors and Awards," preferably in art, but perhaps scholastic as well.

Then, I personally like to see a heading called "Personal Interests." List three. Why? Well, it makes me feel you're human. I've seen some wonderful ones like "cat sitting" and "horror films," which I think are charming and humorous, though the normal "travel," "hiking," "skiing," etc. are fine. I'd suggest that you find something outside of painting, sculpture, etc., since one assumes that and is generally looking for some outside interests that are not art-related. I sometimes find this a helpful point at which to start my interview.

And last is "References: Available Upon Request."

As for the sheet itself, I personally prefer to see a clean, typewritten resume, 8½" x 11", on white, pale beige or pale gray paper, rather than one typeset on lavender. You may stand out -- but negatively. As for designing your resume, I'd think twice about it. What if someone doesn't like the design? What if they don't like the typeface? You may never get a chance to show that person your portfolio. Isn't that more important that having everything rest on your resume instead?
I've seen everything from heavy black borders that looked like someone died, type slanted all over the sheet (I didn't know where to start reading) and all capital letters in 6 point, bold type that was virtually unreadable, to a long, narrow sheet of paper that got lost in one of my file folders. Yes, I do save these resumes, but unfortunately only to use as examples of what not to do.
You might also consider including a separate sheet listing three references in an envelope in the back pocket of your port-folio case. If you're interviewing for your first job, your art teacher or perhaps someone you interned with during a summer vacation would be good reference choices. We're looking for some way to judge your reliability -- do you come to work on time, are you absent a lot, are you trustworthy, etc.? Finally, carry a dozen or so resumes in the front portfolio pocket, in case someone requests more copies to pass along to other department heads or colleagues.
Keep everything short and clear with no personal data. It's illegal for anyone to ask your age, sex, marital status, etc. It doesn't belong on your resume. Nor does working as a lifeguard, waitress or the like. As impressive as your personal data or non-art jobs may be, your prospective employer is interested in

what you can do on the job and is looking for your qualifications in art, so you can help lighten his workload.

Also, do I have to add that it isn't a good idea to begin your letter with "Gentlemen" or "Dear Sir?" These salutations still come across my desk. I also suggest you save your own calling cards as possible portfolio pieces only. Prospective employers wouldn't logically carry your card around in a wallet, so it serves little purpose to send them one.

GETTING THROUGH THE INTERVIEW PROCESS

As for your interview, I suggest that, if possible, you confirm your appointment. You never know when someone was simply unable to come to work that day, was called out on a last minute appointment that superceded yours, etc. Be on time -- neither early nor late. If you are stuck in traffic somewhere in a tunnel, relax. It happens to all of us. Call the company as soon as you can, apologize and ask if you could set up another appointment. Don't assume that the person has no other appointments and is just sitting there waiting for you. You might be lucky and the person will say, "come on up," but then, you might not be.

Try not to explain your work. It should speak for itself.

Don't ask about benefits at your first interview. If you really want to know about them, ask someone in the Personnel Department.

Take any negative comments with a grain of salt and try to learn from them. But don't keep changing your portfolio at the suggestion of each interviewer. Since everyone has a different opinion, your portfolio will end up in a shambles! You have to weigh each criticism and decide which are valid. After all, it's your book and your work. And it's you who must answer for it in the end.

Most important is to be yourself. That's who we hire -- someone with talent, but someone we also feel we can work with.

SOME THOUGHTS ON YOUR PORTFOLIO

Keep the ring binder (which is preferably 14" x 17") or your box portfolio (to hold 14" x 17" boards, preferably) simple. It's your work that should be impressive, not the case you're carrying. It might well detract from your work, a negative you can do without.

If you're using a box, keep all the mattes uniform in size, wrapped in acetate with neat backings. I suggest you keep your boards black. It shows off your work to its best advantage. If the background of your work is black, then consider putting a narrow white edge or border around each sample and then adding a black matte.

Wrapping each board in a lightweight acetate will protect it from frequent handling. And remember that the back of the board should be as neat and clean as the front. If you put acetate only into the windows of your matte and leave the black mattes as they are, then consider putting a thin strip of black tape around the edges of each board to keep them from fraying after frequent handling.

You should have approximately twelve to twenty samples of your work. Your first sample should be your best; your last, the second best. Hopefully the level of art will not fall off too much between the two! If you have published samples, they might not be your best work -- you may well have had to compromise. Therefore, put them in the back of your book (even in the back pocket) and concentrate on showing the best samples, published or not.

Obviously, your book and all your work must be spotless. And when in doubt, leave it out. I can tell from your very first sample all that I need to know: your design ability, your rendering ability, your knowlege of typography, your color sense, your originality, your neatness, the way you think, etc. The remaining samples are there only to confirm that initial judgement and show a variety of work.

Remember, too, that finished samples alone don't show your initial thinking. I'm most impressed with seeing a few neat thumbnail sketches (smaller than actual page size) in a variety of layouts, then an actual, final, page-size, magic marker layout of one of the thumbnail sketches and finally, a more finished layout (a comprehensive) of that same thumbnail.

Make sure that your hand lettering is clean and accurate and do include those magic marker layouts in your book. A great many firms work in this medium and you should know how to do it. Also, include two mechanicals, neatly done, in the back of your portfolio. Some prospective employers consider this mandatory.

Slides and films are inadvisable. There's generally no time to view them, no room and they're not easy to see. And finally, leave out your nude figure drawings and the pencil renderings you did in your early school years, no matter how good you think they are. They don't belong in a professional portfolio.

OTHER WAYS TO LEARN ABOUT OUR PROFESSION

Some of the publications you should be reading in order to acquaint yourself more thoroughly with this professiona and to keep yourself apprised of the happenings in the industry are: Communication Arts, American Artist, Art Direction, Print, Graphis and Upper and Lower Case (U&lc). (These and more are listed in Appendix B of this volume -- Ed.)
I would also suggest that you consider joining one or more of our professional societies (as a student member) in order to make friends and some contacts, hear about possible available jobs in town, work for our profession (what you give you also reap) and generally learn more about the profession you hope to become a part of. The major magazine publishing and advertising

associations are listed in Appendix A.

Continue to add to your "inspiration" or "swipe" file. Local art stores are generally well-stocked with necessary supplies and excellent books relating to our profession. Look at the annual art club books for inspiration as well -- they show the best examples of award-winning work done during each year.

There's also an organization called the Joint Ethics Committee, which adheres to a Code of Fair Practice for everyone in our profession. It was organized in 1945 and now has six of our major professional organizations as sponsors. The Committee meets every month, reviews problems that come up in our profession and tries to solve them, either by mediation or arbitration. There's no fee involved and the Committee is made up of volunteers -- ethical people from our profession who care enough to spend the time to help those in trouble.

I write a column on the Committee's proceedings for Art Direction magazine. If you get a chance to read some of them, they might help you prevent some problems of your own before they happen. If you ever do need help with an art problem, consider writing the Committee (PO Box 1789, Radio City Station, New York, NY 10163). They'll do their best to help.

GETTING STARTED IN PUBLICATION DESIGN

If you do select publication design as your professional goal, here are the specific steps I suggest you take to reach it:

Direct your portfolio entirely and exclusively to publication design. This means inventing two or three specific magazines and designing realistic covers. This should include not only the masthead, but an indication of photo(s), placement of copy lines, and the date and price (one of the most difficult problems in cover design).

I suggest inventing a new magazine rather than re-designing an existing one, because then too much focus is placed on a comparison between the two designs. Using an existing masthead generally shows me less of your promise and talent than I prefer to see.

In addition to the cover, design a table of contents (it's a most interesting challenge to get this exciting and readable), two single-page solutions and two double spread solutions. Either cut the latter in half and place the halves against the rings of your binder or place the layout on end as a full spread.

Use some of your neat little thumbnail sketches (perhaps four to a page) and you will have ample samples to show in your portfolio. I count seven or eight per magazine. Create three imaginary magazines and you will have the 24 samples -- six pages of thumbnails, three cover layouts, three table of contents layouts, six single-page layouts and six double spreads.

Your prospective employer may be so impressed with your work that you might be placed in a design/paste-up position, the

generally accepted entry-level point,   ready to eventually work
your way up to Art Director.

    This means you will be working on the editorial layouts of
the magazine only. (You will have no say in the advertising sections.)   You will undoubtedly be designing the lesser challenges
to begin with and then eventually get to work on celebrity articles,   selecting illustrators and photographers to illustrate
articles and stories and designing the covers (sometimes even
re-designing the masthead itself).

    There may be travel involved -- fashion shoots in the Carib-
bean, Europe or the Far East, celebrities wherever they may be,
etc.   It can all be very glamorous, very exciting and also very
exhausting! Mostly, though, it can be very rewarding and satisfying.

    Especially if you work on a magazine you believe in, it's a
challenge to get your audience to read those worthwhile articles.
A pretty or clever design isn't always functional. In my estima-
tion,   a good Art Director is one who can create an exciting
design and yet make it readable -- make people want to read it
and able to read it.

    This is true of all design. How many times have you seen
this type of "award winning" ad: a beautiful photograph, a beautiful model, a beautiful dress -- only she's standing on top of a
cliff,   is approximately one inch high and the fog is rolling in
so you can barely see her or the dress you're supposed to buy! To
me, this is _not_ an award winning ad.

    One of my favorite examples of what _not_ to do: The subject
is having a sundae on a Sunday...already a dubious editorial
idea, yes? Now picture this. A group of people are dressed in
old-fashioned clothing and standing on a lawn. Only they're on a
slant, tilting sideways because someone shot the photograph with
a strange lens. In front of the group is a long table with an
antique, white-lace tablecloth on which someone has put all kinds
of food -- cheese. fruit, finger sandwiches, ice cream, etc.

    Shining down on top of this poor group of souls and all
that food is a broiling sun that appears to be of such intensity
that you just _know_ it's 120 degrees in the shade.

    And in the middle of all this is a great big empty sky with
just a glimpse of a few smokestacks sticking up into it, giving
the impression that the photo may well have been taken across
the street from some steel mill.

    You are now convinced that all of these people must be suf-
fering from food poisoning, because the sun _must_ have spoiled all
that food. That's, of course, why they're standing on a slant --
they're about to fall over in a dead heap!

    Finally, along the right-hand side of this double spread,
full-color photo is a narrow column of type describing the article.   The heading reads "Sunday sundaes." A pink ribbon or rule,
approximately 23 in all, appears under each paragraph.

    Have you gotten the picture? Now I ask you: Wouldn't this
have been far more effective if it had simply shown a beautiful
photograph of a scoop of delicious-looking ice cream plopping in-

to a frosted glass? Eye-catching, mouth-watering and you wouldn't have had to guess what was happening.

This is only one example out of a tray of 140 slides, magazine page reproductions I use to illustrate the dubious design concepts I'm trying to describe in words. Other examples show spreads of white type dropping out of a black area, so you can't read it (and probably don't want to); words superimposed over a photo (both are in living color and, of course, so totally illegible that you wonder if the Art Director wasn't totally mad; feet cut off; a photo with out-of-scale items that makes a razor look as big as a vacuum cleaner. There is so much poor design that one wonders now it could ever get published -- or how the Art Directors could ever have gotten paid to produce it.

SOME FINAL ADVICE

Hopefully, these points will better prepare you for your entry into our profession. But each job is different. Be ready, be willing and be as able as possible. You will be taught most of what is expected of you on the job. And I suggest that you stay at that job as long as you're learning and enjoying it -- hopefully for at least a year. It takes at least that long to train someone, so do have the respect to return the investment your company made in you. Resumes that show "job-hopping" are not popular. Nor will you be.

Finally, develop a good sense of humor and be strong. It's those who strive beyond the expected who are ultimately considered life's great achievers, not only because of what they get out of life, but because of what they give to it. "Failure will never overtake you if your determination to succeed is strong enough."

If you want to reach for the moon, then dare to be different -- be an individual, break the rules, and follow your own instincts in your work. I really feel that if you don't achieve what you want in this profesion, then you really didn't want it badly enough.

I've always believed that we all have a destiny, but I also believe that you have to sometimes help it along a bit and earn those pluses.

Good luck and my very best wishes to you all.

* * *

In addition to her responsbilities on Good Housekeeping, Ms. Schultz is also Graphic Designer for the Hearst Corporation, publisher of Good Housekeeping, Cosmoplitan, Redbook, Connoisseur, Town & Country and many other well-known popular magazines.

She is extremely active in the graphic communications industry. She was elected the first woman President of the Art Directors Club in its 60-year history, after a long history of involvement in numerous other positions, and is now Chairperson of the Club's Advisory Board. She was also the first woman Chairperson of the Joint Ethics Committee.

She has served in a variety of capacities at The School of Visual Arts, Fashion Institute of Technology, the School Art League, Society of Illustrators, Graphic Artists Guild, Society of Publication Designers and many more professional organizations. She is a well-known and well-travelled lecturer and educator.

Not surprisingly, Ms. Schultz has won numerous awards for both her service to her profession and her graphic skills. She is the designer of a new typeface called "Eileen Cursive."

She received her BFA from the School of Visual Arts, with continued studies at Columbia University, the Art Students League and the Academie des Beaux Arts in Paris.

CHAPTER 10

How To Prepare Your Portfolio

By

Shinichiro Tora, Art Director
Popular Photography

Art students who have just finished art or design school and have started looking for their first jobs must be prepared to show interviewers a portfolio book that expresses their talents and skills. Assembling your first professional portfolio should be considered your initial, tentative step into the professional world of design.

Why is the portfolio so important? Because it presents your talents and skills in visual form without any further explanation. Employers are always looking for creative talents who will help their businesses. While viewing a portfolio, the employer can objectively weigh each young's artist's potential to perform productively. The portfolio is the only way you can prove your artistic talents. It's your sales kit. As such, a neat, well-organized portfolio, showing talent and professional skills, is the best way for any artist to promote his talent to potential employers and land that important first job.

Before putting your portfolio together, you must first know something about the business side of the creative world and the types of positions available. Commercial, creative art and design is a large and varied field. Professionals may work in advertising agencies, publishing companies, printing companies, design and photo studios, package design studios, architectural design offices, construction companies and almost any other industry. Jobs may be found in many different departments -- Art, Promotion Art, Creative Arts, Planning Design, Editorial Art, to name a few. As a designer, you can specialize in numerous areas -- fashion, graphics, editorial, industrial, architecture and many more.

Given all these choices, the first step may be the hardest -- selecting the particular industry or area in which you want to work. Otherwise, you'll be unable to set up a portfolio which will demonstrate the abilities and skills you possess that are necessary to get an entry-level position in that particular field.

The portfolio should, therefore, be carefully focused to highlight only the kind of work endemic to either the industry or specific job you're pursuing. Even if you are multi-talented -- skilled in a number of disciplines and styles -- you can't show off everything in a single portfolio. And you shouldn't try. I've sometimes interviewed persons who have shown me such "unfocused" portfolios. I find them confusing. A person who does a little bit of this and a little bit of that fails to perfect any specific artistic skills. Such portfolios don't provide sufficient samples in my specific areas of interest. So if you have a variety of talents, create a separate portfolio for each major category -- design, illustration or photography.

PUTTING TOGETHER AN ILLUSTRATION PORTFOLIO

If you are looking for a job as a staff illustrator in an Art Department or contemplating freelance illustration, this kind of portfolio is what you need.

First, select your best original drawings, reproduction prints or proofs (if you have them), about 20 to 30 in all. (That's, I think, the best size for a portfolio presentation.) If your paintings are unusually large (bigger than 30" x 40"), you should make smaller, photographic copies. Otherwise, you probably won't even be able to carry your portfolio and, if you do manage to drag it along, interviewers won't have enough room in their offices to spread it out and go through it. You might consider making photographs of any canvas paintings, even the small ones. Canvas is just too bulky to fit comfortably in your presentation case.

The photographic copies you intend to use in your portfolio must be faithful, good-quality reproductions. Use black & white film for black & white drawings, color prints or transparencies for color materials. If you plan to make 35 mm slides, use slide protector vinyl sheets. They're available at any photographic or art supply store and hold 20 slides each.

Unfortunately, slide projectors are sometimes unavailable and viewing 35mm slides on a light table is an injustice -- they're really too small to view the details. I prefer using 8 x 10 or even 11 x 14 color prints or, if you must use slides, 4 x 5 color transparencies for reproducing illustrations. (But, unless they're too large or are 3-D or computer-graphic illustrations, I personally would really rather see the original illustrations, rather than photos.)

You should mount each drawing, printed proof or photo print on white or black illustration board of uniform size. This will give the portfolio a neat appearance. The preferred size is a maximum of 24 x 18. If you have many small illustrations, you may group more than one on a single board. If your drawing was made on illustration board, don't mount it again, but do try to maintain a uniformity of board size.

When mounting an illustration, leave at least two inches of space all around it. This will protect the painting from fingerprints. You can also put your credit in this border area. In order to protect the painting fully, lay a clear acetate sheet over each board.

The credit for each painting -- your name, address, telephone number and, preferably, the title of the illustration -- should always appear <u>somewhere</u> on every illustration. If you want to use a rubber stamp, that's all right (though I prefer the title with each in the border area). Paintings may be held for a rather long time and could easily become mixed up with other artists' work, so such identification is mandatory.

PUTTING TOGETHER A PHOTOGRAPHIC PORTFOLIO

The student of photography, who is probably aiming to become a professional commercial photographer, an art photographer or a photojournalist, needs to create a different portfolio.

There are two ways to break into the professional photography ranks. One is to start as an assistant to an established photographer or in a commercial photo studio. Either job will teach you the special techniques and skills you need to know to sell your work directly to magazines, ad agencies or stock photo houses.

The second way is to avoid such an apprenticeship and become a professional freelance photographer immediately. I don't recommend it. You need not only quite a bit of talent but several lucky breaks to even have a chance.

Whether you choose commercial or art photography, you must develop a solid foundation of photographic skills. Shoot, shoot and keep shooting. Practice as much as you can. Photographs can be of a single subject, a series or any other variation, but they must be sharp, clear images. Then select the best shots from each series or group for your portfolio.

Today, most professionals shoot color, which most advertisers and publications prefer. But black & white prints are still used and a selection of black & white photos should be included in your photographic portfolio. Prints or transparencies are acceptable.

Advertising agencies, generally speaking, tend to prefer large-size (4 x 5 or even 8 x 10) color transparencies; fashion photographers usually use 2¼ x 2¼ film. Magazines are generally flexible as to format. Stock photo houses prefer 35 mm slides.

There are two ways to present a 35 mm color portfolio. One is simply to utilize the slide protector sheets mentioned earlier. The other is to organize your slides in a carousel tray, ready for projection, of anywhere from 80 to 140 slides.

A maximum of 10 sheets or one carousel tray is probably sufficient for any presentation. If you lean towards the tray method, however, make sure you arrange to have a slide projector available when you make an interview appointment.

To display large size transparencies, cut black matte board to uniform size. Use 8½ x 11 boards for 4 x 5 film, 11 x 14 for 2¼ x 2¼ or 8 x 10 transparencies or films. "Gang up" 12 of the 2¼ shots per board. Use one board for each 4 x 5 or 8 x 10.

To prepare a 2¼ presentation board, draw four rules on the back of the board, 1½ inches from each edge. Draw three boxes horizontally, four vertically, each separated by ½ inch spaces. Now cut out these box windows. You can then make as many such matte boards as you need.

Put each 2¼ transparency in a plastic sleeve and tape each photograph to the back of the matte board so the image shows through the windows you've created. In a similar manner, cut out a single window in the center of the board to mount 4 x 5 or 8 x 10 transparencies. It's also better to mount prints rather than just leaving them loose. Mounting will protect them from fingerprints and other damage and display each photograph in a attractive way.

As previously discussed, make sure each slide or print is fully identified with your name, address and telephone number, especially if you are sending your work to a stock photo agency. Since they handle millions of photos a year, one unnamed slide can very easily get lost in the shuffle. Use 20 to 30 mounted shots in one portfolio case.

PUTTING TOGETHER A DESIGN PORTFOLIO

If you're looking for a job in advertising, editorial or graphic design at an ad agency, magazine publisher, design studio or similiar media arts firm, you will need to put together a design portfolio. There are two types, depending on where you want to work and the specific kind of design with which you want to be involved -- an **advertising design** portfolio and an **editorial design** portfolio. They are distinctly different categories and, therefore, not at all interchangeable. A portfolio designed for advertising should not be used if you are applying for a publishing job, and vice versa.

An advertising design portfolio should contain concepts for as many of the following as possible: newspaper and/or magazine ads (single ads or entire campaigns for consumer, business or trade publications), annual reports, booklets or brochures, sales kits, direct mail pieces, record jackets, packages, calendars, letter heads, Point-of-Purchase materials, corporate identity programs, a sample TV story board and posters. In other words, sample ads for all the various media and various collateral pieces an agency utilizes in its attempt to sell its clients' products or services.

An editorial design portfolio should concentrate on editorial page and layout designs, cover design, book design and some typographic designs that would be used for presentations.

If at all possible, I would recommend you "customize" each portfolio before the interview with the specific art director you're scheduled to see.

To prepare either type of portfolio, start by collecting as many interesting magazines -- new and old -- as possible. These will provide you with the raw materials necessary to create your own sample ads or editorial designs. Using these ads and stories as a base, recreate various designs your way. At this stage, work freely and don't worry about size and space limitations. Once the concept design is worked out, sketch out each of your ideas and, finally, pick the best ones. Using general magazine sizing and layout formats, turn your sketches into finished mechanicals. If you are working on editorial designs, you must furnish keyed layout sheets for the text column format (2, 3 or 4, generally) you are using. This is an important element in editorial design and should, therefore, be carefully prepared and certainly not omitted.

Now find the photographs or illustrations that fit your designs, either from the magazines you've culled or your own selection of original illustrations or photographs. Advertising agencies especially like to see such original artwork in a design, rather than pictures from cut-up magazines. Set actual headlines by using press type, which is available in a wide variety of typefaces and sizes at most art supply stores. Text can be neatly cut out from your magazine pile. (If you can't find a text section that's long enough for a particular design, just cut out what you have, photocopy it and add the two together.)

If you have some experience in darkroom techniques, you can try 3-M color key processing for color lettering on clear acetate, tacking it over the photographic print or illustration. You can also create drop-out lettering on a black background by first using press type on clear acetate and then making a direct print on photo enlargement paper. This can also be colored with magic markers. These and other creative techniques will make your overall presentation far more attractive.

Your paste-up should be neat and clean. Remove all excess cement. Trim the finished work to magazine size and mount it on uniform-sized white or black boards. For two-page spreads (whether for advertising or editorial), mount them on a single board, just as they would appear in the magazine.

Ten to twenty designs are probably sufficient for a solid presentation.

Finally, with portfolio in hand, you start making the rounds, looking for an appointment with the right Art Director.
Good luck!

* * *

In addition to his responsibilities at <u>Popular</u> <u>Photography</u>,
Mr. Tora is an active member of the Society of Publication Designers, the Society of Illustrators and the Art Directors Club.
Since 1974, he has coordinated annual shows in Japan for the
latter two organizations. He has chaired numerous association and
professional committees. He has received a variety of awards for
art direction, illustration and design <u>annually</u> <u>since</u> <u>1973</u>,
including the 1974 Gold and 1977 Silver Awards from the Society
of Publication Designers; the 1980 Gold, 1982 Silver and 1981 &
1985 Distinctive Merit Awards from the Art Directors Club; and
the 1984 Silver Award from the Society of Illustrators.

IV
Circulation

CHAPTER 11

Have I Got A Job For You!

By

David H. Foster, President
David Foster & Associates

Several years ago, I helped organize a "career day" in New York for students from Bryn Mawr and Haverford Colleges. Of the 60 or so students who attended, about fifteen expressed an interest in publishing, so I made arrangements for them to spend a day talking with top executives in the publishing division of CBS, my then-employer.

Before the day began, I asked them to tell me what jobs they would be most interested in learning about. Without exception, they all wanted to know about being Editors. In fact, none of these bright and otherwise worldly students seemed even remotely aware of any other type of position in a publishing company. It had never occurred to any of them that editing is just one facet of a very complex business.

After speaking with Publishers, Advertising Directors, Production people, Office Managers, Newsstand Sales Managers, Subscription Circulation Managers and executives from a number of other departments, they were amazed by the number of skilled people necessary to get the printed word in the hands of interested readers.

Before their career day, there really was no reason to expect that any of the students would have had any interest other than editing. After all, magazine editorial is what we are all most familiar with. Before the publication of this <u>Career Directory</u>, there was simply no way for most students to learn about all the functions necessary to actually produce a magazine -- other than by actually being in the industry.

Most people who have experienced publishing as a business happened upon it by accident. Some have a slight idea of what it's like and want to be Publishers. A few make the conscious decision to sell advertising space. But I have yet to meet anyone who began a career in publishing yearning to be a circulator. Nevertheless, Circulation is the most complex part of publishing and one of the most intellectually challenging careers in all of business. The people who are responsible for finding a magazine's potential readers and for making sure it gets into their hands are referred to as "circulators," of which there probably are fewer than 2,000.

THE ROLE OF CIRCULATION IN THE MAGAZINE INDUSTRY

According to a recent estimate provided by the United States Postal Service, there are over 37,000 publications in the United States that qualify for second class mailing privileges. These periodicals come from cities and towns located all over the country. However, there are heavy concentrations of publishing companies in New York, Chicago and Los Angeles.

The largest magazines, measured by the number of people who buy or receive them, usually are consumer magazines of either general or special interest. In the United States, there are just over 500 publications that are members of the Audit Bureau of Circulation (known as ABC). ABC is an industry organization that certifies the Publisher's claim about how many people buy or receive each issue. This information is essential for member advertisers and advertising agencies who must decide which publications they want to use.

Another thousand or so magazines belong to the Business Publication Association (commonly referred to as BPA). This group performs a similar role for magazines that are distributed largely to individuals in an industry, business group or trade association -- such as chemicals, lumber, medicine, teaching or electrical engineering. It can safely be said that there exists a publication devoted to every identifiable field of human interest. There is even a magazine exclusively about the weather.

In order to reach people who want to read them, all of these magazines undergo a complicated process of being written, edited, manufactured and shipped. Only a small percentage of the people working for a particular magazine are actually responsible for composing it and getting it to the printer.

Companies differ in the way they are organized to publish. A small company that puts out three or four issues a year of a single "title" may have one person who performs all the jobs from editing/design to distribution. More frequently, however, a number of people are involved.

At large companies that publish many magazines, there are separate departments responsible for each function. A diagram showing a typical organization chart for the Circulation Department of a large company can be found on page 100.

Large or small, every publishing firm must reach its readers. To do so, the following steps always happen:

1. Defining the editorial concept
2. Writing
3. Design
4. Advertising sales (if it accepts advertising)
5. Layout
6. Printing
7. Marketing to customers
8. Distribution

"Circulation" refers to the marketing and distribution functions. While the number of people actually assigned to do these jobs as a specialty is small relative to all those in publishing, the importance of this function can be measured in a number of ways.

According to industry statistics, about half of the revenues of a magazine are generated through circulation. An annual survey of a sample consisting of 154 magazines, conducted by Price Waterhouse on behalf of the Magazine Publishers Association, established that the magazine industry currently generates about $4.1 billion in revenue, $ 2.0 billion of which comes from advertising. The other $ 2.1 billion comes from circulation.

The impact of magazine marketing affects far more "bottom lines" than those of the publishing companies. There are over 125,000 outlets across the country that sell consumer magazines. These retailers and the jobs they provide depend on publications for a significant portion of their revenues, both directly from the magazines and from the consumer traffic they generate. This channel of distribution -- from the publishing company to the wholesaler to the retail outlet to the customer -- is called the "newsstand network." It accounts for roughly 1/3 of the distribution for consumer magazines (and is covered in more detail by Peter Armour in Chapter 13 -- Ed.).

Nearly all other publications are sold through mail, broadcast or telephone solicitations and get to their readers via the United States Post Office or UPS (United Parcel Service). These include the other consumer magazine copies, trade and business publications, general interest periodicals and specialty publications. (See Chapter 12 by Stephen Bernard for a detailed discussion of subscription sales -- Ed.).

IS CIRCULATION FOR YOU?

The first responsibility of a Circulation Director is to meet his <u>rate</u> <u>base</u> at the highest possible profit. Meeting rate base means delivering the number of copies that the Publisher has promised advertisers will be delivered -- regardless of whether a publication is distributed free of charge ("<u>controlled</u>" <u>circulation</u>) or is purchased by its readers (<u>paid</u> <u>circulation</u>).

Circulation Department Organization Chart
Large Company

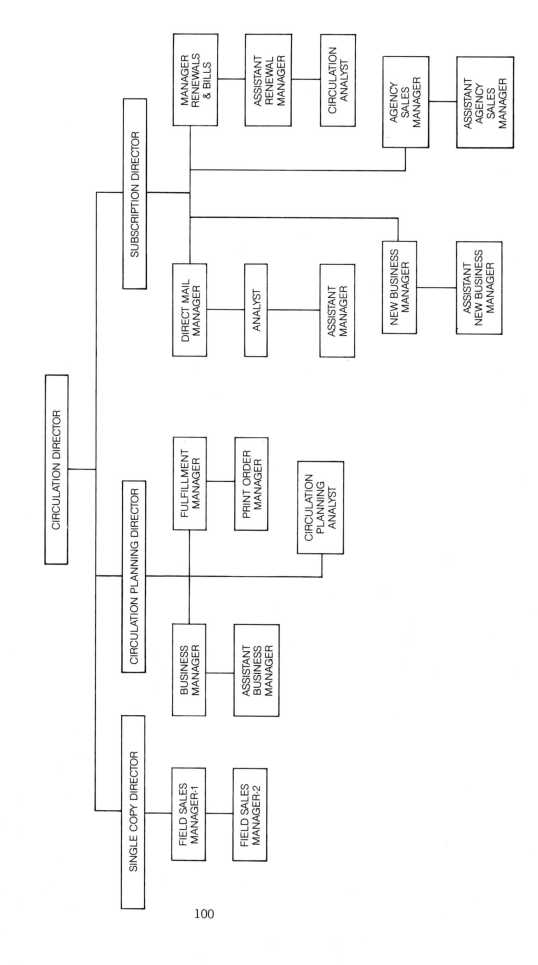

It is important to note that the need to meet rate base often conflicts with pressures to do so at the highest possible profit. The reason is that it costs money to locate those who may be interested in reading your publication and in convincing them to take it. Some people, the "_core group_" or best prospects, are easy to locate and relatively inexpensive to attract. Others who have only marginal interest, are harder to find and more expensive to bring in. Delivering the right number of copies of each issue at the right cost is as complex a balancing act as conducting a symphony orchestra. The difference is that the Circulation Director has to write the score at the same time as conducting it.

Consider, for example, magazines that are sold on newsstands. There is no guarantee that a person who buys one issue will pick up the next one. For magazines that have subscriptions delivered through the mail, there is a constant flow of people whose subscriptions have expired, as well as people in the process of renewing their subscriptions, paying their bills or being added to the subscription list for the first time. Whether a magazine is controlled or paid circulation, business- or consumer-oriented, does or does not take advertising, it is the job of the Circulation Director to coordinate all these different flows as each issue rolls off the printing press. The circulator must insure that the proper number of paid or qualified customers have been persuaded to accept the publication and that they receive it in compliance with the standards set by the auditing agencies.

What makes the process complex is that there may be as many as 40 or 50 sources for obtaining the magazine that a Circulation Director must keep track of. Each source, whether it's sending out direct mail pieces, ads that appear on television, telephone solicitations or renewal notices being sent out, has its own marketing strategy, level of response and number of subscriptions or newsstand sales to generate.

What makes the job possible is that every source is subject, within limits, to laws of statistical probability that lend a degree of predictability and control to the business.

What makes the job exciting is that probabilities don't always work because the market in each source changes constantly. A Circulation Director has to be able to read trends and anticipate those changes in time to do something about them.

What makes the job fun is inventing new ways to attract people to a publication. There is an enormous amount of creative energy that goes into developing television commercials, telehone scripts and direct mail packages that will acquaint potential customers with the benefits your publication has to offer and persuade them to give it a try.

What makes the job challenging and worthy of consideration as a career is the variety of skills you have to develop and draw upon to do it well. Furthermore, there is a never-ending panoply of things to learn in technology and marketing. A circulator can never get bored. Financially, Circulation can be rewarding -- top circulators in major companies may earn over $100,000 per year.

And the reason there are openings for bright young people like you is that the job opportunities for people who have been trained in Circulation are unlimited. This is because the advertising and entertainment industries have recognized that the combination of creativity, insight, facility with numbers, ability to communicate in writing, coordination of complex multi-variate tasks and people-management skills that being a circulator demands is one of the finest training grounds for higher management positions.

As Peter Armour makes clear in Chapter 13, however, to succeed you need the drive and commitment that comes from a love of what you are doing. To rise in Circulation, you must always be able to tackle the job at hand.

Not all Circulation jobs are the same. As we have pointed out earlier, different companies may be organized in different ways to handle all the necessary tasks. In addition, Circulation is integrally related to other industries.

Circulation draws upon both marketing and distribution. But different parts of the business use these broad areas differently. Newsstand sales, as Peter Armour points out, depends upon retailers to reach customers. While a lot of marketing decisions go into the sale of magazines at retail (including cover price, cover design, point of sale promotions, support advertising, publicity and the like), the backbone of the business is a network of warehouses, trucks and wholesalers. They are the ones who have set up business systems to make sure the right magazines get to the right racks at the right time. The remarkable coordination of placing 2,000 different publications week in and week out is a world quite different from subscriptions.

The basis of subscription circulation is direct marketing. Here, a circulator reaches a customer through the mailbox or over the airwaves. Success of these efforts (which may include direct mail pieces, participation in agency sweepstakes, calling people on the telephone or enticing them to respond to a print or television advertisement) depends on the willingness of a sufficient number of people to be persuaded to respond.

The other side of direct marketing is that subscription circulators depend upon subscription fulfillment houses for processing orders, maintaining an accurate list of subscribers and their proper status along the continuum of renewal, term of subscription and payment, as well as for supplying them with the statistics and information they need to make operating decisions.

ARE YOU FOR CIRCULATION?

Some time ago, the President of the Publishing Division of a major media conglomerate asked me what the ideal background would be for the Vice President of Circulation he was attempting to find. Without hesitation, I replied it would be a major in either

English or Mathematics, with a minor in the other. (Our candidate actually turned out to be someone who had majored in Accounting as an undergraduate and studied English in graduate school).

Given the wide variety of tasks and jobs that circulators perform, a number of skills are required. Among the most important are these:

1. **Marketing sense**. A circulator needs to know whether a marketing effort is going to appeal to the potential reader. It does no good to send out a glossy direct mail piece if it doesn't have a message that will compel the target audience to respond. Similarly, it does no good to spend $50,000 on a television commercial that won't pull enough orders to pay for itself.

You get marketing sense through a lot of experience, trial and error, hearing what works for other people in the industry and by designing tests that can be read with statistical validity.

While marketing sense can be trained and learned, you can tell whether you have the inherent raw material by seeing how well you do in those classes where you need to have an intuitive feel for subject matter related to how people think and react. It helps, for example, to be able to feel in your gut what an artist has accomplished.

2. **Analytical acumen**. The best intuitions in the world are those that have been trained. Direct marketing and newsstand sales both require the ability to absorb a wealth of information that allows your judgments to be informed. That capacity can be achieved only by knowing how to organize knowledge gleaned from test results, and how to read the story that lots of numbers reveal. Unless you can read a trend line and recognize its significance, you won't be able to fit everything in Circulation together.

3. **Initiative**. Circulation is much too complicated for one person to have all the answers. People who can interpret the significance of a body of information and figure out a course of action that will protect or enhance the profitability of their particular publications are worth their weight in gold as circulators.

4. **Intellectual curiosity**. Circulation is something that changes all the time. In order to keep up with it and to be on top of your job and your profession, you need to be a person who is curious, who always wants to know more. If you don't enjoy learning, then the tides of the marketplace, as well as the innovations in technology and marketing techniques that occur every day, will pass you by.

5. **Personal integrity**. In order to succeed at selling, you have to be able to faithfully represent your product. You have to believe in it and be able to talk about it convincingly to other people. Whether you are guiding the creative process for direct mail copy or running a challenge competition for wholesalers, people all along the line have to know what you stand for. If you

say the wrong things in the promotions that you send out, eventually you will confuse your market and hurt your profitability.

With the suppliers you will come to depend upon and with the team of other managers in the company where you work, your ability to do your job will depend upon the trust they have in you.

6. <u>Organization</u>. Once again, successful circulation management requires the coordination of many parts moving all at once. In order to get your renewals out on time or send your direct mail on the date it is scheduled, you have to be able to have the copy written, the envelopes printed according to the appropriate specifications and have everything show up at the mailing house at the right time. To perform these and other functions well takes someone who is personally well-organized. For you will have to make sure a lot of other people are on schedule.

7. <u>Ability to manage and get along with people</u>. Circulation is much too complicated to do all by yourself. You depend on suppliers -- printers who print your direct mail pieces, copywriters who compose the contents of your promotions, designers who create attractive pieces, list brokers who assist you in selecting who to mail to, fulfillment houses who open your mail and supply the reports that are the lifeblood of your business. If you are in the newsstand business, the cooperation of the wholesalers, as well as the truckdrivers who deliver your goods to the stores and put them out on racks for your customers to look at, is essential for reaching the sales and "bottom line" goals you want to attain. Any circulator must be able to respect and work with all kinds of people.

You must also meet the challenge of getting along with people in your own company. There will be a Publisher to report to, as well as a General Manager and perhaps even a President. They all expect their Head of Circulation to know the business, represent it to the rest of the company in a clear, professional manner and be able to understand and respect the jobs that each other member of the team has to do. Leadership ability is just as important for a successful career in Circulation as in any other. And no matter how smart you are, you can only achieve your full professional potential when you are able to understand what the person across the table from you is saying...and appreciate it.

WHAT ABOUT SPECIFIC TRAINING?

Entry to this profession is strictly by on-the-job training. Newcomers generally learn Circulation by their own mistakes and from others who have done it before them. There are no schools for Circulation and there are no courses one can take as an undergraduate or graduate student that will prepare you to step right out and become a Circulation Director.

You <u>can</u> become exposed to what Circulation is all about prior to actually being hired by a publication, however, by enrolling in the publishing courses taught each year at Harvard and

Stanford Universities. Courses are also offered throughout the year by various institutions in the New York metropolitan area, such as New York University and The New School.

After being hired by a company, people generally find it helpful to attend seminars in Circulation offered by FOLIO:, a key trade publication for the magazine industry. They sponsor seminars held in cities around the country on all aspects of publishing. If you join a company that is a member of the Magazine Publishers Association, one benefit is the seminars and training sessions offered on issues related to Circulation. In addition, the Direct Marketing Association sponsors events that teach skills needed for subscription circulation.

Many companies use consultants to assist in training new employees. In addition, courses are often provided by those who service Circulation Departments, such as printers and subscription fulfillment houses. Perhaps the best way to learn about the strategies of Circulation is to attend seminars in Circulation Planning and Modeling offered by the Policy Development Corporation, Lighthouse Publishing Models or 3M Media Services.

No one who hires you as a beginner will expect you to have mastered the intricacies of direct marketing or newsstand sales. But there are certain attributes you can bring to the party that will help you get hired in the first place. You can hone these in college, and show during interviews and through your resume that you have them.

First, you need to have developed a good capacity to communicate both orally and in writing. If you failed to pay attention when the rest of the class was learning spelling and basic grammar, you can be certain it will catch up with you the first time you are responsible for a direct mail piece. There is nothing more embarrassing than to send out a million pieces of misspelled mail to people all over the country, with your signature prominently displaced at the bottom of the letter. Courses you have taken in writing, English, art and design will prove to be especially helpful.

Second, there is no substitute for being able to understand basic arithmetic. As a circulator, your performance will be measured at least monthly by the statement of profit and loss you generate. You need to be able to understand how those numbers came to be and explain why. You don't have to have a degree in higher math, but you do need to be familiar with logic and with basic calculations. You will find that any courses you have had in mathematics, economics, statistics and the like will be invaluable.

Third, the computer. There is no avoiding it. As a circulator you will be asked to report at least monthly on the performance of your newsstand sales or your promotion campaigns or your overall profitability. The number of pieces of information you have to bring together in order to satisfy the reporting requirements of a modern Circulation Department is staggering. It cannot be done effectively without a computer. Eventually, you will <u>have</u> to gain computer skills. If you can bring those to the job in the first place, you will be way ahead in the learning curves you will have to climb to be a circulator.

Finally, you will find that you have entered into a social organization. As a former Political Science major, I found that the courses I took on organizational behavior and "Politics and Power" were particularly helpful in understanding the corporate environment.

HOW TO GAIN A TOEHOLD

For more information about Circulation, there are several books and periodicals that will help you become more familiar with the industry. These are listed below, along with people to contact.

Periodicals

1. <u>Capell's Circulation Report</u>. Newsletter on Circulation available from Capell's Circulation Report Inc., 51 Chestnut St. Suite 202, Ridgewood, NJ, 07450. Call 201-652-0635.

2. <u>Circulation Hotline</u>. Newsletter on Circulation available from David Foster & Associates, Inc., 360 Hayward Ave., Mt. Vernon, NY, 10552. Call 914-699-9414.

3. <u>FOLIO:</u> Available from Folio Publishing Corp. 125 Elm St., PO Box 697, New Canaan, CT 06840. Call 203-972-0761.

People to contact

David Lee, Vice President, Magazine Publisher's Association 575 Lexington Ave., New York, NY 10022. Call 212-752-0055.

David Foster, President, David Foster & Associates, 360 Hayward Ave., Mt. Vernon, NY 10552. Call 914-699-9414. (Placement Service).

Ron Kops, Miller & Kops, 300 Park Ave. South, New York, NY, 10016. Call 212-986-0001. (Placement service).

Staff Coordinator, Circulation Council, Direct Mail/Marketing Association, 6 E 43rd St., New York, NY 10017. Call 212-689-4977.

Other useful items to read

1. <u>The Handbook of Circulation Management</u>, Barbara Love, Editor, <u>FOLIO:</u>, 1980.

2. Nash, Edward L., _Direct Marketing_, McGraw-Hill Book Company, 1982.

3. Stone, Bob, _Successful Direct Marketing Methods_, Crain Books, 1979.

* * *

Prior to establishing his own consulting firm in 1982, Mr. Foster served as Circulation Planning Director of Times Mirror Magazines, where he was instrumental in planning and executing the reorganization of their Circulation Department. He previously served as the Paperback Book Club Manager at Xerox Educational Publications (now Field Publications) and as Director of Reporting and Analysis for CBS Consumer Publications, where he assisted on the repositioning of _Mechanix Illustrated_, developed business plans for new products and implemented a Circulation Management Reporting System.

Mr. Foster began his career at the Hearst Corporation, where he was Assistant to the President. He is a graduate of Haverford College and received his MBA from the Harvard Business School.

In addition to consulting, he publishes _Circulation Hotline_ (The Newsletter for Managing Rate Bases at Higher Profits). He is a frequent contributor to _FOLIO:_ magazine and a speaker at numerous publishing industry events.

CHAPTER 12

A Circulation Subscription Primer

By

Stephen Bernard, VP-Circulation
ABC Publishing

"All happy families are alike but an unhappy
family is unhappy after its own fashion."

The above quote is the opening line of Tolstoy's <u>Anna Kare-</u>
<u>nina</u>. I find it rather curious that I should immediately recall
this quote just as I sat down to write an article on magazine
subscription circulation. I had just returned from a magazine
circulation function and it occurred to me that most of the seemingly "happy" Circulation Directors appeared strangely similar in
their outlooks and recent circulation experiences. On the other
hand, those Circulation Directors with drawn expressions and less
successful results this year had quite unique explanations for
their disappointments.

The point of this reflection is that, although most of these
same Circulation Directors attend this function each year, they
move quite casually from the "content" to the "malcontent"
groups...and perhaps reverse the process the following year.

I have always found it far more interesting to sit with the
malcontents, for here is where one Circulation Director can learn
to avoid the mistakes made by another. And in a business that
changes as fast and is as complex as magazine subscription circulation, the key to success and rapid advancement is to learn from
others' mistakes.

The purpose of the following discussion is to familiarize
you with the exciting and challenging business of marketing
magazine subscriptions. Hopefully, my remarks will give you
enough sense of what it's all about so that you can avoid falling
into something that may not be for you. Or better, you will be so
attracted by what you learn, that you would consider it a mistake

not to try it out. In that case, this abbreviated record of my own mistakes and early misconceptions might help you avoid some of them in your own careers.

RESPONSIBILITIES OF SUBSCRIPTION CIRCULATION

The first responsibility of the person in charge of Subscription Circulation is to deliver an agreed upon number of paid subscribers to the magazine. Once the Publisher sets a policy that, say, 500,000 people are to be located who can be counted as having paid for a copy, it is the task of the Subscription Director to see that this objective is achieved. How this is done varies considerably from magazine to magazine.

A Subscription Circulator has a large bag of tricks to draw upon. In the trade, they are referred to as "**sources**." A source is the way in which a subscription is entered onto your list of people who are to receive the magazine each time it is printed. Most subscription sources involve **direct marketing** -- any promotion that attempts to directly induce a potential customer to respond to a solicitation to subscribe to the magazine.

Such **direct response** advertising can take a variety of forms. You've probably seen any number of television ads or mail solicitations attempting to get you to subscribe to various magazines. Another variety of direct marketing is the insert cards that attract your attention each time you thumb through a magazine. Even more popular these days are the magazine stamp sheets offered by such well-known **subscription agents** as Publishers Clearing House and American Family Publishers. Typically, each of their mailings includes stamps for 100 or more magazines. All you need to do to subscribe to one or more of the magazines is clip the appropriate stamps, attach them to an order form (on which your name and address are already printed), and send in your selections. In a few weeks, the magazines you ordered will start arriving. And if you're lucky, you may even win one of the sweepstakes prizes the company offered just to get your attention in the first place.

The task faced by the Subscription Circulation Manager is to estimate how many customers each of these sources is likely to generate, compose a promotion campaign for each source and, when appropriate, coordinate the suppliers of copy, art, printing, and mailing services to make sure that the various promotions reach potential customers at the appropriate time to assure the right number of subscriptions for each issue.

Being successful purely from a marketing standpoint isn't enough -- equally important is the level of profit the Subscription Director is able to achieve. A Subscription Manager must continuously evaluate the various promotion vehicles and assign priorities in the source mix. In evaluating various subscription sources, one must consider the renewal performance as well as the initial acquisition cost of each new subscription. In some instances, particularly in the case of larger consumer magazines, the Publisher may actually be willing to incur a loss in securing a new subscriber. In other words, if you have the proper demographics for the publication's advertisers and your interests and lifestyle seem consistent with the editorial content, the Publisher may actually be willing to lose money on your introductory subscription.

Direct mail, for example, may be an extremely expensive source of new subscriptions, but since you can select your prospects, it generally results in an excellent renewal response. Moreover, since direct mail offers the Publisher the ability to target his prospects, it also offers him the ability to control his demographics. We must remember, however, that the editorial content is probably the greatest determinant of any publication's demographics.

While direct mail can be an extremely expensive promotion vehicle to secure new subscribers, subscriptions generated through agency sources usually cost the Publisher nothing initially, since the agent pays the total promotion expense. The large multi-magazine sweepstakes mailings from Publisher's Clearing House or American Family Publishers, for example, are paid for by the agent. The subscribers return their orders to the agent, who then forwards them to the Publisher with a portion of the revenue received.

Since the agent bears the total expense of the promotion, he also retains most of the revenue generated from the orders and remits perhaps 15-25 percent to the Publisher. Since the agent's multi-magazine offer cannot be targeted and usually includes the added inducement of winning a substantial amount of money or prizes through the sweepstakes offer, the subscribers obtained generally do not renew as well as those who respond to a straight offer from the Publisher's own direct mail. Moreover, a subscriber may choose to renew his subscription by ordering through an agent, in which case the Publisher again receives only a small portion of the total revenue.

Obviously, the Circulation Manager would like to produce the greatest number of subscriptions from those sources which generate the best profit per order on the acquisition and the best renewal. Since it is often difficult to achieve both these criteria simultaneously, the Circulation Manager often must sacrifice long-term objectives for short-term profitability. For example, most magazines achieve the bulk of their subscription revenue and profits from renewal business, but those subscription sources which renew best often carry the most expensive new business acquisition cost.

Circulation is clearly an "art" rather than a science. There is no one ultimate solution to acquiring and maintaining circulation. Each possible solution must be considered in light of the overall financial strength or weakness of the publication at a particular time. If advertising revenue is not strong in a particular year, for example, the Publisher might be less likely to invest in long-term circulation strength and instead concentrate on those sources which secure subscribers without high promotion expense. If, on the other hand, the publication relies on extremely selective demographics to lure potential advertisers, the Publisher might have to rely more on targeting his own direct mail, rather than mass mailings from direct mail agents, to achieve his goals.

SMALL VS. LARGE PUBLISHERS -- WHICH IS RIGHT FOR YOU?

Working for a small publication with a two- or three-person subscription sales staff is usually quite distinct from a job with a larger consumer magazine. Each environment offers advantages and disadvantages.

As you might expect, with a small publication the job responsibilities are much broader. Consequently, it's often easier to accelerate your Circulation education and responsibilities.

At a larger company, on the other hand, Circulation jobs are usually much more specific and narrowly-defined. In many instances, for example, a large Subscription Department might be organized by the source of the subscription and the specific function of the Manager. There might be a Direct Mail Manager, for example, responsible for all direct mail solicitations of new subscribers; a Renewal Manager responsible for retaining subscribers on the file and, probably, a Subscription Agency Manager responsible for coordinating and monitoring the sales of other companies or organizations selling subscriptions. In all probability, the larger the circulation of the magazine, the more subscription sources it would utilize, and the more such "sub-departments" it would maintain. (See the Circulation Department Organizational Chart on page 100 for a more complete look at all the possible functions and/or titles such a large Circulation Department could include. -- Ed.)

Since direct mail promotion is usually one of the more expensive vehicles used to attract new subscribers, it is also one of the most visible positions in the Subscription department. In the case of larger, more mature magazines, like _Time_ or **Newsweek**, the prospect is usually already familiar with the publication and has certain, preconceived notions of its value. In all probability, the prospect has already received previous offers to subscribe from various sources, and has elected not to. In this instance, the Direct Mail Manager might try to change the prospect's preconceived notions or offer a better value through a special price offer. Most of us have received various introductory subscription offers that include a free preview issue with the option to cancel, or a free gift which accompanies the subscription. These are just additional methods of discounting the price of the subscription.

As postage and paper costs have risen rather dramatically in the past few years, Publishers have had to rapidly increase their subscription prices to cover the incremental costs. A free gift offer, for example, is often an effective means to hedge a subscription price increase. Another effective means might be to lower the term of the introductory subscription and, thus, the total dollar value. A six-month trial subscription which offers six issues for twelve dollars might perform better, for example, than a full-year subscription (twelve issues) for eighteen dollars, even though the shorter term offer has a much higher price per copy ($2.00 vs. $1.50/copy).

Although the Direct Mail Manager will usually test various offers and copy packages before committing to a large mailing expense, the risk factor is unavoidable. Since the risks are higher, so, too, are the financial rewards and opportunities. In the case of renewal promotion, for example, it is quite easy to attribute the success or failure to the editorial content of the magazine. The Fulfillment Manager is usually most visible when something is wrong. The success or failure of the Direct Mail Manager, on the other hand, is usually considered a direct reflection of that person's abilities and skills. As such, it is usually one of the more attractive and sought after positions in the Subscription Department.

In general, when you consider the relative advantages and disadvantages of working at a small or large publishing company, you might weigh the merits of the broader job responsibilities of the small organization, against the level of sophistication and financial opportunity provided by a larger company. In addition, in evaluating your possible opportunities, you might investigate how much circulation revenue (as opposed to advertising revenue) contributes to that publication's total profit picture. Some magazines depend on advertising for the bulk of their revenues and profits. The most visible positions at those publications exist within advertising sales. Obviously, your opportunities might be greater at a magazine where circulation is, or could be, a major contributor to the company's profits.

ENTRY-LEVEL OPPORTUNITIES IN THE SUBSCRIPTION AREA

As you start your search for an entry-level job in magazine circulation, remember -- you are not expected to have experience. Frankly, few of the recent college graduates with whom I've spoken have ever even thought of the Circulation Department as a potential area of entry-level opportunity. Most of them, when pushed to explain their career objectives, say they want to get into the "business side" of magazine publishing. Yet, as anyone who knows anything about this business would quickly point out, the major portion of a magazine's profit (or loss) comes from selling the magazine (either through subscriptions or single-copy/newsstand sales) and selling advertising in its pages.

The titles of entry-level positions may vary from company to company. Most often, they reflect the functions that a Circulation Department performs. In a small organization where the entire Circulation Department consists of only a few people and responsibilites are wide-ranging for each person, typical titles might be "Assistant Circulation Manager" or "Circulation Manager."

The organization chart for a typical large Circulation

Department on page 100 gives you an idea of the functions that need to be performed at such publishing companies. Entry-level positions are typically titled "Analyst" or "Assistant....."

There are entry-level positions available for people who can demonstrate intelligence, aptitude and a willingness to work hard. Clerical help is often needed -- such jobs can often be landed with just a high school diploma and will pay $12,000 - $14,000. If you're a college graduate, with either a BA or BS, you may qualify for a position as an **Assistant Source Manager**, **Assistant Direct Mail Manager** or **Circulation Analyst**. Those of you with an MBA might wind up with the same entry-level titles, but you would probably command a starting salary in the high 20's, or possibly higher at a major company.

If you were a Math or Accounting major in college, chances are you would start in the Circulation Planning Department as **Assistant Business Manager** or **Circulation Planning Analyst**. Your primary responsibilities would be computer modeling, cost controls and management reporting of circulation results.

If you were an English major, or had a flair for design and creativity, you would probably start as **Assistant Direct Mail Manager**, **Assistant Renewals and Billings Manager** or **New Business Analyst**. In these jobs, your primary responsibilities would be to plan promotional efforts, assist in devising appropriate tests and report the results. Depending on the specific company, you may even be assigned to work with copywriters, designers, printers, lettershops (which mail out the packages) and other suppliers to coordinate the process of getting your promotions out on time. Whether you start in the direct mail operation or in billings and renewals, the process of identifying the target audience, planning appropriate solicitations, executing the plans and reviewing the results is similar.

The compensation you can expect for these positions depends on the area of the country, the company and your level of education. Typical salary ranges in metropolitan-area publishing companies are as follows:

POSITION	SALARY RANGE (New York Scale)
Analyst	$15,000 - $ 20,000
Assistant to...	$20,000 - $ 25,000
Renewals & Bills Manager	$25,000 - $ 40,000
Direct Mail Manager	$25,000 - $ 45,000
Source Manager	$25,000 - $ 35,000
Fulfillment Manager	$25,000 - $ 45,000
Business Manager	$25,000 - $ 45,000
Planning Director	$40,000 - $ 60,000
Subscription Director	$40,000 - $ 60,000
Circulation Director	$45,000 - $100,000++

In talking about salaries, there are several points to keep in mind. First, if you have no experience, you should not expect to be paid top dollar. The upper end of the ranges quoted above are usually offered to people who have a track record in the industry.

Second, if you are looking at jobs outside of the major metropolitan areas, the figures quoted above will sound like a lot -- expect starting salaries to be 25 to 40 percent less than those above. For example, a Circulation Director outside of New York with 7 years of experience might expect to draw a top salary between $60,000 and $70,000. In some exceptional cases, this figure may be higher, but keep in mind, you can live a lot better on a lot less outside New York.

Regardless of where you start, once hired your chances of getting promoted or finding a better or higher paying job will depend on your abilities to analyze, organize, work hard and get along with people.

A BACKWARD GLANCE

Like most businesses, the primary occupational hazard of working in Circulation is the potential for excessive credit in good times and excessive blame in bad times. In either case, however, regardless of the level of credit or blame, the results are usually obvious. Although the more experienced and tactful Circulation Directors can conceal disappointing results temporarily, it is virtually impossible to disguise disappointing performance over a longer period of time.

As a result, performance is usually the ultimate criteria for appraisal and reward, unlike many other fields where individual accomplishments or failures are difficult to assess within overall performance. Circulation often offers the opportunity to run your own business within the goals and framework of a larger organization. Responsibilities and accountabilities are obvious. So, too, must be the resultant praise or blame for performance.

Overall, I've always felt that a career in Circulation offers a rare degree of personal control over future advancement and opportunities. In my case, that has been its most attractive feature.

* * *

Mr. Bernard earned his undergraduate degree in Economics from the Wharton School at the University of Pennsylvania. In a rather radical departure from most proven Circulation career paths, he went on to earn graduate degrees in English Literature from New York University. Prior to his current position, Mr. Bernard spent ten years in the Circulation Department at **Newsweek**, where he held a variety of titles ranging from Direct Mail Manager to Circulation Director.

CHAPTER 13

Newsstand Circulation

By

. Peter Armour, Circulation Director
Conde Nast Publications

In its simplest form, newsstand circulation is the science of placing the right amount of properly displayed magazine copies in the right places at the right time. Unfortunately, the many levels of the distribution channel make it more difficult to realize this seemingly simple goal than you would think.

THE NEWSSTAND DISTRIBUTION CHANNEL

First of all, let's discuss the overall channel of distribution. The first "link" in the distribution chain is the publishing company, which, of course, produces the magazine. Each issue is shipped to the <u>magazine wholesaler</u> -- the second link -- by the printer.

For the most part, the 500-odd U.S. and Canadian wholesalers (or <u>distributors</u>) are independent businesses specializing in the sale and marketing of periodicals. Each wholesaler controls the distribution of magazines in a specific geographical marketplace. In other words, all of the magazines displayed at your newsstand, drugstore, supermarket, etc. come from one source -- your area's magazine wholesaler.

The specific area that each wholesaler covers varies quite a bit. Two wholesalers, for example, cover the Greater Chicago marketplace. In New York, one wholesaler covers Manhattan, Staten Island, the Bronx and parts of northern New Jersey; another distributes to retailers on Long Island, Queens, Westchester and southern Connecticut. Brooklyn has its own distributor. Three others cover the rest of northern and central New Jersey.

A wholesaler can be small, servicing only a few retailers.

Fort Dodge, Iowa, for example, has its own magazine wholesaler. So does Dunkirk, New York.

Whatever their size, all magazine wholesalers essentially perform the same services -- they deliver magazines to the retailers in their area on the publisher's national "on sale" date and collect and credit any unsold magazines. Wholesalers are thus billing and collecting agents for the publishers. They may also provide some marketing and merchandising expertise. For these services, they receive a brokerage fee for each copy sold.

As you can well imagine, magazine wholesalers must deal in "tonnage." There are anywhere from 1500 to 2000 magazine titles published yearly in the U.S. for newsstand distribution. Wholesalers handle all of them, but the allotments per title could range from a few copies to many thousands.

But there isn't room for all these magazines at the retail level, the third link in the distribution chain. So retailers, especially the large chain accounts, have the ultimate say as to which magazines are sold in each store. At most stores, buyers select the magazines that will be displayed at the checkout stands and on mainline fixtures based on their estimates of each title's sales potential and each store's demographics.

Given the abundance of magazine titles and the increasing competition for retail space from other General Merchandise product categories, both publishers and wholesalers are placing increasing emphasis on marketing. Simply put, you can't buy what you can't find. Magazines that aren't properly displayed will never be able to maximize sales and profits.

Some large publishers, including Conde Nast, have their own sales and marketing staffs to work with their many wholesaler and retailer accounts. I think any publisher prefers to have their own experts out in the marketplace looking out for their interests. A publisher's representative can concentrate more on different sales areas of opportunity and better direct the wholesalers' marketing efforts.

Those publishers without the capital or ability to oversee national distribution themselves generally utilize one of the eleven national distributors as their own sales and marketing arms. Unless a publisher is large enough to employ their own field staff or employs such a distributor, staying on top of 500 wholesalers, 100,000 retailers and 2000 magazine titles is an impossible task.

The national distributor, with a field sales staff of one hundred or more, plus office and computer support staff, provides the needed "eyes and ears" at the wholesaler and retailer levels to make certain that any given magazine has the opportunity to maximize sales.

The distributor reviews all aspects of newsstand sales and marketing. His field sales staff usually does everything from reviewing each magazine's allocation at the retailer and wholesaler levels to visiting retailers in order to improve existing displays and make formal presentations to obtain new authorizations for more or better-positioned display space.

Since there are only eleven national distributors to service some 2000-odd magazine titles, the time one of them will spend on any given publisher is allocated based on sales and billing potential. More often than not, the publisher feels that not enough time is being spent on his behalf.

At Conde Nast, we invested in our own field sales staff because of the size of our newsstand circulation and the difficulty in obtaining the needed attention from the national distributors' field staff to our titles. Many of the larger publishers have created their own field staffs for similar reasons.

JOBS ON THE FIELD SALES STAFF

A good way of understanding the job responsibility of a national distributor's field sales staff is to liken it to that of an internal auditor. Except for major presentations to "chain buyers," there really isn't any "hard selling" on the newsstand side of circulation. Whether you're working for one of the national distributors or directly for a publisher, service and auditing will be the basic responsibilities of your position.

The job descriptions for either's newsstand sales force are essentially the same, though specific job titles and applicable salary levels may vary somewhat. In almost all cases (and at all levels), a company car and expense account are usually included as part of the salesperson's compensation package.

City Sales Manager

This entry-level position pays between $14,000 and $16,000 a year. The responsibilities include reviewing allocations at both the wholesaler and retailer levels, making the necessary adjustments to ensure maximum sales and placing point-of-purchase materials and merchandising copies at the stores.

Some publishers require counting "on-hand" copies at each store for sales estimating purposes. Specific accounting/bookeeping requirements will vary quite a bit and be different depending on whether you're working for a publisher or distributor.

Regional (District) Sales Manager

This is the next step up the field sales ladder and pays between $19,000 and $26,000 a year. Much of the same responsibilities of a City Sales Manager are included in the role of the Regional Sales Manager, but with two important differences.

The first is that there can be a considerable amount of traveling involved, because your sales territory may include magazine wholesalers in two to four states. Depending on the company, the position could require 50% travel. And believe me, it's not always to very exciting places.

Second, the position could also require managing other

people. Usually, the City Sales Managers report to the appropriate Regional Sales Manager.

Divisional Sales Manager

This is the top field position and can pay anywhere from $30,000 to $45,000 per year, depending on the individual's experience and the size and location of the territory to be managed. Depending on company policy, these supervisory personnel will be located in a field office or at company headquarters.

Both the Regional and Divisional Sales Manager positions require experience. Don't expect to graduate and walk into a $30,000 a year job. How long it takes to get the appropriate experience depends on you. Conde Nast has promoted people with only a few years experience on to the next level of responsibility because they showed us that they had the requisite desire and willingness to work hard and learn.

THE QUALITIES YOU NEED TO SUCCEED

The overall business of newsstand circulation is not complicated. Neither are the terminology or basic techniques. Remember, it's simply a matter of placing the right amount of properly displayed copies in the right places at the right time.

But it takes a highly motivated self-starter to succeed. As with any field position, there's a great deal of freedom and flexibility inherent in the job. Your superiors could be hundreds or even thousands of miles away. It's not only up to you to be responsible for your own "work ethic," but to be able to identify the areas of sales opportunity in a given marketplace and take the necessary and correct actions to take advantage of them.

Doing this successfully -- proving your sense of responsibility and taking control of the marketplace you're in -- will advance your career.

As far as a "Home Office" or "Headquarters" position is concerned, next to the Circulation Director, who has responsibility for both newsstand and subscription sales, the Newsstand Sales Manager is the most important position. The salary range is usually $50,000 - $75,000. A staff of internal support people, including the field sales staff, report to this individual.

The Newstand Sales Manager is totally responsible for the worldwide sales and marketing programs for the company. Establishing the national print order, determining where a given publication is to be displayed on the magazine fixture, pursuing supermarket checkout exposure, and overall budgeting and strategic planning are his primary responsibilities.

Usually he will have key people in support positions functioning as Department Heads. Support people in Marketing, Allotments and Distribution, plus those who handle the many administrative details, are all part of the Home Office operation. Salaries for these support positions will depend on prior experience and/or education.

THE BACKGROUND WE'RE LOOKING FOR

Let's spend a few moments discussing education. Publishing is definitely looking for people with college educations. Any recent hiring we have done at Conde Nast to fill City Sales Manager positions has been as a result of recruiting at the college level, primarily recent or soon-to-be graduates. Those with Marketing or Accounting degrees get first priority.

Of course, there are exceptions. Prior work experience is also considered, especially in the area of bookkeeping and/or retail.

A suggestion for those not planning on attending college is to contact the local magazine wholesaler and inquire about entry-level positions on their field staff.

There's nothing wrong with even starting in a wholesaler's warehouse and working your way up. I did it for several years during summer vacations from college. It was invaluable experience.

I have been the Circulation Director for Conde Nast Publications for the past two years. Before that I was Newsstand Sales Manager, before that a Sales Supervisor. I have worked for a wholesaler, national distributor and a number of small publishers (some so small and poor that the lights were literally turned off on us. Really!) But it was all great experience, real learning experiences.

To be honest, the newsstand side of Circulation is somewhat talent thin. We need more bright, aggressive and creative people. We need people who aren't afraid to ask questions, who won't just accept things "as is" if the reasoning isn't logical.

We need professionals. We need people who can talk about gross margins, return on investment and direct product profitability. Magazines are sold at the retail level today just like any other product. We need people who can sit down and talk to buyers and merchandisers about the viability and profitability of magazines. We need thinkers.

Earlier we noted that space on retailer's shelves is at a premium. The situation is not improving. We need people who are willing to address this problem and work hard to improve this situation.

Lastly, a word of caution. Don't accept a job in newsstand circulation if your ultimate goal is to be an Editor, Art Director or Advertising Director. It doesn't work that way. It is very unlikely that any major company would transfer and/or promote you from one major department to another.

Rather, enter the world of newsstand circulation with the intention of becoming a Newsstand Sales Manager or Circulation Director. You'll certainly be able to obtain all the necessary subscription sales and other circulation-related knowledge youll need to advance within the Circulation Department.

But you'll never be Editor-in-Chief.

Newsstand circulation is a highly visible, challenging and

fairly well-paying career to enter. Almost any publisher can offer you numerous advancement possibilities.

But, like anything else, you have to work at it. The logic of placing the right amount of properly displayed copies in the right place at the right time is simple. It's the application that becomes interesting.

* * *

In his eight years at Conde Nast, Mr. Armour steadily progressed from a supervisor in the Circulation Department to Field Force Manager, Newsstand Sales Manager and, two years ago, Circulation Director. He was previously Circulation Director of Working Woman magazine, Newsstand Sales Manager for New Times magazine and a Sales Manager and Promotion Director for Curtis Books. He started his career at Curtis as an Account Executive for Curtis Circulation Company.

Mr. Armour attended the University of Pennsylvania. He has lectured at both the NYU and Radcliffe Summer Publishing Courses. He is active in a number of industry associations, including the Magazine Publishers Association Newsstand Task Force, and is a member of the Board of Directors of the Periodical Institute.

V
Editorial

CHAPTER 14

Finding An Entry-Level Job On A Consumer Magazine

By

Judith Nolte, Editor
American Baby

Breaking in. It's hard to do. But once you've found a job in the magazine business, especially on the editorial side, you'll never want to leave.

How do you get the first chance, the first job, that entry-level position that seems so elusive yet must be so plentiful? As a veteran of some 20 years on two publications and an editor who's hired over 50 people throughout those years, I think I can offer some helpful advice and some suggestions that will get you your first interview and -- we hope -- your first job. (While much of Ms. Nolte's descriptions and discussion applies to all magazines, she is writing from a consumer magazine background. For a more complete discussion of editorial at business publications, see Chapter 16 -- Ed.)

The Editorial Department creates the magazine, from the cover to the fractional space at the "back of the book." All the articles, photos and design features are the province of Editorial. Depending on the size of the magazine, its frequency and its budget, the work is either done on staff or freelanced by outside writers, or it's a combination of the two. At most publications, the writing is done by freelancers and edited by on-staff editors. The photographs are taken by freelance photographers, and the pages and the "lqok" of the magazine are designed by the on-staff Art Department.

EDITORIAL DEPARTMENT STRUCTURE

What are the jobs in editorial? Again, depending on the size and frequency and budget of the magazine, the editorial/art staff can range from six to over 100. Generally speaking, the department is divided in the following way:

The top Editor (Editor-in-Chief, Editor, etc.), who supervises all activity, manages the staff, and has final approval (or disapproval) of all material;

Managing Editor, who supervises the daily work assignments and work flow of the department and often assigns and edits articles;

Senior Editors, who edit and assign articles -- sometimes concentrating on particular subject matter only -- and do short writing assignments such as headlines, blurbs, cover lines and mini-features;

Assistant Editors/Editorial Assistants, who work on all phases of the magazine, usually assisting some particular editor and often working on only one subject or one task; and

Copy Editors, who work over the writing style, grammar and punctuation in each article.

Most editors also read proofs and galleys and sometimes mechanicals of all the material that's going into an issue.

The Art Department designs and physically lays out the issue and prepares it in mechanical form for the printer. If the magazine is large enough, or if the subject matter necessitates it, there will be a Research or Fact-Checking Department. A large staff might also include secretaries who answer reader mail, read unsolicited manuscripts and generally pitch in and do any task required of them. The larger the magazine, and the more often it comes out, the more support people it will have in the Editorial Department. And this is where some of the best opportunities exist for entry-level jobs. More about that later.

Some Editorial Departments also include large groups of editors who work only on a specialized subject, such as a Fashion Department that includes a coat editor, shoe editor, beauty editor, handbag editor and so on. Or a news magazine may have departments for science, arts, technology, entertainment, features, news and many more.

THE BEST PREPARATION FOR AN ENTRY-LEVEL JOB

With all of these jobs and the constant demand for good people to work on them, how to you get started in your search and how should you be preparing right now for a job in the Editorial Department? If you're still in school (either high school or college), my best advice is to study and learn the language -- grammar, spelling, punctuation and writing skills. Most students graduating today have a shockingly low level of skill when it comes to English, and if your skills are good, you'll have a real advantage over your competitors for jobs. Knowing how to write a clear and concise English sentence should be taken for granted if you're applying for an editorial job, but you'd be surprised at how often the job applicant can't pass even the simplest copy test. So study -- and if you like to write, practice on your own time so you'll become even better at it.

If you have a love for a particular subject -- such as sailing, tennis, babies, news -- you can use this knowledge and interest when applying for a job on a magazine that covers this subject. While you're still in school, learn as much as you can about the subject, and get some hands-on experience. All of this background will give you impressive credentials when you start your job hunt. While being a mother doesn't necessarily qualify a woman to edit a baby magazine, it certainly doesn't hurt to have some first-hand experience.

The ideal job candidate for an entry-level job on most magazines:

A) **Is** **familiar** **with** **and** **interested** **in** **the** **magazine** he **is** **applying** **to**:

This may sound self-evident, but you'd be surprised at how many applicants have never even seen or read the magazine -- not very flattering to the editor. And it should be embarrassing to the job candidate to know or care so little about the product he wants to work on.

B) **Has** **good** **writing** **and** **editing** **skills**:

Again, if you want to be in the communications business, you should perfect the basic communication skill: writing.

C) **Is** **eager** (**and** **I** **mean** **eager**)...

...to work and do almost anything to get the job, including getting coffee for your boss, if that's required, or other low-level tasks. I call this paying your dues -- being patient and willing to do almost anything just to be around and learn the business, and being willing to stick it out even though it can get pretty tedious at times. On my first job I had to iron wedding dresses for photo shootings -- I wasn't very good at it, but my tenacity and willingess eventually paid off when it came to getting a promotion.

D) **Is** **"with** **it"**:

By this I mean someone who is tuned in, focused, is a good listener, pays attention to directions, isn't always trying to make an impression but rather is trying to learn, and knows a little bit about what is going on in the world -- both in the news and on the cultural scene.

Much of what makes a good editor is a level of general knowledge, interest in and curiosity about the world at large --

especially the subject matter of his magazine. It's out of such curiosity and focus that great story ideas are born. I'll give you an example. An editor friend of mine got sick, and during his illness, he had a lot of time to think about what had made him sick, how he was being treated and how he would get well. This led him to wonder what it would have been like to be sick back in the early part of the century, and that led to even more speculation about illness and treatment in centuries past. When he finally recovered, he turned his speculation into a major story about the history of medicine in America, and that led to a magazine award for outstanding journalsim. Now that's what I would call a good editor.

Finally, I personally lean toward the job applicant who tells me what he can do for me rather than what I can do for him. I don't want to be a teacher anymore; I'm paying for a person who can bring something to the job and who can learn fast -- I'm not paying to teach someone something that he or she should have already learned.

ENTRY-LEVEL SALARIES

Pay. Of course, money is an issue to all of us who work. But if you're interested in making a lot of it, editorial is not the place for you -- at least not in the beginning. Entry-level jobs usually pay very little since there is supposedly a great demand for these jobs. Therefore, demand exceeds supply, and when that happens, you can buy talent "cheap." Anywhere from $12,000 to $20,000 is the range, but most entry-level jobs start at about $13,000 or $14,000 a year in New York City (probably less elsewhere). But if you stay around, work hard and get promoted, you can makes six figures some day in a top editorial job in a large company.

EDITORIAL CAREER PATHS

What kind of work will you actually be doing in an entry-level job? Again, the answer depends somewhat on the size and budget of the magazine. If it's a highly departmentalized staff where a group of editors work on one narrow subject matter (science, for example) or skill (copy editing), then a beginner's job might also be very narrow, and you just might find yourself doing rather menial tasks like typing, proofreading, opening mail, answering phones, setting up appointments for other editors and fact-checking.
If it's a small staff where everyone is very busy doing many different jobs, then your job could be fairly challenging and demanding, and you could be thrown into a busy job with little or no preparation and expected to "sink or swim."
At my magazine, for example, the staff is quite small, so everyone works hard and does many different jobs. An entry-level job, called editorial assistant, includes everything from opening

the mail to proofreading, fact-checking and writing an occasional article for the magazine. We don't delegate jobs as much as we share them, so even the top editors on the staff are doing some entry-level jobs from time to time. The best part of being on a small staff is that you learn by doing. The advantage of a large staff is that you have time to learn and absorb the job before you have to plunge in and do it.

A lot of junior editors wonder how long they should stay in a job before moving on. I'm not necessarily the best person to answer this question since I've been in my current job for 16 years. I don't think there is any standard answer except to stay as long as you are happy and challenged and to leave when and if a better opportunity comes along. Usually, you are rewarded for staying in the same place for three or more years. But if you don't see any chance for promotion and want to move into another company or job, then I'd say do it. Nobody will think you're impatient if you leave a job after two years, especially if you've worked hard, learned a lot and are getting a better job.

Where can you expect to be in three to five years after you start? It's not so important that your job title change but that your job description change. If you're doing the same thing two years after you started, then it's time to ask for more work or a different kind of work. Growth on a job is important, and if you're not doing new or different or more challenging tasks, then you're not growing. In any job you should be eager to take on a new assignment. Volunteer your services, ask for a more complicated assignment, come up with an idea that takes a lot of work on your part or initiate something that will make your job more difficult and more interesting. This is how to make your job more fascinating and challenging while staying with the same company for years.

The best part of working on an editorial staff is that everyone is creative, ideas are the major output of the department and no matter what your title or job description, if you have a good idea, you'll be praised, encouraged, welcomed, and some day, you'll see your idea come to life in the magazine.

The excitement and challenge of putting out a magazine every week or month is, in my view, unmatched by any other kind of work. Since a magazine is both an information and entertainment medium, there's a chance to impart some serious information but also have some fun while doing it. Magazines are not books -- they don't last forever, and they're not the Holy Bible. They're a quick, entertaining, lively and informative way to learn about something or contemplate something or just be amused by something. They're timely, and they're visually stimulating.

If you have a real interest in a subject or a special skill in editing or writing, magazines are the place for you. If you're patient and stay with a job that might be a little boring right now, you'll be rewarded some day either in money or advancement. But nothing matches the special pleasure of watching one of your ideas come to life on the page and knowing that somewhere out

there a reader is chuckling, getting choked up or just sitting
back and enjoying a good read.

* * *

In her 16 years with <u>American Baby</u>, Ms. Nolte has helped
turn it into the leader in its field. She has also helped to
create other publications for American Baby, Inc., including the
successful annual, <u>The First Year of Life</u>. She helped launch and
is now the Publisher of <u>Childbirth Educator</u>, and she is Editorial
Director of <u>Childbirth 85</u>.

Before assuming this myriad of responsibilities at American
Baby, Inc., she was Fashion and Merchandising Editor at <u>Bride's</u>
magazine, a Conde Nast publication.

She is active in a number of professional and charitable
organizations, including the American Society of Magazine Editors, where she serves as Vice President and a member of the
Executive Committee, and the March of Dimes Media Advisory Board.

Ms. Nolte is a graduate of the University of Minnesota. She
received her MA from New York University.

CHAPTER 15

Is Kermit *Really* A Yuppie Frog?

By

Art Cooper, Editor-in-Chief
GQ

The experiences during my first year as Editor of GQ proved that the job was everything that I'd dreamed it would be. They also proved that nothing, absolutely nothing, in my professional life could have prepared me for the daily drama of a fashion magazine. Let me illustrate this with an anecdote:

One morning, shortly after I got to GQ, I was on the phone with literary agent Candida Donadio negotiating for the rights to Joseph Heller's new novel, God Knows. **This is what editing a monthly men's magazine is all about**, I thought. **If Harold Ross could only see me now.**

I was snapped out of my reverie by a fearsome commotion outside my office. I got off the phone and looked up to see people from the Fashion Department and people from the Art Department, like Laurel and Hardy, trying to squeeze through the doorway. There was, of course, a problem. A serious problem.

We were planning a major fashion story called Great Couples, which was going to be shot with real people -- Dick Cavett & Carrie Nye, Jules Feiffer & Jennifer Allen, people like that. One of the couples the Art Department wanted to shoot was Kermit and Miss Piggy.

The Fashion Editors objected and they were crying emergency. They questioned whether Kermit was really a GQ man. Was he really a Yuppie frog or merely a blue-collar frog with pretentions to style? I had never seen Kermit at the Four Seasons or Elaine's, but he is, after all, a movie star with his own TV show.

Movie star or not, heterosexual or not, Kermit did not belong in GQ. That was my decision. But no matter what my decision, I now realized I was in a world only Lewis Carroll could have invented. And, besides that, who could I have got to make a little green suit for such a teeny frog?

These might sound like trivial concerns to you, and they once would have to me, too. But GQ is, after all, a fashion magazine, and reconciling the fashion coverage with serious journalism is the purpose of my job. I've always been moderately interested in fashion. At least I try to leave the house each day without looking like a TV test pattern. But now I'm as obsessed with clothes as those people whose lives revolve around Bloomingdale's. I know about mackelsfield and loden, about the history of the necktie and the trenchcoat. I know the Big Four are not Lawrence Taylor and his fellow New York Giants linebackers. That's what a year can do.

WHAT A DIFFERENCE A YEAR MAKES

When I arrived at GQ in August of 1983, the magazine's biggest problem was that it was perceived as a gay fashion magazine. The perception was wrong. The problem was really not one of style, but of substance -- GQ was not a smart magazine. If you looked, you could find articles in the magazine. But they were badly done and editing was an afterthought. A movie column, for example, more often than not turned into a restaurant review with recipes. So we went out to change the intelligence and bring substance to GQ.

Editorially, GQ's appeal had been "artsy elitist." We wanted to broaden the appeal, make the magazine tougher, livelier, more entertaining and more immediate. What success we've achieved is due to four factors: (1) Writers; (2) Staff changes; (3) The new look of our fashion pages; and (4) Covers by Richard Avedon.

And underlying all of this was the commitment and support of Si Newhouse and Alexander Liberman. When I was discussing the job with Si and Alex, I suggested that we put real men rather than male models on the cover, and they agreed. My first week on the job, Alex asked me what I needed. I told him I'd like eight more pages in the well and run-of-the-book color. Twenty minutes later he phoned and said I had eight more pages in the well and run-of-the book color. And Richard Avedon to shoot our covers. 20 minutes. Now I've worked in companies where if you wanted a packet of pencils you had to submit a five-year plan.

GREAT WRITERS MAKE GREAT MAGAZINES

I've always believed that great writers make great magazines. If you publish the best writing, readers will find the magazine, no matter what magazine it is. So I went after the best writers around, many of whom I'd worked with at Penthouse and Family Weekly, others whose books I'd reviewed kindly at Newsweek. Writers never forget good reviews.

The day in mid-June I accepted the GQ job, I phoned David Halberstam and said, "Please do a piece on the legacy of John F. Kennedy and get it to me by August 15 for the November issue." He did. Following issues contained articles by Garry Wills on Henry Kissinger, Jesse Jackson and the 80's...We sent Roy Blount Jr. to

130

a health spa, an experience that transformed Blount and gave us an amusing piece. He's written several other humor pieces and a profile of Bill Murray. We've published humor and fiction by Bruce Jay Friedman. And we've published fiction by Thomas Berger, Gore Vidal and Joseph Heller.

The November (1983) issue was the first one I had any real involvement with. My first day, we reformated the front-of-the-book with regular departments, and set about enlisting regular columnists. These columnists, more than anything else, have given GQ its tone. The first recruit was Wilfred Sheed to do an At Large column. Next came novelist Mordecai Richler to do the Books Column. Aside from infusing their pages with wit and style, Sheed and Richler served as magnets attracting other top writers. The pleasure of their company helped us get Ron Powers to do our TV column, William Henry III Movies, economist Michael Evans Money, Ben Fong-Torres Music, and Nick von Hoffman's Area Code 202, which is a serial novel, a roman a clef about Washington that Nick writes to deadline each month.

We also attempted to bring stature and style to our service articles and the Travel and Wine & Spirits features by assigning pieces to such writers as A.E. Hotchner, Jan Morris, Clifton Fadiman, Dan Wakefield, Stephen Birmingham and William Styron.

But the column that has attracted the most attention -- and the most mail -- is All About Adam, a monthly turn sometimes laced with wit, sometimes with vitriol, about men, but written by a woman. I started the column because there was no female point of view anywhere in the magazine, and I believe that men like to read what women think of us. So writers like Blair Sabol, Anne Roiphe, Marilyn Sokol and Kate White are telling readers what women think of men as lovers, husbands, helpmates and fashion plates. The column touched a nerve and the mail began pouring in. Especially with Blair Sabol's piece, "Where Have All the Real Men Gone?," a plaintive cry that American women were drowning in a sea of wimps. Oh, the letters! Men, without exception, cried foul. They said they were trying to become new men, sensitive, able to shed a tear. They asked, "What do women want anyway?" Women, without exception, said they wanted the same kind of man Blair did -- someone who enjoyed football and beer, someone more like Clint Eastwood than Alan Alda.

AND SO DOES THE RIGHT STAFF

Which brings me to my second point: staff changes. When I arrived, the top editors of the existing staff, for some reason, thought the magazine would be run democratically, by majority rule, and that I would have one vote in any decision. And they thought I was there sort of "on approval." When they heard and saw what I intended to do, they said they did not approve. They said it strongly and to anyone who would listen. "And," they said, "Please send him back from whence he came..."

The editors who replaced them are some of the most talented I've ever worked with. Eliot Kaplan came with me from Family Weekly, and with him came the writers he edited there: Halberstam, Wills, Sheed and Robert Ward. Rochelle Udell came on loan from _Self_ magazine to organize the Art Department, bring in the best photographers and help give GQ its new look. In September, Jonathan Black came over from _TV Cable Week_. Jon's importance there was obvious. The day after he joined us, _TV Cable Week_ folded. Next came Paul Scanlon with a wealth of writers and a wealth of experience gained during a decade as a top editor at _Rolling Stone_. More recently, Ellen Stern, of _Best Bets_ fame, came to us from the _East Side Express_. Ellen came in to discuss a freelance assignment and I wouldn`t let her leave the building until she agreed to join the staff. And Mark Goodman, formerly of _Time_ and _New Times_ and an about-to-be-published novelist, joined us as Senior Writer.

Once we were all together, we did what magazine editors do...we took meetings. In my favorite book about our business, _The Years with Ross_, James Thurber wrote that the _New Yorker_ never had meetings. God bless Ross and I don't know how he did it. We have formal meetings, informal meetings and ambushes. An ambush occurs when I venture out of my office and am spirited away to the fashion closet to spend hours among the mackelsfield and loden. We have weekly operational and planning meetings. We have bi-weekly editorial lunches in my office where the quality of ideas seems directly related to the quality of the food. We have, it seems, daily meetings with writers and photographers to discuss assignments. And there are all those meetings with the Art and Fashion Departments, which have resulted in (point 3) the changing face of our fashion pages.

FASHION FIRST - SOME THINGS DON'T CHANGE

One thing that hasn't changed, and never will, is that GQ is a fashion magazine. Many readers buy us for the clothes we show and how we show them. When we added pages to the magazine, we also increased our fashion coverage. Now we run about 40 pages of fashion each issue, sometimes more. A year ago, much of the fashion was avant garde, the presentation heroic and narcissistic.

That _has_ changed. Now the clothes are more accessible and more relevant to our readers and the lives they lead. And the presentation is more natural. The pages reflect the reality of men's lives and how they dress. Our fashion stories are photographed in board rooms, law offices, restaurants, the theater, at airports, aboard ships, in resort hotels.

The men who wear the clothes in our pages have changed too. The models are less "modelly", more human. They look more like real guys. They don't have to be prettier than the women models anymore. We're also using more older models who are more appropriate for the clothes and the situations.

But we decided that the best way to get real-looking men into GQ was simply to use real men. Earlier, I mentioned the Great Couples portfolio. We've also shot fashion on jazz musicians, medical residents, architects, Wharton Business School graduates, artists and writers. And on athletes and celebrities like Joe Theisman, Bernard King, Vitas Gerulaitis, Greg Louganis, Ben Cross, Jeff Bridges, Howard Rollins and Marvin Hamlish.

I don't think fashion should be intimidating. So we try to have some fun with it, such as in our regular feature, "Why I Wear What I Wear," and occasional fantasy spreads like the "Watergate Makeover," an illustrated reunion with Nixon and all his men elegantly attired in designer clothes.

Besides modelling clothes inside the magazine, Joe Theisman was the first non-model we put on the cover. That was the November 1983 issue. That issue did exceptionally well, especially in Washington where it sold off the stands. The December issue, with Michael Caine on the cover, was our first Dick Avedon cover.

THE INVALUABLE PRESENCE OF RICHARD AVEDON

How important is Avedon to us? Very. Dick's lighting, his white background and his magic have given us a distinct look. Although going from white to dark gives us a monthly fit with coverlines. And beyond his genius, Dick's reputation helps get us cover subjects I'm sure we would not have gotten otherwise. James Garner is one. Garner grants one major interview a year, and he had turned me down on other magazines for six straight years. So I tried again, and when Garner's wife heard that Avedon would shoot the cover, she persuaded Jim to do it. Because of Avedon, there seems to be a cachet to being on GQ's cover.

A cover ought to be a strong statement of personal style and the most important editorial page of the magazine. So after Avedon shot five celebrity covers, we decided to try a non-celebrity, someone from the businessworld. We took a risk and put Donald Trump on the cover of our May (1984) cover. The issue sold very well, and not only in New York. In New York, Trump himself made sure we had a healthy newsstand increase. Trump hated the profile. Mostly, he hated his own quotes. He thought they made him sound like a hustler. Trump did not want GQ on the newstand in Trump Tower. So when the issue was delivered to Trump Tower, Donald Trump bought them all. We sent more. He bought more. If he had kept buying we would have gone over the half-million mark.

Our August (1984) issue was also risky business. That was our Joseph Heller cover. While Heller is well-known and in the mirror of his mind a dead ringer for Paul Newman, he is also a Jewish novelist, has grey hair and was the oldest man we'd had on the cover. The worry over that one gave me a Heller-like mane. I need not have worried. The issue sold even better than Heller assured me it would.

ISN'T IT NICE WHEN IT ALL WORKS?

So the changes at GQ during my first year were somewhat radical and the results were very pleasing. According to Simmons, our total audience went up 25%, to 3½ million readers. Our readers per copy jumped from 5.3 to 6.3. And those readers had become a bit older and a bit richer. Circulation went up 9% on the newsstand and 9% on subscriptions. And our September, 1983, issue was the biggest in our history -- 470 pages, 309 advertising pages. It was the first issue of <u>GQ</u> to surpass 700,000 total circulation.

In 1983, <u>GQ</u> set a record for men's magazines with 1,452 ad pages. In 1984, we carried more than 1,900 pages, an increase of about 40%. I'm lousy at numbers but those are easy to remember.

* * *

Arthur Cooper was named Editor-in-Chief of <u>Gentlemen's Quarterly</u> in August, 1983, becoming its third top editor since the magazine was founded in 1957. Mr. Cooper was previously Editor of <u>Family Weekly</u>, where he published the original work of Pulitzer Prize-winning writers James A. Michener, Arthur Schlesinger, Jr., and Robert Coles. He also conducted and published exclusive interviews with Presidents Jimmy Carter and Ronald Reagan and former President Richard M. Nixon.

He has worked for <u>Penthouse</u>, <u>Newsweek</u> and <u>Time</u> magazines. He began his career in 1964 with the <u>Harrisburg</u> (Pennsylvania) <u>Patriot</u> as a political reporter.

Mr. Cooper lives in New York City with his wife, Amy Levin, Editor-in-Chief of <u>Mademoiselle</u> magazine.

CHAPTER 16

The Business Press:
Do More Than Write Obits!

By

Anthony J. Rutigliano, Editor-in-Chief
Management Review

For many about to earn their degrees in Journalism, trade magazines seem like a trade-off. The parochial interests of a trade journal hold none of the glories of a national news weekly. The advocacy position of a business magazine is a far cry from the iconoclastic investigative reporting of the Washington Post. What's more, when asked by their fellow graduates where they found jobs, few Journalism majors are eager to reply, Turkey World, Pizza Today or American Cemetery.

However, I would like to advocate your strongly considering an editorial career in business journalism (as we prefer to call it). Those looking for opportunities to be Woodwards or Bernsteins should not overlook the fact that there are many reporters on newspapers and consumer magazines who write obituaries, wedding annnouncements and stories about local field hockey teams. There are many who work as fact checkers and researchers. In short, a lot of dues must be paid before the glory days of consumer journalism are enjoyed by most reporters.

The business press, on the other hand, generally offers a short apprenticeship spent performing unchallenging and thankless duties, and usually provides you an opportunity to write challenging stories at a relatively early time in your career. Business journalism gives you the difficult, but rewarding, task of writing for an audience that knows more about the subject than you do. (Compare that to a career in the consumer press). And, last but not least, it usually offers a more accelerated career and salary track.

Granted, there are many days in the life of a Junior Editor that are positively deadly. But, unlike fact checkers, researchers and obit writers across the land, Business Editors have the chance to give American businesses the means by which they, well, talk to themselves.

Business journalism presents an opportunity to be an expert, to become the eyes and ears of an industry. How many consumer journalists have you seen address a group as _the_ most distinguished expert on a given topic? How many consumer journalists had the inside track on Coke's dubious decision to put the word "new" on its bottles -- I expect the Editors at _Beverage_ _World_ did. How many consumer reporters can be their own bosses within a few short years? Those of you who answered "few" or "none" to these questions are correct: These are distinctions claimed by the business press.

Well, that's enough advocacy journalism. Now, I'd like to try to give you answers to some of your most pressing questions.

GETTING STARTED

Recruiters for the countless business magazines in America generally are looking for Journalism graduates or those with Business degrees who happen to have some writing skills. Besides the diploma, recruiters want experience.

Internships

I would strongly advise undergraduates to seek summer employment on local newspapers or magazines through apprenticeship programs. All of the publishing companies with which I'm familiar welcome qualified interns. (See Chapter 00 for a list of internships and training programs at major consumer and business publishing firms -- Ed.). Usually your duties will consist of opening mail, writing up new product announcements, proofreading and other such thankless tasks. However, most editors will feel obliged to provide you the chance to do a by-lined article which will look just dandy in your portfolio.

If you are unable to secure such an internship or any other publishing-related summer employment, you should make every effort to build up a portfolio through other jobs or means. Be an active staff member of your college newspaper. Attempt to sell some of your articles to magazines. Most recruiters look for experience -- the portfolio is your way of demonstrating professional writing ability.

The Interview

It is a good idea, when contacting recruiters, to include copies of your clips with your resume. Job applications for any opening quickly pile up. What distinguishes them is not the resume, but the quality of the writing on the enclosed clips. If you have actually sold pieces to a magazine or newspaper, all the better.

If you are able to secure an appointment for an interview, go prepared. When you schedule the interview, ask the recruiter to send you copies of the magazine(s) published by the company.

Read the publication(s) thoroughly and come up with a list of questions. Notice the names on the masthead, note the number of articles each person has written and formulate some questions about individual job responsibilities.

If you are not interested in the subject matter of the magazine, don't go on the interview. Nothing is worse for the applicant or the employer than a qualified candidate lacking interest in the subject matter. If you are interested, then be prepared to say why. Better yet, do some extra reading that will enable you to ask the recruiter, and, assuming you get that far, the Editor, some intelligent questions. (I suggest some questions of my own later in this chapter, so read on.)

A DAY IN THE LIFE

So, you got the job! Now, just what will you be doing?

To be honest, your life will be extremely boring at first. Most of the magazines on which I've worked are divided roughly 50/50 between features and news stories and what is known as "back of the book" material. The latter consists of: product announcements, industry news (earnings, losses, staff changes), calendars of events and other material that is generally as dry as the paper it's printed on.

How'd you guess? This will be your job: writing, filing, sorting, tracking, editing and hating "back of the book." Some companies specialize in making it even more hideous than it sounds by requiring headlines for each product. Think of how you'll feel after writing such things as, "Beach Balls Fold Flat for Easy Storage," or "Chair Allows User to Sit Down, Stand Up." Frequently, you will ask yourself, "Just what am I doing here?"

The answer is most often up to you. Unlike the lowly researcher at <u>Forbes</u>, checking facts on Malcolm's editorials, you'll be able to take some initiative in suggesting assignments for yourself. You'll most likely be able to suggest "field trips" for securing stories. You'll be able to attend industry events to get a feel for the business and what its participants think about. In addition, you also will have your share of duties that are even less glorious than "writing products." There's opening mail, filing, keeping track of correspondence to freelancers and other contributors, logging out copy to the typesetter, logging in galleys, logging in artwork, logging out artwork, etc.

ADVANCEMENT

As I mentioned earlier, trade journalism represents a relatively fast career track. You'll start out as a "grunt," and a low paid one at that. Entry-level <u>Assistant Editors</u> or <u>Editorial Assistants</u> can expect to earn $13,000 - $15,000 a year. But if you're talented, you'll quickly rise through the ranks. And at the top end of the scale, there are a lot of business publication editors who make $60,000 or more.

At companies with which I've been associated, the career

track goes something like this: Editorial Assistant or Assistant
Editor...to Associate Editor...to Managing Editor...to Editor.
Many companies throw in other functional titles like Field Editor
-- generally someone who devotes all his time to reporting,
sometimes for more than one of the company's magazines -- or more
illustrious ones like Senior Editor, Executive Editor, even
Editor-In-Chief. Many of these titles, quite frankly, are for
people who deserve promotions but, unless such a new title is
given them, can't be given one.

     Having joined Management Review only recently, I spent the
first nine years of my career at Gralla Publications, which has
some 21 magazines in almost as many disparate fields. A short
look at my own career at Gralla demonstrates how fast the career
track can be.

     I joined the company in August 1976 as its first editorial
trainee (Title 1). After spending eleven weeks filing, writing
products, proofreading and learning the ins-and-outs of the
company, I joined Meeting News as Assistant Editor (Title 2).
This was a very rewarding job in that I was involved -- for the
only time in my career thus far -- with a brand new magazine.
Quite an exciting time. After one year spent doing grunt work,
but also traveling all over the United States, I became Associate
Editor (Title 3). Here I was relieved of a great deal of the
less-than-challenging jobs on the magazine and given more opportunity to write and manage the new Assistant Editor.
     After eighteen months of that, I outgrew any available
positions on Meeting News, and was named Field Editor for the
company as a whole (Title 4). In this position I covered three
industries for three different magazines: travel and hospitality
for Meeting News; food retailing for Supermarketing; and health
care for Health Care Week. How's that for diversity! After only
30 months on the job, I was covering three industries, writing
upwards of six feature-length stories every month! What's more, I
was required to perform no clerical duties nor write any products.
     This was followed by my move into management, the crossing
of the "We/They" line. My rite of passage came as Assistant
Managing Editor of National Jeweler (Title 5). On this job, I was
in charge of the day-to-day operation of a bi-monthly magazine
with an Editorial staff of eleven and an Art staff of four. Above
me was only the Editor -- who was basically an industry personality -- and the Managing Editor -- who spent most of her time
coming up with enough assignments for this huge magazine.
     Soon, some new magazine acquisitions -- and the resulting
personnel shifts they necessitated -- allowed me to become Managing Editor of the same magazine in a very short time (Title 6). I
can honestly say that I learned many invaluable management lessons in this position. Think of it -- I was in charge of 15
people in my fifth year on the job!
     One year later, I was Editor of my own magazine (Title 7) --
American Building Supplies. This was followed by a challenging
stint as Executive Editor (Title 8), soon Editor/Associate
Publisher (Titles 9 & 10) of Health Care Systems.

To those of you considering a career in journalism, I might add that my salary moved upwards even more rapidly than my title.

WHAT'S THE CATCH?

There's more than one. Business journalism might very well be the highest-turnover field in the country. I saw countless numbers of people come and go. Some staffs, in fact, were revolving doors. Obviously, everyone wasn't as happy in business journalism as I have been.

Why?

There are many answers, all of which fall into the following four categories:

The publishing company itself: The philosophies of business publishing companies vary widely. Some companies are content to publish "rags" that do little but tout advertisers and cheer on even the least savory members of the profession. There are magazines that do this. They are the ones primarily responsible for the occasionally tarnished reputation my business enjoys. However, many other companies -- like Fairchild, Chilton, Cahners, Crain, Gralla and others -- keep a sharp line drawn between the editorial and advertising interests of the magazines they publish. At still others, the line exists but is just occasionally forgotten.

At the companies that produce the "rags," editors are strongly encouraged to call on advertisers, write "fluff" stories about advertising accounts, endlessly press the flesh at trade shows, etc. I asked an editor at one such company about these distasteful (to me) tasks he was required to perform and he proudly proclaimed, "We are not in the journalism business, we are in the publishing business."

That is very unfortunate for those working for him who may value their editorial skills and principles.

The field the magazine covers: Many editors find that they don't mind the idea of business journalism or the company they work for, but can't stand the field about which they write. There are some industries in which it is impossible to get sources to talk. I personally have found this true of many retailing fields, in which competition is cut-throat and industry members are loathe to give away trade secrets.

Self-realization: Many people quit because they realize: A) they just can't be happy in the field of business journalism, or B) they can't write or interview well enough to progress in journalism. For years, we lost many people to law or business school, people who simply realized that writing would always be too much of a struggle for them.

The call of consumer journalism: Many talented people with whom I've worked have left trade journalism to go into the more glamorous consumer magazine world. Several have done well, advancing to relatively high positions on some prestigious publications. Many others, however, have floundered and are still toiling away thanklessly in Research Departments.

STRAIGHT TALK

What you want from your employer when you are considering where you want to work is some straight talk about many of the issues I've discussed. Many people are intimidated during interviews and feel that they're there to answer questions, not ask them.

Well, nothing could be further from the truth. You must know how the company you're considering is run, according to what journalistic principles it operates and how it treats its staff. Here are some questions you should ask and some tips on how to evaluate the company's answers:

1. How old is the youngest Editor-in-Chief at your company?

If the answer is "50," then you are looking in the wrong place. This indicates that there is little possibility of upward mobility and, probably, that the company has neither acquired or launched any new publications for quite some time.

2. What can a talented candidate expect to be doing in five years?

Go ahead, give Personnel Directors a taste of their own medicine! You should try to determine the type of responsibilites you'll have in the future. You don't want to be opening mail or writing products five years from now, do you?

3. How are your stories developed?

Does the staff visit trade shows? Take field trips to visit sources? Or are most of the stories developed over the phone? You want to work for a company that gets its staff out into the world about which it writes. You don't want to work for a company unwilling to invest funds in story development.

4. How many magazines do you compete against? Where does yours rank?

Unlike the world of consumer magazines, in business journalism the best, most helpful, most well-written magazines are those most read and receiving the highest number of ad pages. Some good examples are Progressive Grocer, Home Furnishings Daily (HFD) and Chain Store Age, all well known and all successful.

5. How large is the editorial staff?

If the answer is "four" -- on a magazine with 100 pages of copy a month -- think twice. You'll be overworked.

6. Do you promote staffers from one magazine to an opening on another?

Hopefully, the answer will be "yes." This will give you more opportunities to advance without the hassle of changing companies.

7. How autonomous is the editorial staff?

You want to work at a company in which talented editors are left alone to do their jobs. Usually a great deal of centralized control indicates the editorial content is being compromised.

8. What are the average yearly salary increases?

The ideal company will have a range of increases to recognize differences in achievement. The high end of that range should be at least twice the rate of inflation. Again, you want to be on a fast track from the rather dismal starting salaries you'll receive in this business.

9. Does the company generate its own research?

If a magazine is to become or remain an authoritative voice in its industry, it must have a Research Department that produces quality, exclusive materials quoted not only in the industry, but by general business magazines and publications like the Wall Street Journal. I've found that companies without Research Departments don't have the highest regard for the editorial content of their products.

10. What is the circulation of the magazine?

The higher the circulation, the higher the advertising page rate, the higher the budget. That's a fact of life.

IS IT FOR YOU?

After reading all of this, you're probably still saying to yourself, "Gee, I never wanted to be a trade journalist, but I have to start somewhere, and what this guy is saying sounds okay, but Pizza Today...?"
I have to agree that my field has more than its share of less than glamorous jobs. I was probably in a much worse position than you when I entered it. I had a Bachelor of Arts degree, consisting of 90 credits in literature -- including Latin and Ancient Greek -- some other humanities courses and one math course. But, from doing all those term papers, at least I had learned to write.
Now, the field has narrowed to such an extent that I probably wouldn't hire my younger self to be my assistant editor. You've undoubtedly been studying journalism to secure yourself a

job on a newspaper or consumer magazine, and here I am trying to convince you that a job in business journalism can be rewarding.

Well, it's not for everybody. But, even for those of you who long to be on _Time_ or _Newsweek_, it can provide valuable experience. What's more, many of you will find that becoming truly involved in an industry, learning its ins-and-outs, developing sources and breaking important stories can be very, very exciting.

But you must choose a company whose principles are as high as yours are right now.

* * *

In his current position, Mr. Rutigliano is responsible for supervising the editorial staff and directing the development of _Management Review_, the official publication of the American Management Association. He spent 10 years with Gralla Publications, where, as he so graphically explained, he averaged a new title every year.

He is a graduate of Hunter College of the City University of New York.

Mr. Rutigliano, as his article demonstrates, is quite happy as a trade magazine editor and considers the area of consumer magazine publishing to be "foreign territory."

VI
Production
(Manufacturing & Distribution)

CHAPTER 17

There's Nothing "Typical" About Production!

By

Dale Schenkelberg, Production Director
Meredith Corporation

Backbone, backing up, bad break, base, blanket, bleed, blow-up, blueprint, body, brightness, burn, catching-up, creep, cut-off, dot, drop-out, dummy, enamel, feeder, fixing, flat, flow, fog, form, grain, gutter, hickeys, impressions, jog, justify, key, makeup, mask, mat, mechanical, packing, picking, point, positive, ream, register, run-around, score, screen, scum, sharpen, signature, skid, spine, staging, stone, tack, tooth, trapping, undercut, vehicle, wash-up, web and wrinkles.

All familiar words, right? Not quite as familiar as you might think once you enter the world of Publishing Production.
Those of you who like to run know what "jog" means. But in Production, "jog" means to align sheets of paper into a compact pile. How about a "hickey?" To those of us in Production, it means spots or imperfections in printing, usually due to dirt on the press or paper particles.
Another case in point? The word "point." That's a unit of measuring used primarily for designing type sizes. For example, there are twelve points to a pica, approximately 72 to an inch.
There are, of course, completely different "Production meanings" associated with all those "familiar" words up there. If you're interested in a Production career, you have to learn a whole new vocabulary...and a few other things, as well.

WHAT'S PRODUCTION ALL ABOUT?

Why would somebody choose a Production career? Well, in my own experience, I've found that each day is different. Every day, someone, somewhere, will offer you a new challenge -- reducing costs, getting magazines produced earlier, improving reproduction quality or a myriad of other possibilities.

At Meredith Corporation, I think our Production Department is unique, because we find ourselves working on a lot of areas other than the production of magazines. We also get involved producing brochures for the Circulation and Book Divisions, custom publications for outside customers (through the Meredith Publishing Services Department), hardbound and softcover books, envelopes, letters, inserts, reprints and more.

We also are responsible for the Electronic Text Processing Department, which works closely with our Editorial and Art groups to manage the flow of text through our electronic text processing system.

We also have a warehousing facility, which mainly ships books to the customers of our Book Division. All of this in addition to magazine production, the subject you thought you'd be reading about.

I must repeat myself: The most interesting parts of a Production person's job are the many daily challenges. And not just daily -- there are many late-night and early-morning press checks that have to be done to ensure the customers get exactly what they want out of the material they supplied.

We get daily questions on cost containment. Everything that we do usually affects our customers' bottom lines. It's up to the Production Department to schedule our presses as economically as possible and to check all the invoices from our own outside suppliers for accuracy and adherence to contracts. We are always looking for ways to reduce costs and, at the same time, maintain a top-quality product.

Another challenge we face each day is dealing with the variety of customers we have to serve -- from Publishers and Editors to artists and advertising agencies throughout the United States. Many of these customers don't understand printing, nor should they have to. So we have to learn how to communicate the many technicalities of our job without getting too technical.

During a meeting a few years ago with one of our top executives, I was explaining our production schedule, noting specifily the dates when "turn to's" had to be supplied to the printer. The executive had been in publishing for a number of years, but finally had to ask me, "What's a turn to?" Well, a "turn to" is simply the words that appear at the bottom of a story that's to be continued, asking the reader to "turn to page ---." Now there was no need for him to know that, but it was a term so commonplace in Production that we assumed everbody knew it.

Agency production personnel always provide challenges because they, too, are looking for the best possible reproduction of their customers' materials. No two agencies work the same, mainly because of the individual personalities and talents involved. I can say without hesitation that there are no good guys or bad guys out there -- only good communicators and bad communicators. The good communicators are those with a solid understand-

146

ing of the printing process. Those without it, of course, aren't
as good.

Other customers we serve are the editors of all our products. They and the art directors know exactly what they want out
of the photographs that accompany a particular story. In our
Production Department, we like to let the customer -- the artist
or designer himself -- follow along through the whole process,
from photo selection right to the point where the ink hits the
paper. Because they've lived with the story right from the beginning, they're more sure of exactly what effect they are trying to
achieve. With a little luck, they tell us so we get it right before we go on press.

I learned that lesson many years ago, when I first started
at Meredith, on a 2:00 AM press check.(Why do press checks always
seem to occur at 2:00 AM!?) Anyway, I had brought the press
sheets that I'd okayed back to the office. The customer took one
look and, with an unhappy face and in no uncertain terms, told me
I had not achieved the desired reproduction quality. Once he'd
calmed down, I told him very politely that I would be more than
happy to pass up the 2:00 AM press checks and could suggest that
the plant call him instead.

They never did. And we got along much better after that.
However, we also communicated more before I went to do "color
OK's" so I had a better understanding of what he wanted...in
advance.

I've mentioned often the customers we serve. I think that's
an important word, perhaps the basis of the philosophy of the
Production Department. We do not generate revenue, only costs. So
our basic product is service.

Is the customer always right? Of course not! Most of them,
as I've also mentioned, simply don't know enough about the
limitations of the printing process. But never tell the customer
he's wrong...in so many words. Instead, try to lead him down the
path you think is best.

MY OWN ATYPICAL CAREER PATH

While the Meredith Production Department is itself unique,
my own path into Production is like no one else's in the field! I
began as a radio announcer, took a job in Meredith's Circulation
Department (some 21 years ago) and, after 13 years, was tabbed as
the head of the Production Department. It was at that point that
I had to learn what a "hickey" was and the difference between a
"point" and a "jog."

While I didn't have a wealth of production experience to
bring along with me, I had learned one very valuable thing in my
past jobs -- how to count. At the radio station, in my position
as News Director, I had to know how many words per minute each
announcer could read, so newscasts would take up precisely the
allotted time. In the Circulation Department, I had to know how
to add, multiply and divide to make sense out of things like

147

renewal response, test mailings, credit collections, budgets, net-per-copy, etc.

When I first started in Production, we had no "bottom line," no way to measure from month-to-month how the department was actually doing. We have since set up a number of bottom lines, in order to measure such things as magazine delivery, how our magazines' quality compares to each others' and the competitors', financial reports for our customers, budgets and strategic plans. So, somewhere, somehow, I believe you need a measurement of the work you're doing -- whether it's the number of ad units handled per person or the number of pages handled per Makeup Supervisor.

WHERE ARE THE JOBS?

While _my_ path to the head of Production was certainly unique, there are many entry-level positions that will prepare you for a more normal career in Production. One of these is **Associate Makeup Supervisor**. These people are charged with putting the magazine together, determining the most economical press and placing the ads and editorial in the most desirable configurations. You would work closely with both the Advertising and Editorial Departments.

Another entry-level position is **Advertising Material Technician**. That's the person responsible for ensuring that all the advertising film sent by agencies reaches us before deadline, is the right size and, most important, the right **ad**. All this information is relayed constantly to the printing supplier so the entire production process is coordinated.

There is a lot of technical work involved in both these jobs, as well as a lot of phone-time to obtain accurate information. The challenge of working with a number of customers and staff members is always there, along with ample doses of frustration -- no matter how hard you try, you may not get accurate, complete information or be able to locate needed materials.

Other positions -- a step or two above these two -- generally require more actual printing experience. Such titles would include the **Quality Control Managers** and the **Magazine Production Managers**. The customers are the same, but the responsibilities vary. A deeper knowledge of both the printing process and financial analysis is necessary to move into these areas.

But career paths vary. There is one young lady I know who started as a secretary. She now heads up one of the Customer Service areas for our Printing Group. Another young lady started as a secretary in the Financial Department and is now the Manager of Magazine Makeup, with four Makeup Supervisors reporting to her.

THE "TYPICAL" DAY OF A PRODUCTION DIRECTOR

In all the jobs we've discussed, including my own, there is no such thing as a "typical" day. No two magazines are ever

alike.   The number and size of ads always change from month to
month.   There is always a challenge to make sure competing ads
don't wind up facing each other,   position requests are met,
editorial doesn't conflict with an adjacent ad,   colors don't
clash and, heaven forbid, a coupon doesn't back another ad.
Finding a spot for the inevitable late ads is a constant problem.
Schedules are constantly shifting as on-sale dates are set or if
the Publisher needs to get copies into the hands of subscribers
earlier than usual.

So what's _my_ day like?

The ad that was promised to arrive "no later than the 20th"
didn't, of course, but it _was_ sent and now nobody knows where it
is. When it does finally arrive, it contains a coupon, and the
insertion order said "no coupon."

The Publisher wants to change paper stock at the last minute
and there's none in inventory.

A card to be bound in the magazine arrives at the printer
not printed to your specifications. It may not fit in the magazine.

Film supplied for an ad has not been produced using industry
specifications and the printed result will probably not match
what the advertiser wants (and expects).

An editor's story has somehow been re-routed by the computer and is floating somewhere between the bits and bytes.

A flurry of late business forces a change in book size,
press configurations and a re-do of the magazine makeup.

Then an ad _cancels_, causing a change in book size, press
configurations and a re-do of magazine makeup.

Another call from the Publisher: Is there any way to cut
$1,000,000 from his production costs...without hurting quality???

A call from an agency Production Director wanting to know
why his client's ad in last month's issue did not print up to his
expectations.

The Financial Department must have revised book size estimates for the next twelve issues by tomorrow.

The lost ad is found, but contains an incorrect key number.

The computer that prints out how the regional portion of the
magazine is to be printed blows a chip, so everything has to to
be figured manually.

Due to an unexpected influx of orders, the Circulation Department wants to know if we can get more copies printed.

Advertising Services calls to let us know an ad in the last issue got printed upside down (it happened once).

Another agency calls requesting an extension of the due date for materials. But you'll be off-press by the time they want to get you the ad.

The latest delivery report arrives -- your average arrival date has slipped two days. Why?

The boss calls to remind you that budgets are due in two days, strategic plans in two months, standards of performance next week, performance appraisals for each employee as soon as possible. And don't forget the forecast meeting at 3:00.

Then comes a call from Career Publishing asking you to write an article describing a "typical day" in Production!!!!

HOW TO GET STARTED IN MAGAZINE PRODUCTION

What do I look for when I hire someone for my own department? Depending on the position, experience and reliability will always be paramount. But two other criteria always come to mind -- enthusiasm and an innovative spirit.

Most colleges don't offer courses to prepare anyone for a career in Production. Business Administration or Journalism majors are probably the best choices, but you will be starting at the bottom anyway, learning the printing process. There are, however, some excellent schools out there that do offer courses in Print Production. One such is the Rochester Institute of Technology (Rochester, NY). A complete list of all such schools is available from the Magazine Publishers Association. They will also be able to help you -- along with the information in Chapter 29 -- find summer jobs and internships in various magazines' Production Departments.

Of the many departments most major publishing houses have in common, the Production Department is the least glamorous, even though we have such a significant impact on our customers' bottom lines. The anonymity that we sometimes enjoy is not because the department is unimportant, but because we all seem to share a tendency not to "blow our own horns," if you will. One reason we are shy is because we are not bringing in any revenues for the company. This is changing, however. As costs continue to escalate, the importance of the Production Department and its people will continue to grow as well.

So, if you're interested in a job in Production, be prepared to be challenged, frustrated, rewarded and expect the unexpected -- especially in today's world, where technology is rapidly

changing the way most Production Departments are being run. This
new technology -- and understanding how it will benefit your
company - is the biggest challenge all of us in Production face.
     But then, it's virtually impossible to really predict what
the future holds. And if you could do <u>that</u>, you wouldn't want a
job in Production anyway.

                              * * *

     In his current position, Mr. Schenkelberg is responsible for
manufacturing costs and quality control for all of Meredith's
magazines, books and promotional materials. He is also in charge
of their electronic text processing and the Publishing Group's
processing center.
     Prior to attaining his current title, Mr. Schenkelberg --
who has been with Meredith for 21 years -- held several positions
with the Circulation Department, including Subscription Sales
Manager for <u>Better Homes and Gardens</u>, its flagship publication;
Director of Subscription Sales; and Circulation Marketing Director.
     He is Chairman of the Magazine Publishers Association Pro-
duction Committee and active in a variety of other publishing and
marketing trade associations.
     A native of Spencer, Iowa, Mr. Schenkelberg attended Drake
University in Des Moines, majoring in Journalism.

CHAPTER 18

If The Phone Isn't Ringing, Everything's Fine

By

Irving Herschbein, Director of Manufacturing and Distribution
Conde Nast Publications

Magazine Production is one of the old terms used in our industry. In recent years, it's often been replaced by Manufacturing Department or, more frequently, Manufacturing and Distribution. This change in nomenclature is not frivolous or just window-dressing. It's a more accurate description of what we are doing today to get magazines printed and distributed.

Magazine production as it is actually practiced today covers a far broader area than it did even ten years ago. It includes not only putting together the editorial and ad content of each publication, but typesetting (sometimes through an in-house system), the negotiation of printing contracts, paper purchasing and the distribution of the magazine to both subscribers and newsstands.

So, for purposes of this article, I'll refer to "M & D" instead of Production, since this area now includes these additional responsibilities over and above the "production" of the magazine itself.

Most people, when they think of magazine publishing, think of the glamorous editorial jobs, the interesting promotional activities or the rather heady sale of advertising to the big ad agencies. Production Departments were traditionally looked upon as somewhat akin to the "backrooms" of the Wall Street brokerage houses. We're the people who labor behind the scenes, and actually get the magazines printed and distributed, but there doesn't seem to be as much glamour or excitement in what we do.

Those of us who actually work in this end of the business, though, find it continually fascinating, never dull and hardly routine. As my colleague, Dale Schenkelberg, explained in the previous chapter, there is no such thing as a "typical" day for us. For years I've complained that I've never had two days in a row that were the same. And I have a good many years in the business. We have many challenges, many opportunities, some great successes and, occasionally, some real bombs!

HOW WE RELATE TO THE REST OF THE PUBLISHING OPERATION

Before I go into more detail on what we do in M & D and why it might interest you as a career path, let me explain a little about how we relate to the rest of the publishing operation. Because the Manufacturing and Distribution Department is really the central link to all the other departments in a magazine publishing operation.

We're the focal point for problem solving. We work with the Editorial Department, providing them with the space they must fill in each issue and with the typesetting and engraving facilities they need to actually create the pages.

Simultaneously, we work with the Advertising Sales Department, receiving the "film" from the ad agencies for the ads the salespeople have sold and ensuring that those ads are properly placed in the magazine.

The Circulation Department feeds us the details of their promotion efforts so we can establish a print order for each issue. This single print order is further broken down into the number of issues which will be shipped to individual subscribers or newsstands or used for the magazine's own promotional purposes.

Because of the vast sums of money for which we're responsible, we are deeply involved in budgeting, accounting, invoice checking, contract negotiation, etc., all of which requires us to work closely with the Finance Department.

We also must work with the printer, various freight agencies and the post office to make sure each issue reaches the newsstands on the correct "on sale" date and that the subscribers get their copies at the proper time.

THE MONEY WE SPEND

There's an old saying that the game doesn't start until the sale has been made. That's true, but once the sale is made, someone has to actually produce the product. That's where we come in. A failure on our part in any number of areas could immediately nullify the sale, reduce the profit, or even worse, create a loss.

According to the Magazine Publishers Association, between 46% and 52% of all monies spent by a magazine publisher (it varies slightly from company to company) are spent in the Manufacturing and Distribution area. Quite simply, this means that all the other, more visible areas of operation -- editorial, ad sales, promotion, research, circulation, etc. -- account for one half or less of a company's total budget. We spend the rest.

Given the sheer amount of money for which we're responsible, it's easy to see how poor judgement or a series of mistakes can easily result in less profit...or no profit at all.

Before World War II and for perhaps a decade following, Production Departments were not involved at all in the areas of planning or budgeting. It was only as publishers grew larger and developed better, more professional management that they recognized that what had appeared to be a "minor" department could actually spell the difference between profit and loss.

During the 1950's, more astute publishers began to look for professionals with training in printing, paper, binding, separations, typesetting and other production functions. There weren't too many sources for such people at the time. So the larger publishers spent time and money training people who had graduated from college with majors in somewhat related fields. Many present-day Production Directors, for example, came out of various journalism schools, where they had some, though limited, exposure to production techniques.

As we moved into the "Electronic Age," the manpower pool broadened. Now we could look for people with more scientific backgrounds, especially those with computer or computer-related training or experience. Frankly, it's now generally accepted that we would prefer to hire someone with such a background and then teach them the typesetting and printing skills they would need.

GETTING IN AND MOVING UP

If you wish to come into the M & D area today, the best preparation is a background in the graphic arts, either through one of the many two-year community college courses or, preferably, a four-year degree course. Two of the best known schools for such training are the Rochester Institute of Technology and Carnegie Tech. There are many others, however, that offer good training on modern equipment with knowledgeable, professional teachers.

In addition, the Magazine Publishers Association offers a summer intern program that enables third-year students to join major publishing companies for a 10 to 12 week publishing training program. Nearly all of the people who've participated in this program have opted for jobs in magazine publishing after graduation.

Your knowledge of equipment, systems and theory will stand you in good stead in any publishing operation. Many of the older, middle-level managers did not have a technical background -- they learned on-the-job. So they welcome the more technically-trained recent graduates who can deal with the technological complexities and leave them free to make decisions instead of having to worry about equipment, systems, film, etc.

Years ago, it was not unusual to hear someone say, "well, if you take a job as a secretary, someday you'll become an editor." Actually accomplishing such a move was more the exception than the rule. And it was never true in the area of Production. M & D is a career in and of itself. Very few people have succeeded in using it as a stepping stone to other areas of publishing.

The disciplines required are very different from those necessary for other departments. Until recently, it was so technical that it left little room for growth in the business area so needed by a Publisher or company President. So don't take a job in this specialized area expecting it to be your entree into editorial, ad sales or the executive suite.

If you do take an entry-level position in an M & D Department, you'll probably spend your first couple of years in the traffic area. This means you will be responsible for contacting the ad agencies to get the necessary ad materials (generally camera-ready artwork or film), answer questions about scheduling, placement, mechanical specifications and other semi-technical information.

In a reasonably-sized magazine publishing company, you can expect to move up to the makeup area within two to three years. You will then begin working with the Editorial and Ad Sales Departments to actually put the magazine issues together. Ads and editorial content do not just mix haphazardly in any issue; it is carefully planned by the editors and art directors, who must get editorial and art placement to work with the advertisements necessary to support the magazine.

The makeup people find themselves continually challenged by any number of variables. The Editorial Department will require "X" number of pages to serve their readers. The Ad Sales Department sold "Y" pages of ads. The Business Department, working with the Production Director, has decided that the whole issue can only contain "Z" number of pages (to maximize profitablity). Trying to put together a good-looking magazine while torn in three directions at once is the challenge!

The Makeup Manager must be able to get the editors to supply the necessary amount of content on time. The ads must be received on time. And he must answer to the Production Manager who is, at the same time, working with the printer to make sure the whole magazine is put together and gets shipped on time.

Magazines do not go to the printer all at once. They are usually sent form by form. Each form may consist of eight, sixteen or thirty two pages (depending on the printer's press capabilities). So for very large magazines, the press schedules may extend over two or more weeks. Getting the right materials to press at the right time takes a concerted effort from all the people in M & D.

Production Manager would be the next step up the career ladder. It might take you anywhere from six to ten years to reach this position. In a medium-sized company, the production manager would be responsible for negotiating printing contracts, buying paper (or negotiating for the printer to buy it for him) and engaging and dealing with color separators, typesetters and other suppliers.

Production managers do not always have to work their way up the ladder in a publisher's M & D Department. Quite often, an individual without any publishing experience who has worked for a printing or graphic arts company is brought in to manage the Department. This is because many companies believe that whoever is at the top of the M & D pyramid (especially given the large sums of money for which he's responsible) should be extremely familiar with the functions of the whole manufacturing process. This has also led to increased areas of opportunity for the college/university-trained production person. In recent years, the technical knowledge and training of graduates of four-year graphic arts courses have often put them on a par with the more mechanical experience of the printing plant people.

A word of advice about future career moves. Assuming that you are a graduate of one of the major printing schools and are fortunate enough to get an entry-level job with a major publisher, you would be well-advised to pursue an MBA degree after a year, or at most two, on the job. This business training will stand you in good stead as you try to move up through the hierarchy of the company. Being responsible for as much money as you will be in M & D makes it imperative that you understand how to use and handle that money. The MBA training will prove invaluable.

WILL YOU BE HAPPY IN M & D?

If you like details, schedules and numbers, you will probably enjoy the detail-work inherent in M & D. You'll need the ability to juggle several operations at once. You will not create -- you will execute. And you will need to be able to get along with all kinds of people, because you'll be working with every other department in the company and a multitude of outside suppliers and customers.

Your job satisfaction will come from producing a product exactly the way the editors, art directors, advertising director and Publisher conceived it. You will accomplish this on an exacting schedule, dealing with a complex and ever-changing number of variables that threaten to ruin your job.

Quite frankly, if you need to be constantly bolstered with pats on the back, congratulatory notes or profuse thanks for "a job well done" -- you don't want to work in M & D. My experience is that all is going well as long as the phone doesn't ring. Because if the phone does ring, it will not be a complimentary call. It will mean something has gone wrong or is going wrong.

Despite what seem to be a series of negatives, the job can be greatly rewarding and highly satisfying. I've spent my entire business life in M & D. Like Dale Schenkelberg and our peers in this field, I stay in it because I enjoy it.

If you like the series of challenges I've outlined, then M & D is the area to head for. Go to school, get an internship while you're in college, ask questions and eventually you'll join me here with the aspirins and coffee!

* * *

Mr. Herschbein is responsible for the manufacturing and distribution of all Conde Nast-owned magazine publications --

Vogue, _House & Garden_, _Glamour_, _Bride's_, _Mademoiselle_, _Self_, _Gentlemen's Quarterly_ (_GQ_), _Vanity Fair_, _Gourmet_ and the Street and Smith Sports Group. This includes supervision of contract negotiations, paper purchasing, composition and engravings, and the management of all related manufacturing and distribution services.

He attended Brooklyn College and New York University and began his career in the graphic arts at U.S. Camera Publishing Company. He later joined Henry Holt & Company (now Holt, Rinehart & Winston, a division of CBS, Inc.) as Assistant to the President of their Magazine Division. He joined CBS when Holt was acquired in 1967, serving in a variety of positions until he was appointed VP/Director of Manufacturing and Distribution in 1973.

Mr. Herschbein is involved in a variety of publishing and printing industry organizations, is a frequent contributor to printing industry publications and a noted speaker at conferences throughout the U.S. and Canada.

VII
Promotion

CHAPTER 19

Learn Advertising And Sales From The Inside

By

Leslee Lenoff, Advertising Promotion Manager
Scientific American

Magazine promotion is a hybrid career in that it combines elements of advertising, promotion and sales. It is not a career readily considered by a lot of graduates, many of whom are accustomed to thinking of advertising and publishing as distinct and separate career paths. Perhaps this is why it suffers from somewhat of an "identity crisis." It is <u>not</u> as well known as other communications careers -- account executive, art director or copywriter. And yet it combines the skills of all three.

By answering some of the questions most often asked about magazine promotion, I hope to clarify its purpose and give you a clearer understanding of the professionals who specialize in this exciting area of magazine publishing.

WHAT EXACTLY IS MAGAZINE PROMOTION?

Magazines, like all products, must be marketed. Magazine promotion is divided into two basic areas: <u>circulation promotion</u>, in which you market the magazine to potential subscribers, and <u>advertising promotion</u>, which targets potential advertisers. At most magazines, these two functions are performed by separate departments. Since my area of expertise is advertising promotion, I will address this area throughout. (Details on careers in circulation promotion are included in the Circulation section of this Directory -- Ed.)

Through advertising promotion, you provide support for a sales staff trying to solicit advertising for the magazine. This promotional support can take any number of forms:

1. Advertising:

It sounds confusing but yes, magazines do advertise themselves to solicit advertisers. Pick up a copy of Advertising Age, Adweek or Marketing and Media Decisions, to name just a few of the many trade magazines we might utilize, and you'll see a bounty of media advertising.

The purpose of this advertising is to communicate the unique qualities of each magazine -- those that make it valuable to advertisers. There are a number of approaches media advertising can take, but nearly all magazines choose to promote their audience, their editorial content or a combination of the two.

This advertising is part of the Promotion Department's job. Often you will work with an advertising agency that will help you develop a campaign to communicate both the image of the magazine and specific qualities of its readership. In creating the ad campaign, you act as a liaison between the magazine's advertising sales staff and the ad agency. You must first understand the problems your sales staff is encountering on its sales calls, then develop the advertising strategies that will address them and help the salespeople overcome the "objections."

You must also decide where to advertise. Working with your agency's Media Department, you put together a marketing plan that will help you choose the types of media -- print, radio, transportation displays, etc. -- that will most efficiently reach the greatest number of people in your target market.

Media advertising, like all advertising, is an invaluable tool, not a replacement for the magazine's sales staff. Advertising creates an overall corporate image that can help to increase awareness of the magazine, position it within its particular category and, hopefully, "open some doors" for the sales staff.

2. Presentations and Collateral Pieces:

Once the door is open, the sales staff needs further support to actually make the sale. Promotional pieces -- in the form of audio-visual and board presentations, brochures, flyers, media kits, etc. -- are designed in collaboration with outside design studios or agencies. These pieces can be targeted to a specific category of advertising -- automotive, liquor, corporate, etc. Or they can be pieces that speak in general terms about the quality of the magazine's audience or editorial content. Once again, it is the Promotion Department's job to support the sales effort with a dramatic presentation of the facts -- one that communicates quickly and effectively when used by the sales staff.

3. Promotional Events:

These are a popular and effective way to reach a large group of current and potential advertisers in a more personal and relaxed atmosphere. Events range from cocktail parties and sit-down lunches to musical concerts and sporting events. All of these activities generate a great deal of fun and excitement within the industry, and a great deal of work for the Promotion Department. You have to orchestrate all the details of these functions, from designing menus to choosing the door prizes and so on. All of these activities provide additional support for the sales effort by creating publicity, entertaining advertisers and, hopefully, attracting new advertising prospects.

4. Premiums:

From cameras to key rings, golf umbrellas to beach towels, premiums are used throughout the promotion industry as a way of being remembered. The Promotion Department coordinates these merchandising programs, selecting items that are both fun and memorable.

5. Direct Mail:

Sometimes promotion can go to work before a sales call, as in the case of direct mail. The Promotion Department creates a mailing piece that asks for a response. Perhaps it is promoting the latest research on your readers' computer ownership and contains a response card prospects can return for more information. Such a piece could be mailed, for example, to the Marketing Departments of computer hardware and software manufacturers and their advertising agencies. Those that then request more information -- making them potential advertising candidates -- would be new sales leads for your sales staff. Used in such a manner, direct mail can be an effective tool, in that you can reach a much larger number of prospects than your sales staff could ever personally visit.

NECESSARY CAREER SKILLS

Creativity is perhaps the most important single skill. The ability to communicate the qualities of your magazine in an exciting and innovative way is the most challenging task of Promotion. Most often, the facts you are promoting are just that -- cold, hard data. You have to give them a little warmth, make them a little inviting. You have to take the qualities of your magazine and its audience and humanize them, make an advertiser comfortable with his decision to run his ads in your publication and a prospect consider the possibility of jumping on the bandwagon.

But perhaps the most difficult task you will face is getting attention. Clients and agency people are deluged with media messages every day. You have to create promotion that will be heard above the noise, noticed and, hopefully, remembered.

If you're applying for a Promotion job, one of your best assets would be an ability to write. A portfolio of writing samples will help show the way you think, analyze problems and communicate solutions. Writing is nearly always a prerequisite for a position in Promotion.

Graphic design skills or some demonstrable visual abilities are a second important asset, since nearly all the support materials you will be working on have two elements -- the written and the visual. A combination of both copy and art skills will make you an ideal Promotion candidate.

Courses that may help prepare you can thus fall into a number of majors -- English Literature, Creative Writing, Graphic Design, Fine Arts, etc. Any of these areas will provide you with a background to build on. A job in Promotion is in no way limited to the student majoring in Advertising. The abilities necessary to solve creative problems and communicate effectively can be attained through a wide variety of course studies.

In addition to these basic skills, an ideal candidate for the Promotion Department should have two other important qualities. First, the ability to work well with people. The Promotion Department services the sales staff. This means listening well to their input and suggestions, interpreting them and turning their ideas into creative promotional products. As in any service job, you are operating in a cooperative environment. This attitude must extend to the outside suppliers with whom you'll be working as well -- your ad agency, design studios, audio-visual houses, etc. Promotion is a team effort and is, therefore, best suited for team players.

The second quality is versatility. Since promotional support takes such a wide variety of forms, you are required to "wear many hats." And most often you have to wear all those hats at the same time. In the same week, you could be holding a luncheon for a new advertiser, preparing a new audio-visual presentation, breaking a new ad in the trade magazines and writing copy for the media kit.

In other words, you are required to juggle a number of on-going projects at one time. For those who prefer to do only one part of this mix, they would do best looking for jobs at publications with large Promotion Departments, where the work is often more specialized. Generally, however, magazine promotion requires a degree of versatility and will be most challenging and rewarding for those who enjoy this diversity.

GETTING STARTED...AND WHERE YOU CAN END UP

From personal experience, I can attest to the importance of talking with as many people already in Promotion as possible. Even if an opening at a specific company does not exist at the time, meeting with and making an impression upon people in the industry can often lead to a chance at a position further down the road. Obviously, sending out a resume is a necessary first step. But nothing reveals as much about a potential candidate as a personal chat.

And if you are successful in getting to talk with people in the industry, go in prepared. Know their magazine, read it, look at the advertising and try to understand their position in the marketplace. This preparation will go a long way in helping you to talk intelligently with the person across the desk.

What about the future? Where can a career in magazine promotion lead you in three years, five years or farther down the road?

Because it's a career that requires both creative and administrative skills, magazine promotion occupies a unique niche in the communications industry. The job requires the creative ability to conceptualize a problem and its solution, but also the administrative ability to execute that solution, which requires working effectively with your own staff, other departments and many outside suppliers.

For this reason, magazine promotion provides an invaluable background that can be applied across a number of industries. Possible moves outside of magazine publishing could include account work at an advertising agency or communications firm, marketing at a client company or possibly broadcast promotion for radio or television. Whichever path you choose to follow, your exposure to the elements of advertising, promotion and sales will prove a solid foundation on which to build.

*　*　*

Ms. Lenoff joined <u>Scientific American</u> in December, 1981, as an advertising promotion assistant. Prior to that, she spent three years as an Account Executive at Fearon/O'Leary Advertising (now Kaprielian O'Leary), where she worked on promotional campaigns for clients like <u>Business Week</u>, among many others. She graduated from the State University of New York at Binghamton and lives in New York City.

CHAPTER 20

Enjoy A Special Kind Of Power!

By

Barbara Mitchell Raskin, President
Mitchell Media/Marketing

Magazine promotion people -- whether staff members, managers or directors -- enjoy a special kind of power. Not many other careers allow you the privilege of identifying <u>and</u> shaping a published product. Each person on a Promotion staff can contribute greatly to the acceptance, or lack of acceptance, of a publication. So it's fair to say that, by choosing such a career, you will have direct effect on literary history (if you're not opposed to stretching a point).

Now that's a fairly lordly notion when you've spent the past four years concerned with classroom discipline, required reading and mini-careers conducted after-hours or during semester breaks. But magazine promotion offers you the opportunity to be influential from your first days on staff -- and to grow in many directions.

My colleague, Leslee Lenoff, offered an excellent introduction to the concept of magazine promotion and discussed the many functions most Promotion Departments must handle. I'd like to focus a bit more on what <u>you</u> should be like to be successful in Promotion and, finally, offer some of my own advice both as you begin your job search and as you progress in your career in magazine promotion.

THINK SALES. . . AND LEARN HOW TO TYPE

From my point of view, the most valuable qualification for any promotion job is a basic <u>sales</u> mentality. Though the Promotion staff is only <u>indirectly</u> involved in the sales process, it <u>directly</u> affects the <u>success</u> of that process. So, someone who <u>thinks sales</u> will be an automatic asset to any Promotion operation.

Job titles, other than top management spots which will take you a while to reach, go beyond the obvious -- copywriters and artists -- and include Production and Traffic staffers as well as a variety of staff assistant positions not covered by general job identifiers. Remember, as Leslee detailed, Promotion Departments are responsible for conceptualizing and carrying out any number of projects, from a sales meeting with a motivational theme to various kinds of client entertainments (parties and special events) to purchasing premiums for give-aways, running contests and sweepstakes, producing promotional videotapes or films...absolutely everything that might possibly create some excitement about your product -- your magazine.

By the way, please don't be too proud to learn to type. There's nothing demeaning about it and, if your other skills and instincts are where they should be, you have no need to worry about being "stuck" behind a typewriter for the duration. But time is money and, in many cases, faster is better. Typing is a salable skill for a Promotion career at any level and a great boon to efficiency. In my last Marketing Director's spot, the typewriter still lived at my right hand and was used daily. Given two people with otherwise equal qualifications, I would always hire the person with typing skills. Taking the time to learn this skill evidences a willing, hands-on-the-job attitude I like.

In many companies (my last two were typical), entry-level positions were confined to junior-level artists and copywriters (both positions were called assistants) and administrative assistants, who had general office skills and were responsible for a fascinating and diverse list of chores associated with following through on those many projects mentioned above.

There's no truly reliable formula for choosing a first position, because Promotion operations vary so much from company to company. But you can count on excitement, a chance to polish your best skills and practice new ones in an eclectic atmosphere that makes the days whiz by, leaving you with a sense of accomplishment and enthusiasm for the next set of tasks.

PROMOTION'S NOT THE PLACE FOR SELFISH EGOISTS

Successful promotions require teamwork. There's always one very good idea at the root of a project, but it's rare if that idea is fully formed right from its introductory stage. The best promotion managers, in my experience, have little ego about the origin of an idea -- but are great coaches and understand the importance of cheering on the staff that's really responsible for making those bright ideas turn into real products or events. I would suggest, once your career goals and attitude are in the right place, that you interview your manager carefully. He or she should be a constant source of informatiion and motivation, with the ability to help further the futures of all the members of his team. In other words, be cautious in selecting the manager you'll be working for -- and get one who can perform up to this ideal.

A word of warning: Since promotion is first and foremost a

<u>team</u> effort, you should be comfortable working as a member of a team. Promotion is <u>not</u> a single-minded glory train.

When you think about it, a Promotion career really requires a certain selfless dimension that allows you to contribute (somewhat silently, from the background) to the success of the sales staff, whose members are generally compensated on a commission basis. Promotion positions, of course, are usually straight salary.

While the sales staff must provide you with the information you need to do your best work, they are not always "tuned in" to asking the right questions. So you must be imaginative, innovative and, above all, creative. It will all bring rewards in personal satisfaction.

MOVING UP THE CAREER LADDER

That satisfaction -- and the confidence it breeds -- should move you naturally up the Promotion career ladder. If Promotion Management is your goal, all that skill stored along the way and a firm commitment to the teamwork concept we've been discussing will serve you well. As you climb the ladder, your creative abilities become more refined, sophisticated and usable. Somehow, the "possible" begins to sort itself from the "impossible." Practical, budget-wise projects become a main concern, since fiscal management is a large part of any such higher-level job description. Creative control preempts volume creativity -- your staff will be fully capable of generating enough new ideas. More time is naturally spent communicating and coordinating with other department managers -- and dealing, to a degree, in corporate "politics."

The time required to climb this ladder varies, too, from one company to another. Timing, as it relates to career progress, is often (face it!) truly a matter of luck, but given the talent and the right set of circumstances, an investment of three to five years should produce dividends in accomplishments, responsibilities (reflected in your job title) and compensation.

The actual <u>amount</u> of time invested is secondary to your feelings about <u>how</u> the time is spent -- and what rewards it's delivering to your personal advancement. If boredom sets in at some point, discuss the situation with your manager and make some changes -- perhaps adding a few new and challenging tasks -- to alleviate it. One important consideration: Periods of bordeom are <u>regenerative</u> for creative people. They are <u>normal</u> and don't necessarily indicate it's time to change jobs or companies.

It's equally important to understand the difference between <u>temporary</u> <u>boredom</u> and <u>stagnation</u>. The latter is anathema to the creative mentality and indicates that a change is very much in order. Stagnation, by its very definition, precludes the growth of anything positive or career-enhancing, and therefore <u>should</u> cause movement to another level of responsibility, another company or another career altogether.

Given a "good wind," cooperation by your colleagues and managers, and intellectual growth, there are certainly areas you can consider beyond the confines of Promotion. My own suggested target -- for utilization of skills and compensation potential -- would be a position on the advertising sales staff. In that spot, you're sure to use all those well-developed skills honed on the Promotion staff. There are daily opportunities to use -- and benefit from -- great, creative sales approaches. And, certainly not least of all, there are constant opportunities to tap the very necessary resources of the Promotion Department to ensure success with your new account list. What better working tool to possess than the knowledge necessary to draw the maximum promotional support to your own income advantage!?

Where you start on this trail is, obviously and honestly, not nearly as important as where you finish. I would concentrate on the choice of the parent company and the publication -- and less on the actual job title, since that can change with all deliberate speed. Not very definite, granted, but that's the reality of most entry-level Promotion jobs.

It's wise to invest at least a year in any position before making a judgement about its long-term value to your career. Any job worth taking is probably worth keeping at least that long. I have always reacted negatively to "job-jumping" resumes and know that I am not alone in that sentiment. Naturally, it's best to spend more time researching a company at the interview stage and less time regretting a poor choice later. I strongly suggest you prepare for any interview. I am impressed by questions that indicate more-than-average thought beforehand -- and a basic knowledge of my company and its publications.

A COMFORTABLE CAREER PATH FOR THE ECLECTIC PERSONALITY

There is little that specifically qualifies someone for a career in Promotion -- but then there is virtually nothing in terms of academic preparation that disqualifies you either. An MBA, in my opinion, makes little difference in day-to-day challenges, assignments or progress. But, considering the attitude of some corporations, it may make a substantial difference in the contents of your pay envelope.

Courses focused on sales and marketing are helpful. A good sense of budgeting matters, too. And there's always the golden requisite -- the ability to use the English language in "beyond-ordinary" dimensions. A basic command of statistics as they relate to demographic research, etc., will come in handy when it's necessary to interpret and explain research findings relating to sales promotion.

Promotion is a comfortable career path for the eclectic personality. Succeeding, once you count in that magical element of luck we've allowed for, is simply a matter of intelligence, hard work and concentration. Being first to understand the basics means also having the first chance to put them into practice. First chance at trial is also first chance at error. Pure self-starter learning works here.

MY UNMAGICAL YELLOW PAD OF PAPER

My own, very unmagical "tool for living" on the job was an omnipresent, lined yellow pad of paper that I carried with me from the day I entered the magazine business until I felt I could afford to abandon it with a reasonable sense of security in my professional knowledge. On it, I recorded every word or phrase, every situation, every transaction I encountered which was beyond my sphere of understanding. It always contained long lists and was an object of no small amusement to some other staffers.

It was an object of much less amusement to those I approached to shed light on the subjects listed there. Two or three pages of concepts take time to unravel and, Madison Avenue being the world of long executive luncheons and early commuter trains, there was little time to find or develop patient teachers. But I listed and listened and besieged everyone I thought might have the knowledge I needed. I swallowed my pride and just ept asking questions -- I considered it a mission of serious proportions. I just never stopped trying to learn.

Finally, I found a mentor, someone with all the answers and the patience to match. Things went uphill fast. The questions, of course, came easily. But finding the person or people with the knowledge and patience to answer them doesn't. I'm still grateful -- more so every day -- that someone actually took the time to help me.

I've told this story before and "suffered" the consequences. Lots of my own hours after 5:00 P.M. have been spent explaining notes on my staffer's lined, yellow pads. And the questions they come up with, I might add, are a lot tougher than mine ever were! College communications programs have obviously expanded to better prepare their students, though the competition is tougher, too.

Finding an entry-level slot in magazine promotion is definitely worth the effort. You'll be amused and challenged, prepared to move in many directions from a position that allows you to observe and have dialogue with virtually every corner of the operation. A good sense of organization and the ability to switch from one task to another without breaking your stride are important attributes. You'll often be tired, but rarely bored. And, if the job is the right one, you'll certainly learn -- and enjoy.

P.S. If I've left something out, please feel free to forward your questions on lined, yellow paper. It would be my pleasure to answer them.

* * *

After some 21 years in a number of Sales and Promotion positions in the magazine industry, Ms. Raskin formed her own consulting firm in July, 1985.

Previously, she was Director of Marketing for Bride's magazine, where she began as Travel Accounts Sales Manager in 1981. She began her career as the secretary to two junior salespeople in the (then joint) Advertising Sales Department for Harpers and The Atlantic. Eleven jobs and 17 years later, she was Executive Vice President. During that period, she moved comfortably and frequently between positions in both Sales and Promotion.

Ms. Raskin graduated from the NYU School of Journalism in 1964. While at NYU, she was one of the first students to participate in their publishing work/study program and held internships at the New York Times, UPI and the White House Press Gallery while completing her studies for her BA. She later interned at the New York Telegram and the Herald Tribune, as well.

VIII
Public Relations

CHAPTER 21

Influencing How Others See You

By

Phyllis Crawley, Director of Communications
CBS Magazines

"By the year 1990, there will be more than 200,000 new jobs created in mass communications disciplines," projected Dallas Kersey, the Communications Director of Peat, Marwick & Mitchell, one of the "Big Eight" accounting firms. Communications skills, he said in a speech at the University of Georgia School of Journalism, are the skills our economic world will need -- whatever the momentary fluctuations in the job market.

Our society's current, seemingly insatiable appetite for information -- and the corresponding deluge of data created by "space age" communication technology -- point to a rapidly expanding role for the professional communicator. More and more corporations are recognizing the importance of the "image" they present to the world at large, especially to their most important "publics": their customers, stockholders and potential investors.

Even though we in the comparatively small magazine industry forsee no such volume of positions (new or otherwise), Kersey's optimism is still good news for all of us in communications or media. It is particularly heartening for those of us in public relations.

WHAT IS PUBLIC RELATIONS?

In the simplest terms, public relations is communicating (relating) to the public. To go beyond so general a definition, however, requires defining that key term, "public." All firms, large or small, publicly held or private, have various "publics" -- the groups, both internal and external, to which a company must communicate its "self" and sales story in order to operate successfully. Because of the unique nature of the magazine business, we have more than most. In our industry, customers (the most crucial public) are both advertisers and readers, our key income sources. A wide variety of activities, therefore, are involved with "relating" to these diverse publics. The result is an often confusing picture of just what magazine public relations is all about.

The Magazine Publishers Association (MPA) conducted a study in 1982 that revealed eleven different appelations by which PR Departments are known: Public Relations, Public Information, Public Affairs, Communications, Publicity, Promotion, Corporate Affairs, Corporate Communications, Corporate Information, Creative Services and Community Affairs. The majority used the Public Relations title, with Publicity, Communications and Public Affairs next in order of preference. The person in charge of the function, however, had a title that usually included the word "Communications" (as in "Director of Communications").

"Observers of the PR field," the study noted, "in recent years have reported the ascendancy of `Public Affairs' as the preferred description of the activity, presumably because it's more accurate and less onerous than `Public Relations' -- a notion whose validity lies in the eyes of the beholder. Of the top four operative words in the titles, the anomaly is `Promotion,' which is quite different in its methodology, goals and the way it is perceived by the public, as compared to `Public Relations' or `Communications.' Clearly there is some confusion," they conclude, "about roles played by public relations/communications/public affairs vs. those of promotion."

A measure of the confusion is in the title of the study itself. Conducted by the MPA's Communications Committee, it was entitled, "Public Relations, Publicity/Communications."

IN THE UNIQUE WORLD OF MAGAZINES

The one thing no one is confused about is that in the magazine industry, public relations (whatever it's called) is a complex collection of highly-targeted, specific functions, generally hand-tailored to meet the needs of each company, if not, in fact, each magazine. While not all companies assign the same tasks to PR, the following all-inclusive list of general PR functions is an indication of the range and diversity of magazine Public Relations:

1. External Communications/Releases

*Press/Media Relations - Originate and write (or delegate and approve) all news releases and announcements; develop and maintain distribution lists; designate dissemination.

*Act as spokesperson and answer all press queries.

2. General Public Relations/Identity

*Develop overall program, including speaking platforms,

policy speeches, business presentations/speeches and necessary brochures/booklets.

3. Extensions of Editorial Information

*Participate in policymaking. Oversee Rights & Permissions, Licensing and Reprints.

4. Customer/Reader Relations

*Responsible for all "outside" (non-press) inquiries, complaints and, at some companies, Letters to the Editor.

5. Social Responsibility/Charitable Contributions

*Develop and oversee overall program; administer budget; recommend/generate contributions; attend or designate company representation at charitable/community service functions and events.

6. Meetings & Events

*Plan and execute necessary sales conferences, management seminars/conferences, organization parties (Christmas, Picnics, Awards, etc.), community/trade association/industry functions and events.

*Maintain "Calendar of Events" for Editorial and management.

7. Organization Membership Coordination

*For both industry associations (MPA and myriad of advertising industry organizations) and community groups (local Blood Drives, United Way, etc.). Attend appropriate dinners and events as company representative.

*Answer all general (or industry) inquiries to company, in all cases positioning magazine/company as industry leader.

8. Internal Communications

*Oversee announcements of policy and staff appointments for company.

*Write and distribute all staff communiques.

*Create and distribute newsletter (house organ). Provide information to and liaison with corporate (or parent) internal publication(s).

9. Clipping Service

*Maintain files and distribute all press clippings to

appropriate staff.

10. **Resources**

     *Maintain media library, slide presentation files, key Executive biography & photo files, plus various freelancer and vendor lists.

THE PROBLEM OF <u>BEING</u> AND <u>RELATING</u> TO THE MEDIA

     The MPA member survey uncovered several interesting, if not downright bothersome, facts. The first is that only 60 percent of the respondents placed the responsibility for media relations with their PR executive, although some 71 percent of these same executives are the ones writing (or at least initiating) news releases.

     The second is that more than half (58 percent) of the responding companies have no authorized spokesperson and few (only five percent) have an official policy about spokesperson control (i.e., who officially "speaks" for the company).

     There are several likely reasons -- probably stemming from the knotty problems associated with <u>being</u> the media and <u>relating</u> to the media. Certainly it is an indication, as the MPA survey concludes, that the PR function may be poorly understood.

     All other considerations notwithstanding, it is axiomatic that good press relations begin with the designation of an official spokesperson and the maintenance of a clear policy of screening and promptly replying to press inquiries. Therefore, since no industry standard exists, it is important to determine <u>or establish</u> these crucial practices. How effective can you be if other people release all the "good news" or the "big news" and refer the rest to you -- or worse, if you don't know the questions <u>or</u> the answers?

WORKING WITH TOP MANAGEMENT

     An obvious challenge to all PR professionals, especially in the magazine industry, is gaining the confidence of top management. Their support is particularly critical to the success of any significant PR effort. You can often gauge how effective a company's PR Department has been in obtaining this support by finding out to whom the Department Head reports. Working with the Chairman, President or Publisher offers the opportunity to gain understanding and support. If, on the other hand, department supervision has been relegated to a middle manager, it's harder to get the "hearing" (or, for that matter, the budget) it needs to function effectively. "Reporting to", of course, doesn't necessarily mean being privy to confidential or even relevant information. But, as the survey wryly concludes, "it's better being closer to the horse's mouth than to other parts of the organizational anatomy." Hence a supportive relationship is crucial.

GETTING THE FIRST JOB

Entry-level jobs in magazine publishing -- and, I suspect, in most industries -- tend to be low-level spots, often with clerical duties attached. It's easy to figure out which they are -- just look for an adjective like "assistant," "coordinator," or "associate" preceding the main job title, whether it be publicist, writer, radio/TV placement or any other variations on the communications/publicity/public relations functional definition.

It's reasonable, I think, to expect the investment you and your families have made in a college education to pay off and that a return on that money, time and energy will be forthcoming. It will...but probably not as quickly or predictably as you think (or hope). The sign on the wall in one of my colleagues' offices reads, "You gotta have patience and you gotta have lunch."

Reasons for working in magazines are many and compensation is certainly high -- it's fun, often glamorous. Creative, dynamic, intelligent people abound. Challenging problems arise and the exuberance of facing and solving crises is constant. Big Bucks are not -- that's the trade-off. The magazine industry does not pay PR people -- entry-level or otherwise -- as well as other industries do. According to a 1984 study by the Public Relations Society of America (PRSA), the PR Director for a small to medium-sized corporation (non-publishing) can expect to earn from $35,000 to $40,000, up to $20,000 more at a bigger firm. At the top, PR Directors for major, Fortune 500 companies earn anywhere from $75,000 to $150,000. Suffice it to say that magazine PR professionals are simply not in the same range. Entry-level positions in our industry pay anywhere from $12,000 to $18,000. Other industries would tend to start at $18,000 to $25,000.

The most important thing to remember now is that you're in transition -- trying to match your skills, your expertise, your selves to the needs of the "real job world." There are no grades, no "E's" for effort. The track is fast and the competition is stiff. This transition -- from the top of the student world to the very bottom of the working/professional world -- is only the first. Get used to it -- the rest of your working life will be a series of transitions, perhaps every three or four years as you move, or move up through the ranks.

ON THE JOB...AND MOVING UP

There is no such thing as a "typical day" in the PR Department. Given the myriad of diverse functions, how could there be? Some days will be spent writing, others researching, some thinking. But there will always be a need to communicate. Listening is a key.

The "ideal" candidate for promotion through the ranks has virtually the same qualities and characteristics as the "ideal" entry-level candidate -- skills and the wherewithall to use them. The former are far easier to acquire. Key PR skills are writing, organization, typing and persuasively communicating -- talking and listening. Obvious courses of study for developing such skills are composition/grammar, literature, logic/reasoning (perhaps math), graphics and design, public speaking, and any sales training or related studies (persuasion is central to any PR function).

Is an MBA important? Certainly, if management is a career goal. Otherwise, a Bachelor's degree, once merely desirable, has probably become essential because of competition in the workplace and job market. The many specialty magazines in both the trade and consumer areas invite almost any major. A science major, for example, has an excellent chance of getting an entry-level job on a medical or health magazine, whether they want to join Editorial, PR or another department.

The most important thing when you get that job (and you will get that job) is to do it, whatever it is. If you're hired to type and file, it's because the typing needs to be done and the files need to be maintained. For a while, your first job will be less glamorous and certainly more demanding that any job description might suggest.

Successfully moving up the organizational ladder requires no secret formula. All the standard rules apply -- the bright, energetic, capable hard workers succeed...and are promoted. In the PR field, some career paths are easier to see and take advantage of than others. Mobility is a way of life within the magazine industry and most publishing companies. Moving from public relations to promotion, marketing or sales, for instance, is not uncommon; switching from Editorial to PR is the easiest of all. The reverse is seldom, if ever, done. So don't get into PR thinking it will be your entree into the glamorous world of Editorial. The fact is that an uncredentialed journalism student probably has a better chance at landing one of those coveted Editorial jobs than an on-staff PR person with a year or two experience. "Getting one's foot in the door" might mean getting stuck in the wrong room.

Until quite recently, Public Relations has not been considered one of the tracks leading to senior management. While the numbers of company or magazines executives who have come out of Public Relations is on the increase, few publishing company Presidents or magazine Publishers have public relations experience or credentials.

Of some note, however, is the expanding role of finance. As public confidence in business wanes -- unemployment, cutbacks, etc. -- the area of investor relations is a strong career growth area. According to a recent New York Times article, financial background and communications skills tend to be mutually exclusive. So where are companies to find investor specialists? An investment consultant they quote declares: "It's wiser to hire a communicator and have him or her add financial training later, because it's easier than teaching a financial person to communicate." Having dual credentials -- knowlege of finance or business and skill in communicating -- would suggest an edge.

Ultimately, there are just too many variables in the PR profession, especially in a unique and complex business like magazine publishing, to be definitive. Magazine Public Relations is a creative profession in a creative industry. People, ideas, and opportunities are the key elements. The right people, the right time, the right idea, the right place are all essential. The ability to find them -- or make them -- far exceeds any "career path," however well thought out.

1986 will probably not be a boom or bust year for the economy...or for the Public Relations profession. Indications are that PR professionals will face continued difficulties. However, PR is a profession that has not only persevered through several serious economic dips, but continued to grow and advance in stature, responsibility and renumeration. And while it's certainly not a "recession proof" profession, it _is_ "recession resistant."

Frankly, it's growth depends on the talents and energy of those of you who join our belt-tightened ranks.

* * *

In her current position, Ms. Crawley heads a department with responsibility for all aspects of CBS Magazines' internal and external communications. She is the spokesperson for CBS Magazines and manages programs concerning public and governmental affairs, corporate, community, press and industry relations, as well as employee communications and CBS's charitable activities.

Prior to joining CBS in 1979, Ms. Crawley was Vice President, Corporate Communications for Esquire, Inc. During her nine year tenure there, she held a number of positions.

From 1967 to 1970, she was Director of Advertising and Publicity for Pegasus Books. Before moving to New York in 1967, she taught at the University of Nebraska, from which she received a BS in English and Public Address. In 1978, the University of Nebraska named her a Master Alumnus.

Ms. Crawley is active in a wide variety of magazine publishing, public relations and community organizations and has received numerous awards for her professional accomplishments and community service.

IX
Starting Your Own Magazine

CHAPTER 22

Start Up: Thirteen Observations

By

Owen Lipstein, Publisher
American Health

Three years ago, as start-up General Manager and Associate Publisher of <u>Science</u> <u>'81</u>, I wrote an article for <u>Folio</u> about starting a magazine. I now find the article almost unreadable, but unintentionally very funny.

We're all students in this game, as demonstrated eloquently by the recent spate of entrepreneurial and corporate failures. Every launch is different. Anybody who doesn't admit that they're learning as they go along is a liar or unconscious. At best, an article like this is a work in progress, an update. But maybe I'll swear by my words in three years. Who knows?

Here are <u>my</u> "checkpoints" for launching a successful magazine:

1) HAVE AN IDEA.

It's important. It's amazing how many magazines have been started without one. (As opposed to, say, just wanting to start a magazine or wanting to be your own boss, or sharing overhead.) How you develop an idea, is, obviously, a custom thing.

I developed the idea of <u>American Health</u> by nearly getting into a fight with a Washington, D.C., doctor who was, I felt, treating me poorly. (He made me wait in the reception room for an hour.) It turns out I'm not the only person who ever felt this way, which brings me to the next point.

2) GATHER A CONSENSUS

It should be encouraging to the aspiring publisher if other people share his enthusiasm for the idea. (Wives and mothers should be excluded from the poll.) But everybody else should be included. Including a few enemies. Look for support for your idea in the newspapers, in TV commercials, popular songs, everywhere in the culture. For example, in 1981, sneakers were becoming the national uniform. Perrier was (and still is) hot. The Cambridge diet was the rage. When asked why there was no magazine dedicated to this obvious revolution, nobody I polled could come up with a very good answer.

3) FIND YOURSELF A PARTNER.

American Health would not have happened in the form it took without T George Harris. You can assume that during the launch period you will be crazy at least part of the time. The right partner will tend to be crazy at different times, for different reasons, in different ways. Besides the fact that George was thinking about the same idea when I approached him, we have found that our strengths and weaknesses mirror each other.

I've been re-reading Huckleberry Finn and it occurred to me that our relationship (indeed any good publisher/editor relationship) is best compared to Huck and Jim. The big question being, who is Huck and who is Jim? By that I mean, who gets to have adventures, go into town, participate in feuds, and who has to watch the raft? Who needs taking care of? Both George and I have alternately felt ourselves to be Jim, left to mind the raft because right then he seems to be black. The fact is, though, when you start a magazine, you're both on a raft going downstream and you're going to learn a lot about each other along the way. Hopefully, it will be an adventure for everybody.

4) COUNT THE (POTENTIAL) BEANS.

If you come to believe on a gut level that your idea has some merit, a good test is if you can explain it to a ten-year-old nephew in thirty seconds or less and have him understand it. If so, it's worth doing some technical research. Specifically, does your magazine have a natural direct mail universe? (It's always amazing how little time start-up teams spend at a list house.) Is there an endemic advertising marketplace that is not being well served? Can the industry support an annual publication or is it cyclical? Is there a network of information that has not been tapped?

With American Health, we have a grass-roots revolution in health, fitness and nutrition, which spawned a rich variety of lists, powerful industries (pharmaceutical, foods, sports equipment) that do print advertising, and an enormous amount of new data on the body and nutrition. All of which makes things a little easier. As George wrote in a speech about starting the magazine, "Given my druthers, I'd rather be lucky, than smart."

5) CONCENTRATE ON EXECUTION.

When you do your business plan, you should probably assume the worst case. It always takes longer and costs more money. Period. As the Harvard Business School's great teacher of accounting says, "The purpose of a conservative business plan is to make sure that your future surprises will always be pleasant."

But there's an added reason for caution in our business: magazines are not just businesses, they're relationships. It takes a while for people to get comfortable with them. In doing the business plan, keep in mind that it's easier to model a good renewal rate than to achieve one. In fact, most business plans look remarkably similar. It's the execution that is hard. There appear to be whole industries bent on telling would-be publishers that the business plan itself is a major part of the process, and that armed with a plan, you're on your way. But it's just not true. It is certainly true, however, that an entrepreneur will personally spend anywhere from $10,000 to $25,000 for the plan alone -- probably out of his own savings and some of it just to achieve a better level of personal comfort. One of my more mischievous fantasies is to give out new magazine plans for $299 -- first one free. Just think of what would happen to the consulting industry!

My point is that plans and computer models often take the place of serious thought and planning. The ritual must not be allowed to push aside the ·reality of working out a solid new product and a business to sell it.

6) GET YOUR FINGERS DIRTY.

There are three or four critical line functions in any magazine. The more of them you've done yourself, the better you will be at managing and understanding the business. Most good magazine launches were not conceived and certainly not executed by strategic planners. They were started by editors and journalists who know the agony of a blank page on deadline, or ad sales people who sold advertising someone didn't want to buy, or circulation managers who by themselves put out direct mail campaigns.

Put together a bunch of fierce line managers who know their business and are determined to do it right. Having them function independently, yet coherently, as a business is kind of like putting together a rich stew -- every time you add a new ingredient, it changes the meal.

7) GET YOUR EYE ON CASH.

It's the mother of us all. It's the seminal consciousness. The centerpiece of the day for me is getting the bank deposit figure from our fulfillment house. The most sobering part of every Friday is signing outgoing checks. Make certain that you sign the checks (or get somebody who knows enough to think piously about it). Sensitivity to cash, especially the timing of subscription cash receipts, can be an early warning system to both good news and bad news. Signing the checks gives you the illusion that you're spending your own money (even if this is not technically true). It's a quaint ritual which tends to give a certain poignancy to financial and purchasing decisions.

8) HAVE FAITH, INTUITION AND COURAGE.

Pursuing a new idea is full of contradictions (or, perhaps, rich paradoxes). You have to be obsessive about serving your market. You have to know the guts of your business -- Henry Ford was a notorious grease monkey. At the same time, you have to be completely ignorant and deliberately biased. There are always perfectly rational reasons why <u>not</u> to do something. There were lots of reasons why we shouldn't have started <u>American Health</u>. I chose not to explore them. Being a reasonably rational person, this took courage. Courage and drive are possible only if you have a real conviction about what you're doing.

So the basic requirement for starting a magazine is that you know you <u>must</u> do <u>this</u> magazine, not just <u>any</u> magazine, and that everybody might as well go along with you because you're going to do it anyway.

9) DON'T OVER-PROMISE.

As a matter of fact, don't promise at all. Surprise. Your very existence then begins as something of a novelty. The inevitable imperfections become part of your personality, something overlooked. <u>American Health</u> was conceived in February (my fight with the doctor), tested in July, launched in December. Very few people knew anything about it until the Dougherty column on November 20, 1981 (Phil Dougherty's New York Times advertising column -- Ed.). At the heart of the matter is something we all learned as school children -- no one likes unfamiliar braggarts. We all wait for them to fall down and bruise themselves. Sometimes we even trip them up. On the other hand, at the first hint of real success, one should promote it aggressively. <u>You</u> may get bored with the message, but since <u>most</u> people didn't pay attention, they should be reminded constantly. More paradoxes.

10) USE CHARTER PRICING.

It's not just the entrepreneur who requires faith and courage and a suspension of disbelief, if you will. Readers need it and, more obviously, so do advertisers. As an entrepreneur, you will presumably be rewarded for your courage. The same should hold true for other believers. A good way to achieve this for your advertisers is <u>charter</u> <u>pricing</u>. Give them a price break, an incentive to buy. Make them comfortable. You had doubters when you came up with the idea, so will they. Give them a reward for their foresight and bravery. Something tangible to show the media supervisor or their spouse. It's their equity.

11) DRILL A LOT OF HOLES.

American Health is really in the oil business. By that I mean we are constantly testing new things -- a catalog business, a video business, a seminar business or just new ways of developing the magazine. Most of our experiments are failures; but the winners -- and there have been some -- have more than paid for the cost of what hasn't worked out. When you stop drilling holes, when you stop looking for the random gusher, you stop growing as a company.

12) KEEP YOUR EYES IN FRONT OF YOU AND YOUR EARS TO THE GROUND.

One thing that is certain about a launch is that the way things start -- one's perceptions and preconceptions about what the magazine should be -- will change. Put another way, the nice thing about publishing is that every time you publish an issue, you get a negative or positive response. Every renewal is a vote of confidence; every expire is just the opposite. I started American Health with an idea, not a demographic, in mind. I assumed that the magazine would be dual audience. It turned out that the magazine is skewed to female Yuppies. Fine. There's nothing wrong with changing your vision of the magazine, as long as you know your primary boss is the marketplace.

13) BUILD A FAMILY.

It is your repsonsibility to help create a community within the magazine; for that matter, too, with readers and advertisers. This past winter, I called a party for the entire staff. A "February Reeks" party. A fitting enough title for the month. It seems to have struck a chord here, given the attendance. For the lack of better alternatives, I also bring my dog to work. A practical solution for my current lifestyle. There's a limit to how seriously you can take anything when an oversized golden retriever sprawls in the middle of the corridor or attends a staff meeting (listening attentively on your couch). The point, though, is a big one. You're in a war. Without a few laughs and a lot of comradery, it's hard to keep going, let alone fight.

F. Scott Fitzgerald once defined intelligence as the "ability to hold two opposing ideas in your head at the same time and still retain the ability to function." That is, of course, not a bad definition of a paradox, or for that matter, of trying to run a magazine.

* * *

At only 34 years of age, Owen Lipstein has been described by Walter Joyce, a well-known publishing consultant, as "the leader of a new generation of imaginative but bottom-line oriented magazine manager-entrepreneurs." He's founder, general partner, and Publisher of <u>American Health</u>, a magazine that <u>Newsweek</u> has called "one of the most successful (new) magazines of the '80s."

Before <u>American Health</u>, Owen learned his trade as Associate Publisher and General Manager of <u>Science '82</u>. <u>Science '82</u> won the National Magazine Award for General Excellence during Owen's stay at the American Association for the Advancement of Science (its publisher). Prior to <u>Science '82</u>, he was a Circulation Manager and Manager of the Magazine Development Laboratory at CBS.

Through Oppenheimer & Co., he raised the largest amount of venture capital ($10,000,000) ever raised for a new magazine. In three years of publishing, <u>American Health</u> has established itself, according to the <u>Chicago Tribune</u>, as "the bible of the health and fitness movement." In its second year of publishing, <u>American Health</u> was nominated as a finalist in the National Magazine Awards' prestigious General Excellence Category. In its third year, it was nominated and won the National Magazine Award for General Excellence. Other finalists included <u>Forbes</u>, <u>The New Yorker</u>, <u>House & Garden</u>, and <u>Cuisine</u>.

CHAPTER 23

Starting A Magazine
From Scratch...Without Any

By

Tam Mossman, Owner/Publisher
Metapsychology

Owen Lipstein created <u>American Health</u> after years in the magazine publishing industry, using $10,000,000 raised by a major financial house. His magazine is now well-known, award-winning and very successful.

I just recently began publishing <u>Metapsychology</u>, a quarterly, special-interest magazine dealing with a variety of "psychic" subjects. I had slightly less capital with which to begin this venture -- just my own savings -- and, until quite recently, ran it part-time out of my home while I earned my living as a full-time editor for a book publishing firm. Needless to say, our perspectives -- and some of our advice -- are different, based as they are on the inherent differences in our start-up experiences. But I think reading both of these chapters should give any of you considering starting your own magazine some good food for thought.

Someone with little or no experience in magazine publishing is rarely counseled to just jump into the business and create a new publication. But if you can't find a magazine whose slant or subject matter really grabs you, it <u>may</u> pay you to create your own. By founding your own periodical, you essentially create your own entry-level job, and then -- almost automatically -- proceed to create a lot of other entry-level jobs around you. Following are a few of the basic hurdles to overcome.

DIVIDE AND CONQUER

Gone are the days when a single individual could start up a general interest magazine like _Time_ or _Newsweek_, _Ladies' Home Journal_ or _McCall's_. Today, new magazines of this scale are usually spun-off by existing publishing companies with plenty of money, staff, experience and marketing clout to at least increase their likelihood of profit. But as the book _Megatrends_ so succinctly points out, we are entering an age of specialization, and the "little" magazine that aims at a very narrow, but very _distinct_ interest group of the population has a good chance to succeed.

When a magazine goes down the tubes, on the other hand, it's usually because the idea seemed like a good one at the time, and/or because the editors were following "Received Wisdom" to an excessive degree. There's nothing wrong with Received Wisdom _per se_, it's just that everybody else obeys it, too -- so that the more you follow these truisms, the more your magazine is going to resemble the competition, and the more likely it is to suffer from whatever ailment may happen to afflict them.

A perfect example of this syndrome has occurred in the "men's" magazine field. Until the late 1950's, Received Wisdom said that to sell sex, you had to be down and dirty. Hugh Hefner decided to prove otherwise. And so, _Playboy_ spent millions of dollars making sex respectable and carving itself a niche on the newsstands right beside _Look_ and _Popular Mechanics_.

It didn't take a genius to realize that the class-act approach to pin-ups could be cloned, and thus were born _Gallery_ and _Penthouse_ and a host of other imitators who sacrificed some of _Playboy_'s sophistication for a higher ratio of raunch. But ironically, all of these magazines are now suffering a slump, thanks to the proliferation of porno on video cassettes, which are obviously more arousing than a static "pictorial essay."

Yet another -- and really more typical -- example lies in the almost overnight boom and bust that afflicted computer magazines. When the industry first began to take off, there were any number of different personal computers, each with its own distinct capabilities and software. In effect, the consumers were faced with a digital Tower of Babel, and the obvious -- in fact, too obvious -- answer was to match each brand with a magazine specializing in its particular "language."

These dozens of magazines were not competing with one another -- but the computer manufacturers _were_! And so, when the smaller computer and software firms began to fail, and even giants like Apple and IBM took their lumps, the computer magazines were caught in a double squeeze -- declining advertising on the one hand, and on the other, fewer topics to write about.

In biology, a wide variety of genetic diversity assures that at least _some_ individuals will survive any given disease or calamity. In magazines, being distinctive and different will help your effort live through any unforseeable change in circumstances. Your best bet, then, is to stake a claim far beyond where any other publishers may be pitching their tents.

Your first -- and most important -- task is to identify

something that readers presently aren't getting, and then devise a format that will bring it to them. Then think things through in terms of your editorial content and target audience, because your answers to these questions are going to determine the answers to all sorts of other questions such as advertising, print runs, design and many others.

About two-thirds of your brainstorming should revolve around your personal interests and enthusiasms -- because unless you're high on whatever your topic is, there's no way you can communicate with your readers. It helps if you're as much of a buff as they are. For example, the Publisher of Soldier of Fortune enjoys personally field-testing many of the automatic weapons the magazine later "reviews." My fascination with ESP is matched by my passion for contemporary art -- which is why I commission local artists and photographers to provide illustrations for Metapsychology. Being artists and not illustrators, they give the magazine a look that distinguishes it from the rest of the field.

This part of your planning determines what the magazine will be. The remaining one-third of your brainstorming should be completely personal and private -- namely, what you hate about magazines generally, and specifically the ones in your chosen field. This part of your planning determines what your magazine won't do -- and thus, what it will do instead.

To give an example, here's what I most dislike about other magazines in the parapsychology/occult field:

1) No focus -- everything from UFO's to superstitions to astrology.

2) Sloppy layout and ads that insult one's intelligence.

3) No way to view a sample copy by mail! No matter what the ads say, those bills keep on coming, no matter how many times you write "CANCEL" on the invoice.

4) No real build-up from issue to issue. Articles are short, self-contained and do not complement one another.

5) Aside from Letters to the Editor, no real opportunity for reader participation.

To turn my dissatisfactions into advantages for Metapsychology, I decided to:

1) Focus on "channeling" -- Ouija boards, automatic writing, trance material and spirit messages only.

2) Use professional journal-quality page layout, and accept ads mainly from book publishers and associations.

3) Let the undecided order a sample copy only -- at full cover price, however.

4) Not only continue features from issue to issue, but "cluster" articles to cast in-depth focus on given issues.

5) Give subscribers the privilege of submitting questions that may be answered in the "Questions and Answers" section of future issues.

STYLE

No matter who your readers are, demographically, it's wise to talk to them as if they were more intelligent, more wise and more affluent than the average. Few male college students of the past decades have had an encyclopedic knowledge of jazz, a foreign sports car or a $100,000 apartment overlooking the Golden Gate Bridge -- but Playboy talked to them as if they did. Many people who read Scientific American do not understand all the articles, nor does the average reader of Connoisseur or The Magazine Antiques have the funds to purchase even one of the goodies pictured in its pages.

Basically, magazines help the reader define his or her identity, which is why it's such a drastic mistake to talk down to your readers. Yet Esquire did just this in the late '60s and early '70s, allowing its writers to become arch, self-indulgent and smart-alecky. (A photo of Linda Lovelace was captioned, "If you don't know why this woman is famous, we sure as hell aren't going to tell you.") The magazine was sold shortly thereafter and went through several identity crises and changes of Editor before becoming the helpful, supportive magazine it is today. I often characterize Metapsychology as "ESP for Yuppies," and I'm not joking. I deliberately made sure it was something that a law partner could read on the commuter train without fear of embarrassment.

Because of my book publishing background, I used to think of magazines as something that most people read and then throw away, especially the weeklies like Time and People. But in the rare book rooms of various libraries, I had seen treasured copies of old literary magazines, as well as copies of Dickens' novels in their original serialized form. If some magazines were collectable, then why not make Metapsychology obviously worth saving in a "complete run," as the rare book catalogs have it? This way, as my subscriber base expanded, I could continue to go back to press and reprint back issues -- at a far lower unit cost than originally, thus increasing my profits....

FREQUENCY

An essential variable! If you publish once or twice a year, subscribers will probably forget about you, and in certain states, your publication will be subject to sales tax. But publish too often, and the per-issue size dips, and the readers may feel they're being nagged. (How do you feel when yet another Time arrives, and you still haven't opened the last two weeks' issues?) Weekly publication is simply not possible unless you have a four-page newsletter or a sizeable staff. Your best bet is to start with a leisurely pace that you can live with -- quarterly or bimonthly -- and then increase frequency after the subscribers and reveneus have climbed.

None of this was genius-class thinking, but then, a magazine is less a flash of brilliant inspiration than it is a series of common-sense decisions -- lots of common-sense decisions!

SHOULD YOU USE CONSULTANTS?

Yes, but just as you would a prescription drug: in small doses, and then only if you have to. The worst mistake you can make is to give someone carte blanche to do a "marketing survey" or "marketing report." Such projects can cost you thousands of dollars and be practically worthless, simply because no consulant will share your exact preferences and priorities -- and he has nothing to lose if your magazine fails!

At worst, consultants and other well-meaning advisors will play a creative fantasy game of "Let's Pretend" -- "If I were running this magazine, here's what I would do...." When I was finishing my first display ad, a friend who co-directed her own business complained that my ad had "too much copy. You have to keep it simple. My father made a fortune selling slacks by keeping his ads simple." I could not convince her that anyone being asked to pay five dollars for a single issue of a new magazine wouldn't mind reading a little bit about it. (Sadly, her own business has since closed its doors.)

At best, advisers are fonts of Received Wisdom, and so much of the advice you pay for is going to be ill-advised -- if not totally irrelevant. And regrettably, Received Wisdom is often most pernicious when it seems most reliable. So here's how to use consultants effectively: Ask them for facts only, and not opinions. The rules for Second-Class bulk mailings are facts. How you ought to advertise and where, who your audience should be -- these are opinions. As Publisher of the magazine, you want facts on which to base your own opinions. Thus, your questions to a consultant shouldn't be "Where should I advertise?" but rather "Which magazines in the investment field deliver the lowest CPM [Cost Per Thousand]?"

Draw up a list of what you need to know right now. Then show the list to a consultant and settle on a price before he or she does any research. Have the consultant sign a letter of agreement that he is entitled to that figure and no more for providing you with the research or information you're requesting.

Doesn't this approach increase your likelihood of making mistakes? Yes, but you're bound to make mistakes in any case. And from the point of view of learning, it is far better for you to make your own mistakes than to hire someone else to make them for you.

FORMING A CORPORATION

Received Wisdom says that one of the first things you should do is incorporate, so that Your Magazine, Inc., is responsible for any debts and legal liabilities. The truth is that incorporation is like having a baby: It creates a new taxable entity which then must have its taxes filed on at least an annual basis. The corporation's taxes will, of course, have to come out of its income -- and you will pay _additional_ taxes on whatever salary you receive from your company. And should the magazine fold, a corporation is very difficult to "kill." It will continue to live on as a taxable entity, running up needless bills and paperwork.

In my experience, incorporation is _not_ necessary at the very beginning and is too often motivated by an entrepreneur's desire to seem sophisticated and business-like. Let your tax accountant advise you when -- and if -- it's time for you to incorporate. Meanwhile, spend the money you save on something that pays tangible dividends.

BUDGETING, EQUIPMENT AND PRIORITIZING

The rule of thumb is that it takes any magazine at least two years to show a profit (and some of the bigger start-ups, like _People_ or _Sports Illustrated_, can take a decade or more to recoup their initial investment), but that fact is slightly misleading. The start-up costs are indeed high -- but your salary, or personal compensation, is one of those costs! So even if the magazine isn't in the black, you shouldn't worry about starving.

But yes, you are likely to lose money the first year. And so, the question becomes how best to lose it. Too many entrepreneurs I know spend start-up money on attractive, but non-essential items like stationery and state-of-the-art office equipment, which is like buying a corporate Lear Jet before you've hired a secretary. I believe in skimping on everything but the magazine -- therefore, I am still using a rubber stamp for my letterhead, still using stationery trimmed down from a stack of obsolete stationery that my last employer was about to throw away. As long as I can, I'm delaying the purchase of a postage meter and other labor-saving gadgetry, _because they don't make any difference to the reader_.

On the other hand, I _am_ spending on certain things to maintain my own morale. A new desk doesn't come with nicks, scratches and a funny smell in the right top drawer, and it says to my unconscious that I am worth it. After all, if you are going to be sitting in an office for 8 to 10 hours a day (or more!), it better not be a depressing place, but somewhere you can think and create and enjoy the play of words and ideas.

Good lighting is a must -- as is _dependable_ office equipment. It may seem a great saving to buy a used typewriter or word processor, but first, do your homework at a store that sells new equipment. At my last job, my office typewriter (an IBM Electronic 75) had an 7,500-character memory that printed out addresses, frequently-used phrases and entire form letters at the touch of a single key. But it was constantly breaking down, and I must have logged at least two dozen service calls. One repairman told me that the company had been losing so much money on servicing these older typewriters that for a limited time, it offered to replace them with new, wholly-electronic models for a mere $250!

If your magazine is a full-time job, you can't afford to wait for a repair person to show up. That means either having a spare typewriter in case of emergency, or buying one you're sure you can depend on in the first place. The same goes for computers and software. One of today's most popular word processing programs has a serious "bug" that causes it to save a single document as many as three times in a row, which swiftly eats up all your storage space. But the good -- in fact, great -- news is that the new laser printers enable you to type, edit and typeset an entire magazine at home, without its looking homemade. Such printers are currently quite expensive (around $4,000 and up), but as with VCR's and compact disk players, prices are bound to drop once the demand increases and initial production costs are amortized. Eventually, such technology will make the traditional typesetting methods all but obsolete -- and vastly enhance the scope of private publishing.

GETTING GOOD CONTENT

For your first issue, you must have either A) one of the biggest writers or names in the field, or B) an exclusive scoop on a major new development, or -- ideally -- C) both of the above. In my case, I was fortunate to know a number of top trance mediums and to know of quite a few others, so I was able to debut with some fairly heavy hitters. After your first issue, begin to trade up: Dump writers who aren't up to snuff, and get your best authors to write for you exclusively by offering them better pay, larger bylines, their name on the cover -- whatever it takes. And all the while, be on the alert for up-and-coming writers who may be your next headliners.

ADVERTISING

A mixed blessing. On the plus side, ads can offer intriguing graphics, a visual pizzazz and a welcome respite from column after column of print. They provide important information that your readers find interesting -- and actually pay you to run them. On the down side, ill-conceived or just plain ugly ads can run down the image of your magazine: Just take a glimpse into the Automotive Section of any newspaper -- it's not a place where your gaze would care to linger. Many advertisers have no taste or judgement. The "camera-ready" ads they supply will be poorly-worded and look like third-generation photocopies of ads they first ran in 1942.

Thus -- for your first few issues, at least -- it's up to you to screen your ads as carefully as the bouncer at a popular disco screens guests. And use the exact same tactics: Offer "free admission" to celebrity accounts and major firms whose clout and prestige will make you look good. Decline admission to anyone who's not up to your standards -- or, if you have time, offer to rewrite or reset their ads to make them more acceptable.

MANUFACTURING

Printing costs are more or less fixed. That is, the printer charges me approximately $1.40 for each copy of Metapsychology, and that figure is more or less constant, whether I print 1,200 copies or 12,000. But the higher print runs are still more economical, because they help me amortize the costs of illustration, typesetting and paste-up -- which are one-time costs. If these factors cost $3,200, say, they would add $3.20 to the cost of each copy in a 1,000-copy printing -- but only 32¢ to the unit cost of a 10,000-copy run.

DISTRIBUTION

When I began Metapsychology, I assumed that the vast majority of all copies would be sold through subscription. This has turned out to be a self-fulfilling prophecy, of course -- but also turned out to be a wise decision! The main problem with distribution on newsstands and in bookstores is the customary discount of up to 40% that you must extend to these retailers. Your subscribers will be buying their copies at a discount equal to only the cost of mailing and postage.

Another problem is the question of returns. Traditionally, bookstores can return unsold copies for full credit for up to one year after receipt. But at least booksellers return the whole issue, so that you can sell it again. Traditionally, magazine dealers and wholesalers simply tear off the cover or masthead of an issue and send that back for full credit. (The illegal sale of magazines and mass-market paperbacks whose covers have gone back to the publisher for full credit is an ongoing problem.)

My first issue was hardly back from the printer when a West Coast magazine distributor proudly informed me that they wanted to distribute an "initial draw" of 60 copies of Metapsychology and told me their standard terms -- 50% discount, with a ripped-off cover or masthead for credit. I wrote back saying that my terms included a regular bookstore discount (which begins at 20% for orders of up to five copies and escalates to 50% for orders of 99 copies or more). Oh, and to obtain credit, they had to send back the entire issue, in undamaged and resalable condition.

Two months of silence went by, and then the distributor wrote back, stating what his terms were. I replied by repeating my terms, and I haven't heard from him since.

Even if you're able to come to terms about discounts and returns, booksellers have one last hassle up their sleeve -- not paying you. One of the most friendly, cooperative store managers I know is in Baltimore, and he's always eager to sell copies of

<u>Metapsychology</u>.   Trouble is, his store is part of a nation-wide franchise, one of the country's largest booksellers -- and any bills and invoices submitted to a branch store have to be for-warded to the "Mother Church" in the Midwest for payment.

After two invoices had gone unpaid, I wrote my friend to ask if he could gently prod the home office into releasing some $$$. After another few weeks, I received a letter from the company with a "verification" form for me to fill out, asking for my telephone number, street address and other data that were wholly irrelevant to the question of whether their branch store had actually received the copies. As of this writing, I still haven't received payment, and my Baltimore friend is the sad victim of credit hold. Nothing personal, but I can't afford to ship maga-zines to people who won't pay their bills.

Can you afford to skip bookstores and newsstands entirely? That, of course, depends on your subject matter and your target audience.   <u>National Geographic</u> can get away with a subscribers-only policy because their readers settle in for the long-term and aren't impulse buyers -- not of the magazine, anyway. On the other hand, any magazine stressing topical information or recrea-tional and leisure activities (e.g., sports, personal finance, or naked women) has to hit the newsstands, because that's where most customers are going to find it.

To a great extent, bookstore and newsstand sales represent a form of <u>very</u> inexpensive but highly effective advertising. As an example, <u>Cosmopolitan</u> offers no discount to subscribers, who have to pay the going newsstand rate. But doesn't the Hearst Cor-poration make more money on subscriptions? Yes -- but they're more interested in making <u>Cosmo</u> a popular newsstand item, which ensures it preferential display space, which in turn attracts advertising dollars. (With a magazine, everything is synergistic, and success in one area will swiftly show benefits elsewhere.)

Let's restate that: <u>Complete</u> copies of your magazine are a most important form of advertising. But if those copies are stained, torn, with missing pages, they're likely to be perceived as garbage, and ignored accordingly. So not only should you take pains to make your magazine look terrific, but you should also make sure it doesn't get unduly mutilated in the mails.

My solution was to use 10" by 13" white wove-paper enve-lopes. Bought in bulk, they cost around nine cents each, but are more than worth it, acting as the first line of defense against disgruntled postal employees. Again and again, subscribers tell me that these envelopes look as if they've been through a short war, but the magazines inside arrive completely intact.

THE TELEPHONE TRAP

Unless you've already worked in publishing, you don't real-ize how telephone calls can eat into your efficiency. A freelance writer once asked the Editor of <u>Atlantic City</u> magazine what interested her most. "Being left alone," the editor replied, "so I can get something done!" Writers can get lonely at the type-writer all day, and too many of them follow the example of the man who used to mail me long letters, and then call me up to tell me what he'd written. I began by running the magazine out of my home, and I'll never forget the stoned guy from Los Angeles who rang me up at 2:00 A.M. "because it's not even 11:30 yet, man."

Answering mail is going to take up much of your working day, and under those circumstances, the impulsive telephone caller is someone who shoves his way in front of all those people waiting patiently in your In Box. Those who can't yet afford a secretary to screen their calls often get themselves a phone-answering device. Problem is, you then have to call back those you actually want to talk with, and it's on your nickel. I prefer to have an unlisted office number, which I give out only to top writers, family and friends. (This also cuts down on the nuisance calls from salespeople who want you to advertise somewhere, and other total strangers with little to say.)

Sadly, any correspondent who asks for your number is almost certain to abuse it, so always encourage such people to keep their thoughts on paper. If necessary, plead overwork and an already overloaded switchboard. Or give them my firm but truthful line: "Callers always call at their convenience, but letters are welcome at any time of day."

MARKETING

A final few words for once you are launched. No matter how many other magazines throng your chosen field, you must remember one essential fact: You are at war with every one of them. Possibly one of the most valuable books you can read is Marketing Warfare by Jack Trout and Al Reis (McGraw-Hill). They do not advise you to drive your enemy into the sea, but rather, explain how to successfully carve out your niche, and then not only defend it but expand it.

Because you are by definition a specialist, it helps to enlist the fanatics. Any field of interest has them -- the grandmother who's seen The Sound of Music 100 times, the trout fisherman who's out casting the first day of fishing season, the collector who has every Elvis Presley record ever pressed. Usually such buffs travel in packs and attend workshops and conventions -- where you can reach them in quantity. The Encyclopedia of Associations (Gale Research Company) will tell you where they hang out. And by parlaying your expertise into seminars, speaking engagements, workshops and other personal appearances, you can make people curious enough to take their first look at your magazine...

...And one look should be all you need!

* * *

Tam Mossman left his job as Editor at Running Press in November, 1985, to devote his full-time effort to his brainchild,

<u>Metapsychology</u>.   His experience has been primarily in book pub-
lishing rather than magazines -- prior to Running Press, he spent
15 years with Prentice-Hall, beginning as an Assistant Editor in
1967. He was promoted to Senior Editor in 1970. He was Editor of
all of Jane Roberts' "Seth" books,   as well as numerous other
bestsellers, among them <u>W.C. Fields By Himself</u> and <u>The Amityville
Horror.</u>

X
How To Get The Publishing Job You Want

CHAPTER 24

The Job Search Process: Getting Started

Graduation looms. And whether you're in high school, college or graduate school, you must now focus on your next great challenge -- preparing to develop your future -- out there. It can be a daunting prospect. Just how do you decide what to do with the "rest of your life?"

If your school days are already a distant memory, but you're considering a complete career change after years in the workforce, you face the same set of problems, questions and decisions. Whether you like it or not, you're all looking for that "entry-level opportunity."

You're already one or two steps ahead of the competition -- you're sure (<u>pretty</u> sure?) you want to pursue a career in magazine publishing. By heeding the advice of the many professionals who have written chapters for this <u>Career Directory</u> -- and utilizing the extensive industry and company information we've included -- you're well on your way to fulfilling that dream. But there are some key decisions and time-consuming preparations to make if you want to transform that hopeful dream into a real, live publishing job.

Right now, the entire job market is open to you. Confused and intimidated? You have every right to be. But you <u>can</u> take control. There is <u>no</u> reason to end up in a dead-end job, settle for anything less than you really want or miss out on a job for which you're perfectly qualified -- if <u>you</u> take immediate charge of your own job search. Treat it like a military campaign. That means detailed research and analysis, good organization, dedication and, probably most important of all, perseverance.

The actual process of finding the right publishing company, the right career path and, most importantly, the right first job begins long before you start mailing out resumes to potential employers. The choices and decisions you make now are not irrevocable, but this first job will have a definite impact on the career options you leave yourself. To help you make some of the right decisions and choices along the way (and avoid some of the most notable traps and pitfalls), the following chapters will lead you through a series of organized steps. If the entire job search process we are recommending here is properly executed, it will undoubtedly help you land <u>exactly</u> the job you want.

If you're currently in high school and hope, after college, to land a job in a magazine publishing company, then attending the right college, choosing the right major and getting the summer work experience many publishers look for are all important steps. For a complete list of the journalism and mass communications college programs accredited by the Accrediting Council on Education in Journalism and Mass Communications (ACEJMC), write Roger Gafke, Executive Director (ACEJMC, PO Box 838, Columbia, MO 65205) or call 314-882-6362. Write to each school for more information about entrance requirements, fees, etc. In addition, read the section of this Directory that covers your job specialty -- many of the contributors have recommended colleges or vocational schools they favor.

If you're hoping to jump right into the publishing industry <u>without</u> a college degree or other professional training, our best and only advice is -- don't do it. As you'll soon see in the detailed publishing company information included in Chapter 29, there are not <u>that</u> many job openings for students without a college degree. Those that exist are generally clerical and will only rarely lead to promising careers.

These are the key steps in the detailed job search process we will cover in this and the following three chapters:

1. **The <u>Self</u> <u>Evaluation</u> <u>Process</u>**: Know thyself. What skills and abilities can you offer a prospective employer? What do you enjoy doing? What are your strengths and weaknesses? What do you want to do?

2. **<u>Establishing</u> <u>Career</u> <u>Objective(s)</u>**: Where do you want to be five years from now? What do you ultimately want to accomplish in your career and your life? You will continue to research the magazine business until you can define your career choices and objectives as narrowly as possible.

3. **<u>Creating</u> <u>Your</u> "<u>Publisher</u> <u>Target</u> <u>List</u>"**: How to prepare a "Hit List" of potential employers -- researching them, matching <u>their</u> needs with <u>your</u> skills -- and starting your job search assault. Preparing publisher information sheets and evaluating your chances.

4. **<u>Networking</u> <u>for</u> <u>Success</u>**: How to utilize every contact, <u>every</u> friend, <u>every</u> relative and <u>anyone</u> else you can think of to break down the barriers facing any would-be publishing professional. How to organize your home office to keep track of your communications and stay on top of your job campaign.

5. **Preparing your Resume:** How to encapsulize years of school and little actual work experience into a professional, selling resume.

6. **Preparing Cover Letters:** We'll discuss the many ordinary and the all-too-few extraordinary cover letters, the kind that land interviews and jobs.

7. **The Interview Process:** How to make it work for you -- from the first "hello" to the first day on the job.

8. **Fielding the Offers:** Evaluating all the companies that are suddenly offering to hire you. Accepting and declining offers.

9. **School Year and Summer Internships:** Applying the lessons you have learned to the even tougher task of finding an internship (especially a paying one) at a publishing firm.

We won't try to kid you -- it _is_ a lot of work. To do it right, you have to get started early, probably quite a bit earlier than you'd planned. Frankly, **we recommend beginning this process one full year prior to the day you plan to start work**. So if you're in college, the end of your junior year is the right time to begin your research and preparations. That should give you enough time during summer vacation to set up your files and begin your library research.

Whether you're in college or graduate school, one item may need to be planned even earlier -- allowing enough free-time in your schedule of classes for interview preparations and appointments. Waiting until your senior year to "make some time" is already too late. Searching for a full-time job is _itself_ a full-time job! Though you're naturally restricted by your schedule, it's not difficult to plan ahead and prepare for your upcoming job search. Try to leave at least a couple of free mornings or afternoons a week. A day or even two without classes is even better.

Otherwise, you'll find yourself, crazed and distracted, trying to finish a one-hour interview in the ten-minute period between your Principles of Marketing lecture and your Creative Writing seminar. _Not_ the best way to make a first impression and _certainly_ not the way you want to approach an important meeting.

Ultimately, this process _will_ lead to success, clinching the job you want and launching a successful and fulfilling career. While you can certainly get _a_ job without going through the time-consuming process we're advocating, the odds of it being the _right_ job -- the _best_ one for you -- are quite a bit lower.

Now, let's go through each of the steps of our job search process in detail.

THE SELF-EVALUATION PROCESS

Plato had it right -- "Know thyself." This is a critical first step in the job search process and, unfortunately, the one most ignored by job seekers everywhere, especially students eager to enter the "real job world." But avoiding this crucial step can hinder your progress and even damage some decent prospects.

Why? Because you're hoping to identify the companies and jobs that best match your own skills, likes and strengths. The more you know about yourself, the more you'll bring to this process and the more accurate the "match-ups." You'll be able to structure your presentation (resume, cover letter, interviews) to stress your most marketable skills and talents. Later, you'll be able to evaluate potential employers and job offers on the basis of your own needs and desires, giving yourself a better chance of actually finding a company for which you'll enjoy working for a while.

Identifying What Motivates You

Let's start the evaluation process by attempting to identify, in the most general terms, what really motivates you. According to one theory, there are only five primary motivations, only one of which is the main force driving each individual:

1. **Money.** The "Almighty Dollar" is "God." Everything else pales by comparison.

2. **Power.** While power-driven individuals can often become quite wealthy (if they have the talents to go with the drive), making money is an afterthought. High-ranking government officials could command high multiples of their current salaries in private industry. Power is its own reward.

3. **Fulfillment.** Many creative types -- future art directors and editors -- are driven by this need for creative accomplishment. Add future United Way fundraisers and anyone whose credo is "feeling good about what they're doing."

4. **Affiliation.** Individuals who don't care where they work, how much they make or how many bosses they have -- just as long as they like their work, the company environment and, most important, the people they work with.

5. **Fame.** While it might eventually lead to fortune (and even to power), fame is its own reward for those who seek it. They shouldn't expect to lead a traditional, nine-to-five existence.

It's quite possible for two or even three of these factors to seem to be equally strong motivators -- we've met a few power-hungry, money grubbers who say they like people. But, if you examine yourself closely, we think you'll find that one and only one of these factors is the key to your personality.

What does it all mean? If you've truthfully and accurately

assessed your personality -- your "style" -- you are already in a better position to choose the proper career path and evaluate how well you will "fit in" at a particular company. After all, a money-driven person should probably reconsider accepting a job that will not in some way lead to "Big Bucks." When a power-driven personality takes a job, it is imperative for him, more than anyone, to be sure that there is a clear-cut path to the top of the mountain. After all, that <u>is</u> where he intends to find himself in the not-too-distant future. Etcetera.

<u>Creating Your "Self-Evaluation Form"</u>

If you found it difficult to characterize yourself in such general terms, let's try a more specific process. After you've completed this detailed evaluation, you should have no trouble identifying which of the five factors is your primary motivator.

Take a sheet of lined notebook paper and title it "My Self-Evaluation" or your "Self-Evaluation Form." Set up eight columns across the top. Moving from left to right, title the columns as follows: Strengths, Weaknesses, Skills, Hobbies, Courses, Experience, Likes, Dislikes.

Now, fill in each of the columns according to these guidelines:

Strengths: Describe personality traits you consider your strengths, and try to look at them as an employer would) -- e.g., persistence, organization, ambition, intelligence, logic, assertiveness, aggression, leadership, etc.

Weaknesses: List the traits you consider glaring weaknesses -- impatience, conceit, easily bored (i.e., need ever-new challenges), slow, etc. Don't presume that these will be considered negatives by a potential employer. In certain jobs, some of these "weaknesses" may be desirable traits!

Skills: Any skill you have, whether you think it's marketable or not. Everything from basic business skills -- like typing, word processing and stenography -- to computer, accounting or teaching experience and foreign language literacy. Don't forget possibly obscure but marketable skills like "good telephone voice."

Hobbies: List the things you enjoy doing. These are distinct from the skills listed above, and may include activities such as reading, games, travel, sports and the like. We presume if they're hobbies they are, by definition, things you enjoy doing. These are probably not marketable in any general sense, but may well be useful in specific circumstances (if you're offered an editorial job, for example, on <u>Sports Illustrated</u>.) So be ready to refer back to this column to evaluate the details of future job offers.

Courses: List all the general types (history, literature) or specific courses you've taken which may be marketable (computer, business, marketing, economics, etc.), you really enjoyed or both.

Experience: Just list specific functions you performed at any part-time (school year) or full-time (summer) jobs. Entries may include "General Office" (typing, filing, answering phones, etc.), "Sales," "Writing," "Research," etc.

Likes: List all your "likes" that have not previously been listed anywhere yet. These might include the types of people you like to be with, the kind of environment you prefer (city, country, large places, small places, quiet, loud, fast-paced, slow-paced) and anything else which hasn't shown up somewhere on this form. However, try _not_ to include entries which refer to specific jobs or companies. We'll list those on another form. For example, entries might include "friendly people," "outdoors," "soft colors," "quiet," "lack of stress," "museums," "long walks," etc.

Dislikes: All the people, places and things you can easily live without.

Now assess the marketability of each item you've listed. Mark highly marketable skills with an "H." Use "M" to characterize those skills which _may_ be marketable in a particular set of circumstances, "L" for those with minimal potential application to any job. Of the above examples, typing, word processing and stenography are always marketable, so you'd mark them with an "H". Teaching, computer and accounting skills would also qualify as highly marketable. Similarly, if you listed high-energy or perseverance as a strength, any Sales Manager will find it a highly desirable trait. Speaking French, however, gets an "M." While not marketable in all job situations, it might well be a requirement for certain industries (e.g., importing and exporting) or jobs.

Referring back to the same list, decide if you'd enjoy using your marketable skills or talents as part of your everyday job -- "Y" for yes, "N" for no. You may type 80 words a minute but truly _despise_ typing (or worry that stressing it too much will land you on the permanent clerical staff). If so, mark typing with an "N." Keep one thing in mind -- just because you dislike typing should not mean you absolutely won't accept a job that requires it. Many do, especially in publishing.

Now, go over the entire form carefully. Look for inconsistencies. For example, if you did not list "persuasive" as one of your strengths, but were a smashing success during that summer sales job, revise your list of strengths accordingly. After you are satisfied that the form is as accurate as you can make it -- and gotten over the shock of some of your honest answers -- pass it along to a close friend or two. Ask _them_ to check it for accuracy -- you'll not only uncover areas you may have fudged a bit, but learn a great deal about what the rest of the world thinks of you.   After they've completed their assessment of the person you have committed to paper, finalze the Form (for now).

ESTABLISHING YOUR CAREER OBJECTIVE(S)

For better or worse, you now know who and what you are. But we've yet to establish and evaluate another important area -- your overall needs, desires and goals. Where are you going? What do you want to accomplish? Go back to the definition of the Five Motivating Factors. Do you know which one you are yet? If so, that will help define some of the directions you will be charting in this next step. Many of these goals will already be highlighted on your Self-Evaluation Form or grow naturally out of that process.

You'll use these initial entries to prepare your **Five Year Game Plan**, a flexible but straightforward list of the things you want to do and accomplish,   both personally and professionally, during that period.

If you're getting ready to graduate from college or graduate school, the next five years are the most critical period of your whole career.   You need to make the initial transition from college to the workplace, establish yourself in a new and completely unfamiliar company environment and begin to build the professional credentials necessary to achieve your career goals.

It's rarely an easy transition. Unless you've narrowly prepared yourself for a specific profession, you're probably <u>ill</u>-prepared for any real job.   Instead, you've learned some basic principles -- the research and analytical skills necessary for success at almost any level -- and, hopefully, how to think. <u>But that's all</u>.

No matter what your college, major or degree, all you represent right now is potential. How you package that potential and what you eventually make of it is completely up to you. And it's an unfortunate fact that many companies will take a professional with barely a year or two experience over <u>any</u> newcomer, no matter how promising.   Smaller publishers, especially, can rarely afford to hire someone who can't begin contributing <u>immediately</u>.

So <u>you</u> have to be prepared to take your comparatively modest skills and experience and package them in a way that will get you interviewed and hired. Quite a challenge.

<u>Preparing your Five Year Game Plan</u>

To help clarify your personal and career goals, create your **Five Year Game Plan**. On a new sheet of paper, make three vertical columns and title them "1 year," "3 years" and "5 years." Under each heading, list your personal goals within that period. They can be specific personal objectives (get married, have first child),   material possessions you'd like to be able to afford (house, car, plane, boat), job-related objectives (vice presidency, private office), overall career objectives (publish first book) or anything else that's important to you.

Attach your Game Plan to the Self-Evaluation Form. Together, they represent a clear picture of who you are now, who you want to be and the interim steps you expect to take to achieve that transformation.

These self-descriptive exercises are not static, one-time-only events. Continue to update both forms as you proceed on your job hunt. This will enable you to consistently match industries, companies, job descriptions and even actual job offers to the "you" on that piece of paper. Keep track of your career progress as you begin that search, enter the market and, finally, begin your career. Then see how closely your real progress matches the steps you charted.

As you delve more deeply into the career options available to you in this industry, you may well want to add more "function-al" and "job specific" objectives (e.g., sell Account X, write your first bi-lined article, etc.).

Is Magazine Publishing the Right Career for You?

Now it's necessary to test your basic assumptions about the magazine industry. We presume you purchased this Career Directory because you're considering a career in magazines. Are you sure? Do you know enough about the industry to decide whether it's right for you? Probably not. So start your research now -- learn as much about the magazine business as you now know about your-self.

Start with the Introduction and Section I, the four chapters which give you a general "overview" of the magazine business. In the Introduction, John Mack Carter, one of the best-known editors in this business, talks about the recent spate of acquisitions in the industry and what they mean to your chances for obtaining an entry-level job.

In Chapter 1, Sandra Kresch of Time, Inc. further clarifies where the industry is and gives her detailed views on where it's going. Barrie Atkin discusses some of the common characteristics of the people who have found success and happiness in this indus-try (Chapter 2). And Peter Diamandis of CBS Magazines and Adolph Auerbacher of Meredith Corporation give their views of where the industry's heading and why you should consider hopping aboard the "Magazine Express" (Chapters 3 & 4).

Chapters 22 & 23, by Owen Lipstein and Tam Mossman, describe the pain and joy of starting a magazine from scratch. Their need to understand and think about every area of creation, production and distribution should give you a better understanding of the many steps involved in transforming an idea into something you can actually buy at your local newsstand...and may set a few of you to thinking about following in their footsteps.

Other sources you should consider consulting to learn more about this business are listed in the two Appendices.

In Appendix A, we've listed all the trade organizations associated with the magazine and advertising industries (the lat-ter because the two industries are so interrelated that many advertising organizations include magazine professionals, too). While educational information available from these associations is often limited (and, for the most part, already a part of this

Career Directory), write each of the pertinent associations, let them know you're contemplating a career in magazine publishing and would appreciate whatever help and advice they're willing to impart. You'll find many sponsor seminars and conferences throughout the country, some of which you may be able to attend.

In Appendix B, we've listed the trade magazines dedicated to the highly specific interests of the magazine publishing and advertising communities. These magazines are generally not available at newsstands (unless you live in or near New York City), but you may be able to obtain back issues at your local library (most major libraries have extensive collections of such journals) or by writing to the magazines' circulation/subscription departments.

You may also consider writing to the publishers and/or editors. State in your cover letter what area of the magazine business you're considering and ask them for whatever help and advice they can offer. But be specific. These are busy professionals and they do not have the time or the inclination to simply "tell me everything you can about magazine publishing."

If you can afford it now, we strongly suggest subscribing to Advertising Age, Adweek -- the two major "trades" for the advertising industry (though they cover magazines, as well), FOLIO: and Magazine Age, the major magazine industry publications, plus whichever of the other magazines are applicable to the specialty you're considering.

These publications may well provide the most imaginative and far-reaching information for your job search. Even a quick perusal of a copy or two will give you an excellent "feel" for the industry. After reading only a few articles, you'll already get a handle on what's happening in the field and some of publishing's peculiar and particular jargon. Later, more detailed study will aid you in your search for a specific publishing job.

Authors of the articles themselves may well turn out to be important resources. If an article is directly related to your chosen specialty, why not call the author and ask some questions? You'd be amazed how willing many of these magazine professionals will be to talk to you and answer your questions. They may even tell you about job openings at their companies! (But do use common sense -- authors will not always respond graciously to your invitation to "chat about the business."

In other words, make sure you learn what really makes this business tick. Take some notes as you continue your research. What is the magazine business really like? Where are the geographical centers? What's the mix between large and small publishers, trade and consumer? What are the pay scales like? Are there specific jobs that seem to pay a lot more to start or offer superior "down-the-line" potential? Is it a growth industry? Where's it heading? What areas of opportunities do the top people expect to see happening in the next decade? What specialties seem like they'll be in demand? Finally, how well do you, as you defined yourself on your Self-Evaluation Form, mesh with the magazine industry? Does it sound like the kind of business you want to be involved in? Or does long-range career success require skills you don't have and don't particularly care to acquire?

For example, make sure you understand and appreciate how much of the publishing and advertising communities are based in New York City. If you hate and despise New York, that's not the end of your magazine career. But it _may_ mean you have more limit- ed options. Know what effects such industry realities may cause _before_ you make potentially career-limiting decisions.

Is the industry growing and changing in ways that interest you? Is there room for advancement and creativity in the position you believe you are best suited for? Can you work in publishing for a few years and achieve the professional stature necessary to start your own magazine? (Do you eventually _want_ your own pub- lishing business?)

How much money do you want to earn your first year? Three years from now? Are your expectations realistic? Keep in mind, someone with little or no experience, right out of high school or college, shouldn't plan to earn $30,000 their first year. If you prefer to work in a smaller, slower-paced city, are you prepared to earn less money than your New York City counterparts?

Of course, money isn't _everything_. Early financial sacri- fices often pay off in the long run. If you begin your career in a five-person Oshkosh publishing firm, you will probably learn first-hand about many aspects of the magazine business. You'll learn to perform a variety of functions in a number of areas, gaining a broad-based understanding of how all the departments and individuals in a publishing firm function together. This is experience you may not get at a large publisher like Time, Inc. or Conde Nast, where you will probably be working in a specific department and stay pretty much within its confines.

Don't get us wrong. We're _not_ trying to talk you out of a career in magazine publishing! But we _do_ recommend studying the magazine business until you can satisfactorily answer these ques- tions. Only then will you know enough about the publishing indus- try to be sure it's where you want to be.

So Magazine's Are It. Now What?

After all this research, we're going to presume you've reached that final decision -- you want a career in magazines. It is with this vague certainty that all too many of you will race off, hunting for any publisher willing to give you a job. You'll manage to get interviews at a couple of firms and, smiling brightly, tell everyone you meet, "I want a career in magazine publishing." The interviewers, unfortunately, will all ask the same awkward question -- "What _exactly_ do you want to do in publishing?" -- and that will be the end of that.

It is simply _not_ enough to narrow your job search to a specific industry. And so far, that's all you've done. You _must_ establish a specific career objective -- the _job_ you want to start, the career you want to pursue. The general "I want to get into ..." is not enough. It demonstrates a lack of research into the industry itself and your failure to prepare any semblance of a five year plan. Do you want to start as a assistant editor, hoping to work your way up the ladder to Editor-in-Chief, or learn to sell advertising, with Advertising Director or even Publisher your eventual goal? The two entry-level positions are completely different. They require different skills and educational backgrounds. And, of course, lead in completely different directions.

Interviewers will <u>not</u> welcome you with open arms if you're still vague about your career goals. If you've managed to get an "informative interview" with an executive whose company currently has no job openings, what is he supposed to do with your resume after you leave? Who should he send it to for future consideration? Since you don't seem to know exactly what you want to do, how's <u>he</u> going to figure it out? Worse, he'll probably resent your asking him to function as your personal career counselor.

<u>The executives you're preparing to see will not be offering jobs in "magazine publishing" They'll be looking for an assistant editor, advertising salesperson or production assistant. It's that career objective they'll want to hear about.</u>

We've included detailed information on the key departments at most major magazine publishers -- Advertising Sales, Art & Design, Circulation, Editorial, Production (Manufacturing and Distribution), Promotion and Public Relations -- along with an explanation of specific entry-level titles, functions & responsibilities and advice from our expert contributors on how to get that first job and what to expect when you start it. See Chapters 5 - 8 (Advertising Sales), 9 & 10 (Art & Design), 11 - 13 (Circulation), 14 - 16 (Editorial), 17 & 18 (Production), 19 & 20 (Promotion) and 21 (Public Relations).

Remember, the more specific your career objective, the better your chances of finding a job. It's that simple and that important. Naturally, before you declare your objective to the world, check once again to make sure your specific job target matches the skills and interests you defined on your Self-Evaluation Form. Eventually, you will want to state such an objective on your resume and "To obtain an entry-level position as an assistant editor at a major consumer magazine publishing company" is quite a bit better than "I want a career in magazines."

Do <u>not</u> consider this step final until you can summarize your job/career objective in a single, short, accurate sentence.

CHAPTER 25

Targeting Companies & Networking for Success

You know what you want to do. Where are you going to get a job doing it? There are hundreds of magazine publishers, ranging in size from the biggest (Time, Inc.) with thousands of employees and offices throughout the world to the smallest (a plethora of single title firms). Small or large? New York or Oshkosh? Just which of these firms is the right one for you?

YOUR IDEAL PUBLISHER PROFILE

Let's establish some criteria to evaluate potential employers. This will enable you to identify your target companies, the places you'd really like to work.

Take another sheet of blank paper (yes, it's time for another list) and divide it into three vertical columns. Title it "Publisher - Ideal Profile." Call the left-hand column "Musts," the middle column "Preferences," and the right-hand column "Nevers."

We've listed a series of questions below. After considering each question, decide whether a particular criteria **must** be met, whether you would simply **prefer** it or **never** would consider it at all. We've also completed a sample form, which follows immediately after the questions. If there are other criteria you consider important, feel free to add them to the list below and mark them accordingly on your Profile.

1. What are your geographical preferences? (Possible answers: U.S., Canada, International, Anywhere). If you only want to work in the U.S., then "Work in United States" would be the entry

in the "Must" column. "Work in Canada or Foreign Country" might be the first entry in your "Never" column. There would be no applicable entry for this question in the "Preference" column. If, however, you will consider working in two of the three, then your "Must" column entry might read "Work in U.S. or Canada," your "Preference" entry (if you preferred one over the other) could read "Work in U.S." and the "Never" column , "Work Over-seas."

2. If you prefer to work in the U.S. or Canada, what area, state(s) or province(s)? If Overseas, what area or countries?

3. Do you prefer a large city, small city, town or somewhere as far away from civilization as possible?

4. In regard to question 3, any specific preferences?

5. Do you prefer a warm or cold climate?

6. Do you prefer a large or small company? Define your terms (by income, employees, number of magazines, etc.).

7. Do you mind relocating right now? Do you want to work for a company with a reputation for _frequently_ relocating top people?

8. Do you mind travelling frequently? What percent do you consider reasonable? (Make sure this matches the normal require-ments of the job specialization you're considering).

9. What salary would you like to receive (put in the "Pre-ference" column)? What's the _lowest_ salary you'll accept (in the "Must" column)?

10. Are there any benefits (such as an expense account, med-ical and/or dental insurance, company car, etc.) you must or would like to have?

11. Are you planning on attending graduate school at some point in the future and, if so, is it important to you that a tuition reimbursement plan exist?

12. Do you feel a formal training program necessary?

13. What kind of magazine do you want to work for (consumer, general interest, special-interest, trade, professional journal, etc.)?

14. Is there a particular magazine or publisher you want to work for?

In the sample form we've filled out on the next page, we drew boxes around entries which were related. An unboxed entry in the "Must" column has no relation to the "Preference" entry next to it.

PUBLISHERS - IDEAL PROFILE (Sample)

MUSTS	PREFERENCES	NEVERS
Major consumer magazine/company	Time, Inc. Formal ad sales training	

MUSTS	PREFERENCES	NEVERS
Work in U.S. only	NY, CA, FL or IL	NJ, PA, DC

Big City (population less important than lifestyle/culture)	New York, Los Angeles, Miami, San Diego	Any small city

	Large Company (200+ employees)	25 employees

	Travel 0 - 20%	More than 40%

$14,000/year	$18,000/year	

Medical insurance	Dental ins., Co. car, Tuition Reimbursement	

It's important to keep revising this new form, just as you should continue to update your Self-Evaluation Form and Five Year Game Plan. After all, it contains the criteria by which you will judge every potential employer. It may even lead you to avoid interviewing at a specific company (if, for example, they`re In Pennsylvania!). So be sure your "Nevers" aren't frivolous. Likewise, make your "Musts" and "Preferences" at least semi-realistic. If your "Must" salary for a position as an advertising sales rep is $40,000, you may wind up eliminating every magazine out there!

Armed with a complete list of such criteria, you're ready to find all the publishers (in addition to Time, Inc., of course) that match them.

CREATING YOUR COMMAND CHART

It's time to set up another chart. Call this sheet your "Command Chart" or "Publisher Evaluation Sheet." When completed, it will be the summary of all your research, containing all the information on the publishers you've initially targeted. As you start networking, sending out resumes and cover letters and preparing for interviews, you will find yourself constantly updating and referring to this Chart.

Create one vertical column down the left side -- this is where you'll begin listing the publishers you're considering. Then make as many columns across the top of the chart as you need to list all your "Must" and "Preference" criteria so you can "grade" the firms accordingly.

For example, using the entries on the sample form above, we would write in the following column headings and make an entry for each publisher you've targeted in the appropriate space (from those possible, noted in parentheses):

1. **STATE**: (Enter "NY," "CA," "FL" or "IL," the only four you'll consider).

2. **CITY**: (Identify).

3. **PUBLISHER SIZE**: (Number of employees).

4. **FORMAL TRAINING PROGRAM**: (Check if "yes" and note important details -- who's in charge, number of new trainees hired each year, etc.).

5. **BENEFITS**: Leave enough room to list all agency-wide benefits. Circle those especially important to you.

7. **TRAVEL**: Enter percentage anticipated.

8. **SALARY**: You'll probably want to leave this blank until able to enter a specific salary offer, but may want to include anything you discover about that agency's general pay scales, etc.

Since the first entry on our sample Ideal Publisher Profile was "large consumer magazine/company," all the firms or magazines you list should satisfy this criteria -- that is, be large, major consumer publishers. Likewise, because of the next entry, "Work in U.S. Only," we expect they will all be U.S. companies. The information necessary to fill in the first four columns (State, City, Publisher Size, Formal Training Program) is available on nearly 100 top publishers in Chapters 28 and 29. Information on benefits is easily obtainable from each firm. The information necessary to complete the Travel and Salary columns is specifically contingent on a job offer and, therefore, probably won't be filled in until near the end of your job search.

Feel free to combine, add to, alter and use this new chart in any way that makes sense to you. While you will probably set up individual files for the publishers high on your list (after "starring" the top ten or fifteen you like most), this Command Chart will remain an important form to refer back to.

TARGETING THE PUBLISHERS

To begin creating your initial list of targeted publishers, start with Section XI. We've listed more than 300 major publishers. Those listed in Chapter 28 completed questionnaires we supplied, and provided us with a plethora of data concerning their overall operations, hiring practices and important information on entry-level job opportunities. This latter information includes key contacts (names), statistics on 1984 hiring of high school, college and graduate students, the number of entry-level people they expect to hire in 1986, along with complete job descriptions and requirements.

Chapter 29 includes lists of publishers offering salaried and non-salaried internships, or some of each, and publishers with formal training programs for "new hires." All of the detailed information in these two chapters was provided by the publishers themselves. To our knowledge, much of it is available only in this **Career Directory**.

After you have considered these publishers, turn to Chapters 30 ("Other Consumer Magazine Publishers to Contact"), 31 ("Other Trade Magazine Publishers to Contact") and 32 ("Other Professional/Scientific/Technical Publishers to Contact), depending on the kind of magazine you want to work on. These publishers did not provide information via our questionnaire, so their listings are necessarily less complete.

Although there are over 11,000 periodicals published in the United States each year, the majority are small operations -- scholarly journals for a highly select audience or special-interest magazines put together by a single individual or family team. The 300-odd publishers we've listed in Section XI probably account for over 75% of all magazine circulation and revenues. But that's no reason to not consider one of these other companies as a potential starting place. In the next section of this chapter, we will discuss some other reference books you can use to obtain more information on the publishers we've listed, as well as those we haven't.

OTHER REFERENCE TOOLS

In order to obtain some of the detailed information you need to completely fill in your Command Chart, you will probably need to do further research, either in the library or by meeting and chatting with people familiar with the agencies.

R. R. Bowker (205 E. 42nd St., New York, NY 10017) puts out two excellent reference works -- **Magazine Industry Marketplace** and **Ulrich's International Periodicals Directory**. The former details most of the major magazines published in the U.S., the latter nearly every magazine published throughout the world (but with little information on each of the titles, let alone the companies that publish them. A similar, all inclusive volume is the **Standard Periodical Directory** (Oxbridge Communications). All three will probably be available in your local or school library.

More complete information on each magazine (but again, not

necessarily each company) is available through the various editions of <u>Standard Rate and Data Service</u> (<u>SRDS</u>), the bible of advertising agency media buyers

For more general research, you might want to use the <u>Guide to American Directories</u> (B. Klein Publications, P.O. Box 8503, Coral Springs, FL 33065), which lists directories for over 3,000 fields. If you want to work for an association, most of which publish a variety of professional and scholarly journals for their members, they may be researched in the <u>Encyclopedia of Associations</u> (Gale Research Co., Book Tower, Detroit, MI 48226).

There are, in addition, four general corporate directories which may give you additional information on the major publishers. They should all be available in the reference (and/or business) section of your local library:

<u>Dun and Bradstreet's Million Dollar Directory</u> (Dun's Marketing Services, 3 Century Drive, Parsippany, NJ 07054).

<u>Standard & Poor's Register of Corporations, Directors and Executives</u> (Standard and Poor, 25 Broadway, New York, NY 10004).

<u>Moody's Industrial Manual</u> (Moody's Investors Service, Inc., 99 Church St., New York, NY 10007).

<u>Thomas's Register of American Manufacturing</u> (Thomas Publishing Company, 1 Penn Plaza, New York, NY 10001).

Primary sources which should be utilized from now on to complete your research are <u>The Wall Street Journal</u>, <u>Barron's</u>, <u>Dun's Business Month</u>, <u>Business Week</u>, <u>Forbes</u>, and <u>Fortune</u>. Naturally, the trade magazines which you've been studying (and to which you've already subscribed) like <u>Advertising Age</u>, <u>Adweek</u>, <u>FOLIO:</u>, <u>Magazine Age</u>, etc., offer a steady stream of information. Become as familiar as possible with the magazines, publishers, jargon, topics covered and the industry as it is evolving. Write to each to ask about various special issues published which may help. (<u>Ad Age</u>, for example, publishes its "100 Leading Media Companies" issue in June. This might be an excellent research source for anyone seeking a job at one of these major firms.)

NETWORKING FOR SUCCESS

You're now as prepared as any Boy Scout in history. You know not only the field you want to enter, but an <u>exact</u> job title, summarized in a concise career objective. You know whether you're heading for a consumer or trade publisher. And you have a complete preliminary list of firms, with detailed data on each, that reflects your own needs, wants and goals.

It's time to start <u>networking</u>, telling everybody you know and everybody <u>they</u> know exactly the kind of job you're looking for. Faster than you expect, you will begin to develop a <u>network</u>

of friends, relatives, acquaintances and contacts. It is most likely that the skillful use of this network and <u>not</u> the more traditional approach to job hunting -- studying the want ads and sending out resumes to PO Box Numbers -- is going to be the key factor in landing the job you want.

Why? Because on any day of the week, the vast majority of available jobs, perhaps as many as <u>**85% of all the jobs out there waiting to be filled,**</u> are not advertised anywhere. Many of those jobs that are advertised only remain in the classifieds for a day or two. After that, they're pulled and, for the next few weeks, various personnel sift through resumes <u>**while the job is still sitting there, unfilled and waiting for the right applicant to grab it!**</u>

There are some things to keep in mind while you prepare to crack what others have labled "the hidden job market." First and foremost, remember that there are <u>always</u> jobs out there. Nearly 20% of all the jobs in the United States change hands <u>every year</u>, good times and bad. People move in and out of specific industries, change magazines, get promoted. Companies expand. New magazines are started. The result is near-constant movement in the job market, <u>**if only you know where to look.**</u>

Second, people in a company will generally know about a job opening <u>weeks</u> before the outside world gets a clue, certainly before (<u>if</u>) it shows up in a newspaper ad.

Third, just knowing that this hidden market exists is an asset a lot of your colleagues (hereafter, let's just consider them competitors) don't have.

Last, but by no means least, your industry and company research has already made you one of the most knowledgeable graduates out there. This will undoubtedly work to your advantage.

Creating your Network

In order to succeed, you must exploit any and every resource -- people who can help you get a job -- you have. Start with family, no matter how distant the relationship (<u>especially</u> if they work in publishing!), friends, acquaintances (no matter how shaky). You ought to be speaking to your professors, especially those who teach Journalism (but don't exempt the Advertising, Public Relations or English professors -- <u>you</u> don't know who <u>they</u> know). Write to the important trade journals and industry associations. Let them know what you're looking for and, especially, the kinds of preparations you've already completed and the specific publishers you'd like to work for. Ask them for a list of upcoming seminars or conferences you may be able to attend -- these are excellent sources of professional contacts.

Telling everyone you know of your job hunt may lead to a series of informative interviews or conversations with publishing professionals. Such informal meetings may well lead to more formal interviews for job openings at their own companies, either with them or their colleagues. At worst, if they work at one of your target publishers, they may be able to answer some important questions -- Who's hiring entry-level people? Who should you apply to? What's the interviewer like? Needless to say, someone who's actually worked at a firm can supply you with a lot of not-so-public and personal information you'll never find in the hand-out from Personnel.

Once you meet someone or even talk with them on the phone, they are _always_ potential sources of information and future contacts. Whether they've been helpful or not, don't be afraid to ask them for the names of three or four additional people, at their own or other magazines, who might be in a position to help you out.

You're bound to get a lot of "no's" along the way, but that is just the Law of Averages at work. Don't take any rejection personally and don't let a string of rejections stop you from asking for help from yet another new acquaintance. The more contacts you're able to make, the more people you have working, trying to find _you_ a job! As any salesperson will tell you, the average prospect says "no!" five times before he buys. Expect a lot of "no's" to eventually lead to a lot of "yes's".

If you consider such networking to be nothing more than bra-zen hustling and a far too blatant approach, **banish that feeling.** You must be prepared to use these contacts in any way possible. **They are your key to the right job, the right career and, if money motivates you, the Big Bucks.** Fear must be considered an undesirable obstacle. Get rid of it.

_Do_ keep in mind, however, that the request you make to each person should be both legitimate and thought-out. As we've conti-nually stressed throughout this Directory, busy people do not have time for students who just want them "to tell me something about magazine publishing." But a sincere request for informa-tion, politely solicited, is answered more often than you think.

Just as important, don't avoid networking because of some misguided notion that "you need to do it on your own." What will _that_ prove? Especially if you don't get the job you want! Net-working isn't "taking advantage." No matter _how_ many connnections you have on a magazine, no one is going to hire you if you're not qualified.

Expanding Your Network

Just because you're aware of and actively following up on the 85% of jobs that are _unadvertised_, there's no reason to com-pletely ignore the 15% that _do_ show up in a trade magazine or newspaper (like the _New York Times_). Scour the Classified Ad sections of these publications as well.

If your school's career counseling office has a resume for-warding service or files of employers seeking qualified students, use them. This is a major source of entry-level jobs for many students.

Finally, you may consider registering with an employment agency or recruitment firm -- there are quite a few of them, especially in New York City, who purport to specialize in pub-lishing. Frankly, we don't recommend the time or the effort. Most such companies are simply not interested in handling entry-level people (since they rarely are asked to find them). It <u>is</u> a buyer's market out there.

The best way to expand your network will inevitably turn out to be the way you got it started -- persistence, research, sales.

Organizing Your Home Office

With so many other people working for you, you must carefully and completely organize your own personal employment office. If you've already started filing detailed publisher data in separate folders, you're already a step ahead. We suggest preparing a separate folder for each person you're working with, along with a centralized phone list. Throughout your job search, be prepared to keep accurate and organized records every step of the way. Keep copies of your research notes, photocopy every letter you mail and keep detailed notes of telephone conversations. <u>Always</u> send off a timely and polite "thank you" note to those helping out. That simple gesture will demonstrate a degree of professionalism and good manners often overlooked by students.

If you can afford one, consider purchasing a telephone answering machine. An employer who may have seen and likes your resume -- one who's even willing to interview you -- will rarely call more than once to set up an appointment.

As you continue your networking and library research, you'll slowly learn more and more about the publishers you've targeted (and some you've missed). Add new ones to your "Command Chart" as you uncover them and continually update the information on all those you've listed. If you "starred" your Top Ten target publishers, you'll want to at least have individual folders for them. You may also want to prepare a folder for any publisher at which you've interviewed, even if you're not interested in working there, just to make it easy to find the information. Above all, continue to phone and write everybody!

CHAPTER 26

Preparing Resumes & Cover Letters

Your resume is a one- or two-page summary of you -- your education, skills, employment experience and career objective(s). It is not a biography. It's purpose is to sell you to the publisher you want to work for. It must set you apart from all the other applicants (those competitors) out there. So, when you sit down to formulate your resume, remember you're trying to present the pertinent information in a format and manner that will convince an executive to grant you an interview, the prelude to any job offer.

In order to begin preparing your resume, you will need to assemble all the following information:

1. The names, addresses and telephone numbers of all your past employers.

2. The key personnel with whom you worked and a concise summary of the work you performed.

3. Any letters of recommendation from these employers.

4. Awards and honors you have received.

5. Clubs, honor societies and other activities (including any leadership positions held).

6. Marketable skills (typing, word processing, computer literacy, foreign languages, writing, sales, etc.).

7. Your grade point average (include it only if it's a B+ or better).

8. Your major field of study.

9. A concise career objective.

10. Hobbies and other interests.

CHRONOLOGICAL AND FUNCTIONAL RESUMES

The two standard resume formats are **chronological**, arranged by date, and **functional**, which emphasizes skills rather than the sequential history of your experiences. Generally, since students have yet to develop specific, highly employable skills or the experience to indicate proficiency in specific job functions, they should use the chronological format. A bit of sales, a touch of writing and a smidgen of research will not impress anyone on a functional resume. The latter is useful, however, if you have a great deal of pertinent job expertise. On pages 000 and 000 are examples of both.

GUIDELINES FOR RESUME PREPARATION

Your resume should be limited to a single page if possible, two <u>at most</u>. It should be printed, <u>not</u> xeroxed, on 8½" x 11" white, cream or ivory stock. The ink should be black or, at most, a royal blue. Don't scrimp on the paper quality -- use the best bond you can afford. And since printing 100 or even 200 copies will cost little more than 50, tend to overestimate your needs and opt for the higher quantity.

When you're laying out the resume, try to leave a reasonable amount of "white space" -- generous margins all around and spacing between entries. A resume is not a complete biography and anything that is not, in some way, a qualification for the type of position you're seeking should be omitted.

Be brief. Use phraseology rather than complete sentences. Your resume is a summary of your talents, not an English Lit paper. Choose your words carefully and use "power words" whenever possible. "Organized" is more powerful than "put together"; "supervised" better than "oversaw"; "formulated" better than "thought up." Strong words like these can make the most mundane clerical work sound like a series of responsible, professional positions. And, of course, they will tend to make your resume stand out.

Here's a "starter list" of words, some of which you may want to use in your resume:

achieved	administered	advised	analyzed
applied	arranged	budgeted	calculated
classified	communicated	completed	computed
conceptualized	coordinated	critiqued	delegated
determined	developed	devised	directed
established	evaluated	executed	formulated
gathered	generated	guided	implemented

improved	initiated	instituted	instructed
introduced	invented	issued	launched
lectured	litigated	lobbied	managed
negotiated	operated	organized	overhauled
planned	prepared	presented	presided
programmed	promoted	recommended	researched
reviewed	revised	reorganized	regulated
selected	solved	scheduled	supervised
systematized	taught	tested	traced
trained	updated	utilized	wrote

<u>**ONE FINAL SUGGESTION:**</u> When you've completed writing and designing your resume, have a couple of close friends or family members proofread it for typographical errors <u>**before**</u> you send it to the printer. For some reason, the more you check it yourself, the less likely you'll catch the errors you missed the first time around. A fresh look from someone not as familiar with it will catch these glaring (and potentially embarassing) errors before they're duplicated a couple of hundred times.

PREPARING COVER LETTERS

A <u>**cover letter**</u> should be included with each resume you send out. It may be addressed to a particular individual your networking has identified (or with whom you've already met or spoken) or be sent in response to a newspaper ad (even those that refer you solely to Post Office Boxes). Whatever the case, each cover letter should be personalized -- targeted to the individual publisher, executive and position.

Each cover letter should be error-free, neatly typed (<u>**never**</u> handwritten) and correctly formatted. Students, in particular, sometimes send out cover letters reminiscent of letters home from camp, complete with the requisite stains from lunch. That is both unprofessional (you <u>are</u> trying to impress them with your professionalism) and downright offensive to any potential employer. These letters should be business letters. If you are unfamiliar with the correct way to format such a letter, study the examples we've included and, if necessary, go to your local library and study the appropriate books in the business section.

Address each letter to the proper person at the publisher (i.e., don't write to the Advertising Director to find a job as an assistant editor). Individual editors, sales executives and other department heads are generally listed on each magazine's masthead. Some of this information (only the top executives, usually) may be found in <u>SRDS</u>. Use these sources and the listings in this <u>**Career Directory**</u> to make sure you spell all the names correctly.

Some newspaper or trade magazine ads will not include a contact name, but will instruct you to send your resume to a post office box. In this case, "Dear Sir:" is an appropriate salutation. And if the ad lists a series of instructions ("write, don't call," "send letter including salary requirements and (unreturnable) copy sample," etc.), follow them <u>exactly</u>. Failing to do so

CHRONOLOGICAL RESUME (SAMPLE)

JOE COLLEGE
1 Main Street,
Anywhere, MA 01234
(617)555-1111

Career Objective: A position as an advertising sales representative for a major consumer publishing company.

EXPERIENCE:

Summer, 1985: Smith and Jones Associates, Inc. Responsibilities at this local advertising agency included developing copy as well as assisting on account calls. Presented copy ideas to clients, contacted media, researched media placement, screened phone calls. Light office typing, word processing and filing.

Summer, 1984: Committee to Re-elect Mayor Honest Jim. Office intern to the Mayor's Press Secretary. Responsibilities included writing press releases, typing & filing.

1984/85 School Year : The Daily Blast. Director of Ad Sales for the 12,000 circulation student newspaper. Ad revenue increased 21% over previous record year. Supervised staff of three.

1983/84 School Year : Joe's University Book Store. Sold books, helped keep track of inventory, placed orders with publishers and advertising in the University's publications.

EDUCATION : A.B., Journalism/Marketing, University State Klinger, MA, 1985. Grade Point Average - 3.85 (Summa Cum Laude).

PROFESSIONAL MEMBERSHIP : The Advertising Club of New York (Young Professionals Division)

BUSINESS SKILLS : Sales, media placement, typing (50 wpm), word processing, computer literate.

PERSONAL : Age: 21
Health: Excellent
Languages: Fluent (read/write/speak) French.

REFERENCES : Available Upon Request.

FUNCTIONAL RESUME (SAMPLE)

JOE COLLEGE
1 Main Street,
Anywhere, MA 01234
(617)555-1111

Career Objective: A position as an advertising sales representative at a major consumer publishing firm.

SUMMARY

I am completing my degree in journalism, specializing in marketing, at University State. Last summer, I interned as an assistant account executive (with copywriting responsibilities) for a local advertising agency. I also have one year's experience selling advertising space (and supervising a staff of three salespeople) on my college newspaper. Both jobs have convinced me I will be successful in selling advertising for a consumer publication.

EXPERIENCE

Summer, 1985: Intern, Smith & Jones Associates, Inc.
Summer, 1984: Intern, Committee to Re-elect Mayor Honest Jim.

1984/85
School Year : Ad Director, The Daily Blast.

1983/85
School Year : Salesman, Joe's University Book Store.

EDUCATION

B.A. Journalism (Marketing) University State - June, 1985 (Summa Cum Laude).

PROFESSIONAL MEMBERSHIPS AND BUSINESS SKILLS

Member of the Young Professionals Division of the Advertising Club of New York. Skills: Sales, media placement, typing (50 wpm), word processing, computer literate.

PERSONAL

Age: 21; Health: Excellent; Fluent (read/write/speak) in German and French.

References Available Upon Request

could mean you already failed their "pre-screening interview." You'll have lost the job before you even started chasing it!

The Correct Format

 <u>First</u> <u>paragraph</u>: State the reason for the letter, the specific job or type of work for which you're applying and where (or from whom) you learned of the opening.

 <u>Second</u> <u>paragraph</u>: Indicate why you're interested in their company and that particular position and/or magazine and, more important, what you have to offer them. Without repeating information from your resume verbatim, explain the appropriate academic or work experiences which specifically qualify you for the position.

 <u>Third</u> <u>paragraph</u>: Refer him to the resume you've enclosed and add anything else you feel it's important he know about you.

 <u>Final</u> <u>paragraph</u>: Indicate your desire to meet for a personal interview and your flexibility as to the place and time. Try to close the letter with a statement or question which will encourage him to take some action. Instead of "looking forward to hearing" from <u>him</u>, tell him when he should expect to hear from <u>you</u>. Otherwise, be prepared to <u>not</u> hear from him -- publishing executives get streams of letters, and can't answer most of them.

 This is a very general approach to a "standard" cover letter. If you are particularly good at writing a strong sales pitch, you're probably already used to writing such letters. Otherwise, fitting your thoughts into the orderly paragraphs we have outlined should help you prepare better letters.

 Try to personalize each one -- mention the publisher's or magazine's name whenever and wherever you have the chance. Refer to particular articles, major advertisers they carry or anything else your research has uncovered. Executives at the top publishers receive hundreds of applications, letters and unsolicited resumes from students and others looking for jobs...sometimes <u>weekly</u>. Take this opportunity to show them that you are, in fact, serious about working at their company and that you've taken the time to learn something about them. And don't hesitate to demonstrate the fruits of your research in your letters.

 Don't make a common mistake and simply recopy half your resume into the body of the cover letter, which offers you the opportunity to be a little creative, compensate for some glaring weakness or omission in your resume and make a good, professional first impression. If the cover letter doesn't "sell" them, they may never even bother looking at the resume.

 Two sample cover letters are reproduced on the pages that immediately follow. Cover Letter 1 might have been written in response to a small "want ad" in <u>Advertising</u> <u>Age</u> or <u>FOLIO:</u> which didn't name the magazine or publisher and directed all inquiries to a Box Number. Letter 2 is one we'd write to the Advertising Director at a publisher one of our contacts told us might be hiring two or three new people for their Ad Sales Training Program.

COVER LETTER 1 (SAMPLE)

May 6, 1986

Joe College
1 Main Street,
Anywhere, MA 01234
(617)555-1111

Post Office Box 1000
Advertising Age
740 N. Rush St.,
Chicago, IL 60611

Dear Sir:

The entry-level advertising sales position briefly outlined in your May 5th **Ad Age** advertisement is very appealing to me. Please accept this letter and the attached resume as my application for this position.

While majoring in Journalism (with a Marketing emphasis) at University State, I worked on a number of projects which required the analytical skills you specified in your ad. In addition, as Advertising Director for the **Daily Blast**, and a summer intern for a local advertising agency, I demonstrated the sales and interpersonal skills such a position would require.

I am especially excited about the possibility of working on **Spinner**, your recording industry magazine, as your ad indicates this new hiree would. As I was born and raised in Indiana, I am already familiar with and enjoy Chicago. I would like to work there.

I would like to meet with you at your convenience to discuss this position and my qualifications for it in more detail. I will be in Chicago for other interviews the week of May 27th. I will call you Monday, May 14th, to see if we can set up an appointment for that week.

Thank you for your time. I look forward to meeting with you.

Sincerely yours,

Joe College

COVER LETTER 2 (SAMPLE)

May 6, 1986

Joe College
1 Main Street,
Anywhere, MA 01234
(617)555-1111

Mr. James R. Remington
V.P. Advertising Sales
Big Time Consumer Publishing, Inc.
2435 Dyer Street,
Kokomo, IN 46254

Dear Mr. Remington:

I recently met your colleague,. Robert Black, at a seminar spon-
sored by FOLIO:. He mentioned you were considering hiring two or
three entry-level people for your Advertising Sales Training
Program and suggested I contact you.

Mr. Remington, it has been my dream to work at a major publishing
firm on a well-known consumer magazine. If at all possible, I had
hoped to be accepted in a well-respected, formal ad sales training program.

Sir, Big Time is my dream. Your training program is the best in
the industry. And while I certainly don't expect to be given the
immediate opportunity to work on Girltalk! or MEN, two of your
titles I'm most familiar with, your extensive success in consumer
magazine publishing and well-known sales expertise leads me to
believe that Big Time is the right place for me.

And I'm the right person for you to hire. While majoring in
Journalism (with a Marketing emphasis) at University State, I
worked on a number of projects, two of which simulated marketing
problems a hypothetical consumer magazine would have to help
solve for one of its advertisers in order to get their business.
In addition, as Ad Director for the Daily Blast and, this past
summer, working as an Account Services intern for a local agency,
I clearly demonstrated my sales, communication and interpersonal
skills.

Mr. Remington, I will be returning home to Indiana in one week
and would like to meet with you soon thereafter to discuss this
opportunity in more detail. I will call you on May 14th to
schedule an appointment. I look forward to talking with you then.

Sincerely yours,

Joe College

CHAPTER 27

The Interview Process

Well, the days of research, preparation, chart-making, form-filling, and resume-printing worked. You've got eight publishers that want to meet you! It's time to prepare once again -- for the interviewing process that will inevitably determine the job offers you actually get.

Start by setting up a calendar on which you can enter and track all your scheduled appointments. When you schedule an interview with a publisher, ask them how much time you should allow for the appointment. Some companies require all new applicants to fill out numerous forms and/or complete a battery of intelligence or psychological tests -- all <u>before</u> the first interview. If you have only allowed an hour for the interview -- and scheduled another at a nearby publisher ten minutes later -- the first three-hour test series you confront will effectively destroy any schedule.

Some companies, especially if the first interview is very positive, like to keep applicants around to talk to other executives. This process may be planned or, more likely, a spontaneous decision by an interviewer who likes you and wants you to meet some other key decision-makers. Other companies will tend to schedule second interviews on a separate day. Find out, if you can, how the publisher you're planning to visit generally operates. Otherwise, especially if you've travelled to New York or another city to interview with a number of companies in a short period of time, a schedule that's too tight will fall apart in no time at all.

If you need to travel out-of-state to interview with a publisher, be sure to ask if they will be paying some or all of your travel expenses. (It's generally expected that you'll be paying your own way to companies within your home state.) If the pub-

lisher doesn't offer -- and you don't ask -- presume you're paying the freight.

Even if the publisher agrees to reimburse you, make sure you
have enough money to pay all the expenses yourself. While some
companies may reimburse you immediately, handing you a check as
you leave the building, the majority may take from a week to a
month to forward you an expense check.

PRE-INTERVIEW RESEARCH

The research you did to find these publishers is nothing
compared to the research you need to do now that they've found
<u>you</u>. Study each company as if you were going to be tested on your
detailed knowledge of their organization and operations (because,
in a sense, you are). Here's a complete checklist of the facts
you should try to know about each publisher you plan to visit for
a job interview:

The Basics

1. The address of (and directions to) the office you're
   visiting.
2. Headquarters location (if different).
3. Number and titles of magazines published
4. Relative size (compared to other publishers).
5. Annual revenues (last two years).
6. Subsidiary companies; specialized divisions.
7. Departments (overall structure).

The Subtleties

1. The history of the company (including honors and
   awards, famous names, etc.).
2. Names, titles and backgrounds of top management.
3. Existence (and type) of training program.
4. Relocation policy.
5. Relative salaries (compared to other publishers).
6. Recent developments concerning the company or any of
   its magazines (from your trade magazine and newspaper reading).
7. Everything you can learn about the career, likes and
   dislikes of the person(s) interviewing you.

To be <u>this</u> well-prepared for an interview requires a considerable amount of preparation, which you will not be able to . It
accomplish the day before the interview. You may even find some
of the information you need to be unavailable on short notice.

But if you give yourself sufficient time, most of this
information is surprisingly easy to obtain. In addition to the
detailed information in Chapter 29 and the other reference sources we've noted, the publisher itself can supply you with a great
deal of data. A publisher's Annual Report -- which all publicly-
owned companies must publish yearly for their stockholders -- is

a virtual treasure trove of information. Write each publisher and request copies of their last two annual reports. A comparison of income, sales and other data over this period may enable you to infer some interesting things about the publisher's overall financial health and it's growth potential (as well as that of the magazines it publishes). Many libraries also have collections of annual reports from major corporations.

Attempting to learn about your interviewer is a chore, the importance of which is underestimated by most applicants (who then, of course, don't bother to do it). Being one of the exceptions may get you a job. Find out if he's written any articles that have appeared in the trade press or, even better, books on his area(s) of expertise. (Naturally, if he's an editor, reading anything he may have written for his own publication should take priority). Referring to his own writings during the course of an interview, without making the compliments too obvious, can be very effective. We all have egos and we all like people to talk about us. The interviewer is no different from the rest of us. You might also check to see if any of your networking contacts worked with him on his current (or a previous) magazine and can help "fill you in."

QUESTIONS EVERY INTERVIEWER KNOWS

Preparing for your interviews by learning about the publisher and magazines is a key first step. Preparing to deal with the questions the interviewer will throw at you is a necessary second one. **Don't go in "cold."** There are certain questions we can almost guarantee will be asked during any first interview. Study the list of questions (and hints) that follow and prepare at least one solid, concise answer that you can trot out on cue. Practice with a friend until your answers to these most-asked questions sound intelligent, professional and, most important, unmemorized and unrehearsed.

1. "Why do you want to be in magazine publishing?"

Using your knowledge and understanding of the publishing industry, explain why you find the business exciting and where and how you see yourself fitting in.

2. "Why do you think you'll be successful in the magazine business?"

Using the information from your Self-Evaluation Form and the research you did on that particular publisher and/or magazine, formulate an answer which marries your strengths to theirs and to the characteristics of the position for which you're applying.

3. "Why did you choose our company?"

This is an excellent opportunity to explain the extensive

process of research and education you've undertaken. Tell them about your strengths and how you match up with their company. Emphasize specific things about their company or magazines that led you to seek an interview. Be a salesman -- be convincing.

4. **"What unique contributions can you make to our publications?"**

Construct an answer which essentially lists your strengths, the experience that you feel will contribute to your job performance and any other unique qualifications which will place you at the head of the applicant pack. After all, this is a question specifically designed to eliminate some of that pack. Sell yourself. Be one of the few called back for a second interview.

5. **"What position here interests you?"**

If you're interviewing for a specific position, answer accordingly. If you want to make sure you don't close the door on other opportunities of which you might be unaware, you can follow up with your own question: "I'm here to apply for your Advertising Sales Training Program. Is there another position open for which you feel I'm qualified?"

If you've arranged an interview with a publisher without knowing of any specific openings, use the answer to this question to describe the kind of work you'd like to do and why you're qualified to do it. Avoid specific job titles, since they may tend to vary from publisher to publisher.

If you're on a first interview with the Personnel Department, answer the question. They only want to figure out where to send you.

6. **"What are your strengths and weaknesses?"** and 7. **"What are your hobbies (or outside interests)?"**

Both questions can be easily answered using your Self-Evaluation Form. Be wary of being too forthcoming about your glaring faults, but do not reply, "I don't have any." They won't believe you and, what's worse, you won't believe you. After all, you did the evaluation -- you know it's a lie!

8. **"What are your career goals?"**

...Which is why we suggested you prepare a Five Year Game Plan. Quote from the form.

9. **"What jobs have you held and why did you leave them?"**

Or the direct approach, "Have you ever been fired?" Take the opportunity to expand on your resume, rather than precisely answering the question by merely recapping the job experiences. In discussing each job, point out what you liked about it; what factors led to your leaving and how the next job added to your continuing professional education. If you _have_ been fired, say so. It's very easy to check.

10. "__What is your salary requirement__?"

If they are at all interested in you, this question will probably come up. The danger, of course, is that you may price yourself too low or, even worse, right out of a job you want. Since you will have a general idea of industry figures for that position (and may even have an idea of what that agency tends to pay new people for the position), why not refer to a _range_ of salaries, such as "$16,000 - $19,000?"

If the interviewer doesn't bring up salary at all, it's doubtful you're being seriously considered, so you probably don't need to even bring the subject up. (If you _know_ you aren't getting the job or aren't interested in it if offered, you may try to nail down a salary figure in order to be better prepared for the _next_.)

11. "__Tell me about yourself__."

Watch out for this one! It's often one of the first questions asked. If you falter here, the rest of the interview could quickly become a downward slide to nowhere. Be prepared and consider it an opportunity to combine your answers to many of the previous questions into one concise description of who you are, what you want to be and why that publisher should take a chance on you. Summarize your resume -- _briefly_ -- and expand on particular courses or experiences relevant to the company or position. Do not go on about your hobbies or personal life, your dog, where you spent your summer vacation, etc. None of that is particularly relevant to securing that job. You may explain how that particular job fits in with your long-range career goals and talk specifically about what attracted you to their company in the first place.

The Trick Questions

Every interviewer is different and, unfortunately, there are no rules saying he _has_ to use all or any of the "basic" questions. But the odds are against his avoiding all of them. Whichever of these he includes, be assured most interviewers do like to come up with questions that are "uniquely theirs." It may be just one or a whole series -- questions he's developed over the years that _he_ feels helps separate the wheat from the chaff.

You can't exactly prepare yourself for questions like, "What would you do if...?" (fill in the blank with some obscure occurrence); "Tell me about your father;" or "What's your favorite ice cream flavor?" Every interviewer we know has his or her favorites and _all_ of these questions seem to come out of left field. Just stay relaxed, grit your teeth (quietly) and take a few seconds to frame a reasonably intelligent reply.

Some questions may be downright inappropriate. Young women, for example, may be asked about their plans for marriage and children. Don't call the interviewer a chauvinist (or worse). And don't point out that the question may be a little outside the law. Whenever any questions are raised about your personal life -- and this question surely qualifies -- it is much more effective to respond that you are very interested in the position and have no reason to believe that your personal life will preclude you from doing an excellent job.

"Do You Have Any Questions?"

It's the fatal twelfth question on our list, often the last one an interviewer throws at you after two hours of grilling. Unless the interview has been very long and unusually thorough, you probably should have questions about the job, the company, the magazine you'll be working on or even the industry. Unfortunately, by the time this question off-handedly hits the floor, you -- sensing you're almost out of the "hot seat" and looking forward to leaving -- may have absolutely nothing to say.

Preparing yourself for an interview means more than having answers for some of the questions an interviewer may ask. It means having your own set of questions -- at least five or six -- for the interviewer. The interviewer is trying to find the right person for the job. You're trying to find the right job. So you should be just as curious about him and his company as he is about you. Here's a short list of questions you may consider asking on any interview:

1. What will my typical day be like?

2. Given my attitude and qualifications, how would you estimate my chances for career advancement at your company?

3. Why did you come to work here? What keeps you here?

4. How would you characterize the management philosophy of your magazine/company?

5. What characteristics do the successful_____ at your company have in common (fill in the blank with an appropriate title, such as "editors," "advertising salespeople," etc.)?

6. What's the best (and worst) thing about working here?

Other questions about the company, magazine and/or position will be obvious -- they're the areas your research hasn't been able to fill in. Consider asking the interviewer for the answers you feel are important to know . But be careful and use common sense. No one is going to answer highly personal, rude or indiscreet questions. Even innocent questions might be misconstrued if you don't think about the best way to pose them -- before you ask them.

Unless you're interviewing with the Personnel (or Human Resources) Department, remember that most, if not all, of the executives you'll be meeting are not professional interviewers. Which means they might well spend more time talking about themselves than the company, its publications, the position or you. If that happens, use it as an opportunity to create an informal dialogue. Such a "conversational approach" is often a more productive way of finding out important information than a straightforward Question & Answer session anyway.

THE DAY OF THE INTERVIEW

The preparation's done. "I-Day" is at hand.

On the day of the interview, wear a conservative business suit, even if the publisher is notorious for its non-existent dress code. You may be able to wear a T-shirt & jeans _after_ you get the job (but don't bet your first paycheck on it).

It's not unusual for resumes and cover letters to head in different directions when an agency starts passing them around to a number of executives. Both may even be long-gone. So bring along extra copies of your resume and your own copy of the cover letter that originally accompanied it. Whether or not you make them available, we suggest you prepare a neatly-typed list of references (including the name, title, company, address and phone number of each person). You may want to bring along a copy of your college transcript -- especially if it's something to brag about -- and, if appropriate or required, samples of your work (e.g., your art portfolio).

Plan to arrive fifteen minutes before your scheduled time. If you're in an unfamiliar city, or have a long drive to the company, allow time for the unexpected delays that occur with mind-numbing regularity on days like this.

Arriving early will give you some time to check your appearance, catch your breath, get organized, check in with the receptionist and make sure you know how to pronounce the interviewer's name (pronouncing it correctly is, after all, a nice way to start off).

Arriving late does _not_ make a sterling first impression. If you are only a few minutes late, it's probably best not to mention it or even excuse yourself. With a little luck, everybody else is behind schedule and no one will notice. However, if you are more than fifteen minutes late, have an honest (or at least serviceable) explanation ready and offer it at your first opportunity. Then drop the subject as quickly as possible and move on to the interview.

When you meet the interviewer, shake hands firmly. People pay attention to handshakes. Ask for a business card. This will make sure you get his name and title right when you write your follow-up letter. You can staple it to the company file for easy reference as you continue your networking.

Try to maintain eye contact with the interviewer as you talk. This will indicate you're interested in what he has to say. Sit straight. Keep your voice at a comfortable level and try to sound enthusiastic (without imitating a high school cheerleader). Be confident and poised and provide direct, accurate and honest answers to his trickiest questions. And, as you try to remember all this, just be yourself and try to project that you're comfortable!

Interviews are sometimes conducted over lunch, though this is not usually the case with entry-level people. If it does happen to you, try to order something in the middle price-range, neither filet mignon nor a cheeseburger. Do not order alcohol. If your interviewer orders a carafe of wine, you may share it. Otherwise, alcohol should be considered verboten. Then hope your mother taught you the correct way to eat and talk at the same time. Otherwise, just do your best to maintain a semblance of poise.

There are some things interviewers will always view with displeasure -- street language, complete lack of eye contact, insufficient or vague explanations or answers, a noticeable lack of energy, poor interpersonal skills (i.e., not listening or the inability to carry on an intelligent conversation) and a lack of motivation.

Small oversights can cost you a job. Phil Mushnick, a regular sports columnist for the New York Post, describes the seemingly insignificant incident that, legend has it, made Joe Namath the quarterback for the New York Jets football team:

> If not for one rainy night in 1964, Namath might never have become a Jet. On that evening, (Jets owner) Sonny and Mrs. Werblin were entertaining Tulsa University quarterback Jerry Rhome at a Manhattan restaurant. Werblin was also entertaining plans to draft Rhome and build the franchise around him, much the way he would with Namath.
>
> Legend has it that, following dinner, Rhome made a solo dash for Werblin's car, which was waiting outside in the rain, leaving the Werblins to soak while he climbed in first. Friends of Werblin say that episode convinced him that Rhome wasn't the (quarterback) he wanted to lead his team. Shortly afterwards, the Jets traded Rhome's draft rights to Houston for a No. 1 pick, which they used to select Namath.

As the above story demonstrates (even if it's more legend than fact) every impression may count. And the very last impression an interviewer has may outweigh everything else. So, before you allow an interview to end, summarize why you want the job, why you are qualified and what, in particular, you can offer their company.

Then, take some action. If the interviewer hasn't told you about the rest of the interview process and/or where you stand, ask him. Will you be seeing other people that day? If so, ask him for some background on these new people with whom you'll be interviewing. If there are no other meetings that day, what's the next step? When can you expect to hear from them about coming back?

When you return home, file all the business cards, copies of correspondence and notes from the interview(s) with each publisher in the appropriate files. If you obtained some new information, be sure to update your Command Chart. Finally, but most importantly, ask yourself which companies you really want to work at and which you are no longer interested in. This will quickly determine how far you want the process at each publisher to develop before you politely tell them to stop considering you for the job.

Immediately send a "thank you" letter to each executive you met. These should, of course, be neatly-typed business letters, not handwritten notes. If you are still interested in pursuing a position at their company, tell them in no uncertain terms. Reiterate why you feel you're the best candidate and tell each of the executives when you hope (expect?) to hear from them.

FIELDING THE JOB OFFERS

You may face a dilemma after all the interviewing is finished and you're just sitting and waiting for the offers. What if you're offered a job on Magazine B -- your second, fifth or eighteenth choice -- but still haven't heard from Magazine A -- your first choice? Worse, what if Magazine B wants an answer before you expect to hear from Magazine A?

Well, you can call Magazine A, tell them you want to work there but have received a good offer from another publisher. Does Magazine A have any idea how soon they expect to make a decision? You can even ask the interviewer to "rate your chances." Then, if he indicates the chances are good that you'll be offered a job within a week or so, you can hopefully buy that much time from Magazine B.

Of course, it rarely works out so neatly. If you find yourself with too many secondary choices making job offers, while the two or three publishers you really like continue to procrastinate, you probably should accept another offer. None of the "first choice" companies might come through and you certainly don't want to wind up without any job at all!

If your first or second choice does finally come through with an offer you want to accept, you can always call the other firm, apologize and tell them you won't be able to start working for them after all. It is not immoral. In fact, many employment counselors routinely tell their clients to accept every job offer. But publishers do expect a certain percentage of hirees to wind up with other jobs before they're scheduled to start.

So, in general, accept a job offer, unless you are absolutely certain you do not want it. This will give you some security in case no other offer is forthcoming.

FINDING A SCHOOL-YEAR OR SUMMER INTERNSHIP

There are less internships than entry-level jobs, so expect even stiffer competition. Utilizing the same steps outlined for finding an entry-level job, start preparing your search for a summer internship **the summer before**. Many publishers fill their quota of interns by early Spring, so you need to get a jump on the competition.

Internships are rarely, if ever, advertised and, until now, details on most of them were unpublished. In Chapter 29, we've included a list of 65 publishers that offer internships -- salaried, unsalaried or some of each -- and the specific person to contact at each company. In addition, some publishers contact the Career Placement Offices at a number of colleges as internship positions become available, so check with your counselor.

How important is an getting an internship to your post-graduation job search? In a word -- **very**. Nearly every contributor has stressed such experience. And, of the publishers we surveyed, many cited "magazine or newspaper experience" -- meaning some kind of internship -- when asked to list requirements for their entry-level positions.

Should you choose a large, prestigious publishing company, like Hearst Magazines or Time, Inc., or the local publisher near your home or college? The former will be an impressive addition to your resume, but may limit your exposure to a single department or function. The latter may offer you "hands-on" experience in a number of areas but add little to the resume. While we tend to value actual experience over "names," you have to make your own decision.

Given the scramble for _any_ internship, however, we would even more strongly recommend accepting the first one that comes your way, whether it is the one you want or not. You will probably not have a number to choose from!

No job search is an easy one. They all require time, energy, research and more than a modicum of luck. And jobs at magazine publishers are never easy to get. The detailed job search process we've outlined in these chapters is complicated, time-consuming and, we expect, far more involved than most of you will like. None of you will precisely follow each recommended step. But hopefully, you will come to understand why we've made each recommendation and find them helpful in your own search.

Because the extra work you do _now_ will pay off in the long run. The more time and effort you put into your career _now_ -- as you're just starting out -- the more likely you'll end up at the right publisher, on the right magazine, heading in the right direction and well on your way to achieving the personal goals you set.

Good luck!

XI
Your 1986 Publishing Company Databank

CHAPTER 28

1986 Entry-Level Job Listings

There are five chapters in this section. In this chapter, we have listed nearly 100 major publishing firms that answered our questionnaire, providing us with detailed information about their companies, especially their expectations regarding 1986 entry-level job opportunities. In chapter 29, information regarding the internship and formal training programs offered by these firms has been separately listed. In chapters 30, 31 and 32, we have included additional, albeit briefer, listings for publishers that did not return our survey. We felt it important to include these latter companies -- all large enough to offer additional entry-level opportunities -- even though we cannot provide you with the same, detailed information included on the firms listed in this chapter. To make your search through these listings easier, we have segmented these additional publishers according to the types of magazines they publish -- consumer (Chapter 30), trade (Chapter 31) or professional/scientific/technical journals (Chapter 32). (Those publishers who produce magazines in two areas have been listed according to the type for which they are best known).

AN EXPLANATION OF CHAPTER LISTINGS & CODES USED

Each listing in this chapter begins with the **name** (capitalized and bold-faced), **headquarters** **address** and **telephone** **number** of the publisher.

The next entry, separated from those above and below it, is a complete list of the magazines published by that company. It should be apparent from this list whether the company publishes primarily <u>consumer</u>, <u>trade</u> or <u>professional/scientific</u> <u>journals</u>.

The name of the top **EXECUTIVE** is followed by **CONTACT** -- the person at that publisher to contact first.

1984 **REVENUES** lists the company's gross income for 1984 (their figures). **1985** **REVENUES** is a projection each company made prior to the end of the year. Since a great number of these publishers are privately-held companies (who, therefore, are not required to publish revenue or income figures), many of them declined to furnish this information. If the company itself did not provide us with this income/sales information, we have simply eliminated the Revenue headings from their listing.

Under **BRANCHES**, the number following "US" or "INTL" denotes the number of domestic branch offices and/or international offices. **DEPARTMENTS** lists all of the publishing functions that are organized as separate departments. This information should be checked carefully to ensure that the company you're targeting for employment actually has the department in which you want to work! Departments are numbered as follows:

DEPARTMENT CODES

```
 1.................ACCOUNTING/FINANCE
 2.................ADVERTISING SALES
 3.................ART & DESIGN
 4.................CIRCULATION
 5.................DATA PROCESSING
 6.................EDITORIAL
 7.................MAILROOM
 8.................MARKETING
 9.................OFFICE SERVICES
10.................PERSONNEL
11.................PRODUCTION
12.................MARKET RESEARCH
13.................SALES PROMOTION/MERCHANDISING
14.................SUBSCRIPTION SALES
15.................TRADE SHOW/EXHIBITIONS
```

Departments 1-15 were included on the questionnaire, 16-36 were additional departments written in on a small number of surveys. The former should be considered to be departments most endemic to a reasonable-sized publisher.

```
16.................ADVERTISING SERVICES
17.................ADMINISTRATION
18.................BOOK
19.................CORPORATE COMMUNICATIONS
20.................CORPORATE PLANNING
21.................DIRECTORY
22.................DIRECT SALES
23.................EDITORIAL COPY EDITING
24.................EDITORIAL RESEARCH
```

Under **EMPLOYEES** we've noted each publisher's total employment. If the company has no branch offices -- domestic or international -- the single number listed represents the total number of people employed at their headquarters office. If the company has more than one office, the entry will list a series of numbers: "a" - those employed at headquarters; "b" - employment at U.S. branch offices; "c" - international employment; and "d" - total employment in all offices. Example: "a200, b300, c800, d1,300."

On the same line, **EL1984** is followed by the number of entry-level people that publisher hired in the last 12 months (actually mid-1984 to mid-1985). It's noted whether these individuals were hired out of graduate school ("**a**"), college ("**b**") or high school ("**c**"). If the company hired people from more than one level, the total number hired is first, followed by a source breakdown. Example -- " 3 (a1,b1,c1)"; otherwise, "b3" (which indicates "3 college").

Following **EL1986** is the actual number of entry-level people that company expects to hire in 1986. Such numbers are, naturally, projections and may not reflect the total number they end up hiring.

<u>**Note:** A "?" after the 1986 entry means the publisher does expect to hire some entry-level people but could not project a precise figure. In this case, extrapolating from the 1984 hiring totals will probably give you a reasonable indication of their potential 1986 hiring.</u>
Many of the companies expected opportunities for entry-level people to be at least as good in 1986 as in 1984. Yet often, these same publishers showed a marked disparity between the number of people hired in 1984 and those they expected to hire in 1986.
Publishers with a history of extensive entry-level hiring but a low number for expected 1986 hiring may have reasons for such a disparity. They may have hired so many good entry-level people in the last 12 months that they simply need to hire less people now.

Secondly, they may be planning to sell or cease publication of a title or titles, and therefore be anticipating cut-backs in the professional ranks.

Thirdly, they may simply be "low-balling" their estimates so as to discourage an unwelcome rise in employment inquiries.

Lastly, they may have tried to give their best prediction, but really be unsure as to future staffing needs.

The job descripttions listed under **OPPORTUNITIES** indicate the **actual entry-level jobs** those publishers expect in 1986 (if they've indicated they will be hiring new people). If they did **not** indicate their intention to hire entry-level people, then these descriptions are for the positions they consider entry-level at their firm. We asked them to list such positions even if they did not anticipate any actual job openings, so as to give you a better idea of exactly what positions most publishers consider "entry-level."

Even if a particular publisher indicates it does not expect to hire any entry-level people in 1986, if they list the description of a job you want, you can utilize the information they provided to contact the company anyway. Plans change...always...and you might get a job there in spite of their "no hiring" expectations.

If the company listed only "college degree" or "typing" for a particular position, we have noted "no other requirements specified," just so you know that's all the information we have.

The **COMMENTS** entry is a grab-bag. If the publisher had specific hints or suggestions for entry-level people, we reproduced them here. These are set off in quotation marks and include, where available, the name of the person who gave us this information. We've also used this Comments area for notes of our own concerning the publisher or the information it provided.

"NA" is entered whenever specific information was not provided by the company itself. If a publisher had no branches or listed no entry-level opportunities, etc., those entry headings were simply eliminated.

Finally, you'll note that there are some publishers that clearly do not expect to hire any entry-level people in 1986 (although none declare their intentions to not hire entry-level people **at all**). Why have we included these? Because we felt it was just as important for you to know where **not** to look so you could effectively narrow down your target list.

And now, settle down, study the listings, take notes, and go get that job!

A/S/M COMMUNICATIONS, INC.
820 Second Avenue,
New York, NY 10017   (212)661-8080

MAGAZINES: Adweek (6 Editions), Computer Electronic Marketing,
Southern Jeweler, Southern Office Dealer, Southern Pulp & Paper,
Art Director's Index (annual), Portfolio Commercial Production
(annual), Photo District News (monthly), Ad Day (newsletter).

EXECUTIVE: John Thomas, Jr., President
CONTACT   : Helen Gamm, Office Manager
BRANCHES : US: 5 DEPARTMENTS: 1,2,3,4,5,6,7,8,9,11,12,13,14,15
EMPLOYEES: a86, b100, d186   EL1984: b3   EL1986: 0

ALLSTATE ENTERPRISES HOLDINGS, INC.
3701 West Lake Avenue,
Glenview, IL 60201   (312)291-6813

MAGAZINES: Discovery, Mature Outlook (magazine & newsletter
editions).

EXECUTIVE: Robert E. Gorman, Jr., Publisher
CONTACT   : Mary Selover (Associate Publisher)
1984 REVENUES: $300,000   1985 REVENUES: $850,000
BRANCHES : None   DEPARTMENTS: 2,6,8
EMPLOYEES: 10   EL1984: b1   EL1986: 2

OPPORTUNITIES: Staff Writer - College degree; good writing,
editing and interviewing skills. Marketing Representative -
College degree; good analytical skills; personable; a self-
starter.

AMERICAN ASSOCIATION FOR THE ADVANCEMENT OF SCIENCE
1333 N St., NW
Washington, DC 20005   (202)842-9500

MAGAZINES: Science, Science '85 (plus various science books and
films).

EXECUTIVE: Tod Herbers, Managing Director
CONTACT   : Department heads
1984 REVENUES: $15,464,000   1985 REVENUES: $16,573,000
BRANCHES : US:3   DEPARTMENTS: 1,2,3,4,6,8,9,11,12,13,14,15
EMPLOYEES: a49,b11,d60   EL1984: b2   EL1986: 3

AMERICAN BABY, INC.
575 Lexington Avenue,
New York, NY 10022   (212)752-0775

MAGAZINES: American Baby, Childbirth Educator, Childbirth 85,
First Year of Life.

EXECUTIVE: Alan Goldberg, Publisher
CONTACT : Department heads
BRANCHES : US:2   DEPARTMENTS: 1,2,3,4,6,7,9,11,13,14,35
EMPLOYEES: a45, b2, d47   EL1984: b2   EL1986: 2

OPPORTUNITIES: Editorial - College degree; language skills
imperative. Secretarial - Some college; language and secretarial
skills.
COMMENTS: They also produce their own weekly cable TV show.

AMERICAN BROADCASTING COMPANIES (ABC) - PUBLISHING DIVISION
825 Seventh Avenue,
New York, NY 10019 (212)887-8406

MAGAZINES: Over 200 magazine and book titles

CONTACT : Ms. Marion Harmon, Director of Personnel
BRANCHES : US:10   DEPARTMENTS: 1 - 15
EMPLOYEES: NA   EL1984: 2(a1,b1)   EL1986: ?

OPPORTUNITIES: Asst. Fulfillment Manager - College degree;
familiarity with computers (job is in Circulation area). Asst.
Promotion Manager - College degree; copywriting and math skills.

AMERICAN EXPRESS PUBLISHING COMPANY
1120 Avenue of the Americas,
New York, NY 10036   (212)382-5600

MAGAZINES: Travel & Leisure, Food & Wine

EXECUTIVE: Thomas O. Ryder, President/Publisher
CONTACT : Department heads
BRANCHES : US:3   DEPARTMENTS: 1,2,3,4,6,7,9,10,11,12,13,14.
EMPLOYEES: a120, b15, d135   EL1984: b2   EL1986: 2

AMERICAN HEALTH PARTNERS
80 Fifth Avenue, 3rd Floor
New York, NY 10011   (212)242-2460

MAGAZINES: American Health

EXECUTIVE: Owen Lipstein, Publisher
CONTACT : Department heads
BRANCHES : None   DEPARTMENTS: 1,2,3,4,6,7,8,9,11,13,15
EMPLOYEES: 50   EL1984: 6(a1,b3,c2)   EL1986: 1-2

OPPORTUNITIES: Secretary - High school and/or college degree;
detail oriented and good typing. Word Processor - high school;
detail oriented and good typing.

AMERICAN JOURNAL OF NURSING COMPANY
555 West 57th Street,
New York, NY 10019   (212)582-8820

MAGAZINES: The AJN Guide, American Journal of Nursing, Geriatric
Nursing , MCN/The American Journal of Maternal/Child Nursing,
International Nursing Index, Nursing Research, Nursing Outlook.

EXECUTIVE: Thelma M. Schorr, President/Publisher
CONTACT : Ms. Schorr or department heads
1984 REVENUES: $13,000,000   1985 REVENUES: $14,000,000
BRANCHES : None DEPARTMENTS: 1-7, 9,10,11,13,14,15,25,29,34
EMPLOYEES: 130   EL1984: 16(b6,c10)   EL1986: 2-3

OPPORTUNITIES: Editorial Assistant - College degree; writing,
journalism and English skills. Art Assistant - Art school;
experience in graphic arts and knowledge of print. Production
Trainee - Technical training in Production. Advertising Coordinator - College degree; ability to work with people and with
numbers. Administrative Assistant (for various executives) - no
requirements specified, but secretarial skills (typing 50 Wpm,
etc.) should be assumed.

AMERICAN WEST PUBLISHING COMPANY
3033 N. Campbell Avenue,
Tucson, AZ 85719   (602)881-5850

MAGAZINES: American West

EXECUTIVE: Thomas W. Pew, Jr., Publisher
CONTACT : Department heads
1984 REVENUES: $1,639,151   1985 REVENUES: $1,929,370
BRANCHES : None   DEPARTMENTS: 1,2,3,4,6,7,9,11,14
EMPLOYEES: 13   EL1984: b1   EL1986: 2

OPPORTUNITIES: Editorial Assistant - College degree; editorial
skills. Art Director - College degree, some experience in magazine design and production.

ASSOCIATED BUSINESS PUBLICATIONS, INC.
41 East 42nd Street, Suite 921
New York, NY 10017   (212)490-3999

MAGAZINES: Convenience Store Merchandiser, NASA Tech Briefs,
Vegetarian Times. (The company expected to announce a fourth
title as this volume went to press.)
EXECUTIVE: William Schnirring, President

CONTACT   : Patricia E. Neri, V.P.
BRANCHES : US:2   DEPARTMENTS: 1,2,3,4,5,6,7,10,11
EMPLOYEES: a45, b5, c50   EL1984: c5   EL1986: ?

OPPORTUNITIES: Data Entry - High school; typing skills. (With good English skills may be moved to Word Processing.) Editorial Assistant - College degree (Journalism major preferred); typing. New hires for 1986 will probably be in data entry.

BAKER PUBLICATIONS, INC.
5757 Alpha Rd., Suite 400
Dallas, TX 75240   (214)239-2399

MAGAZINES: Living Magazine, Office Leasing Guide, Texas Business Magazine

EXECUTIVE: Ray L. Baker, President
CONTACT   : Doug Yoder, Administrative VP or Mary Schiff (person-nel)
1984 REVENUES: $15,000,000   1985 REVENUES: $18,000,000
BRANCHES : US:10   DEPARTMENTS: 1,2,3,4,5,6,7,10,11
EMPLOYEES: a70, b90, d160   EL1984: 0   EL1986: 1-2

OPPORTUNITIES: Clerical - High school graduate. Editorial - Associate or Bachelor degree; proofreading & copy editing skills. Art/Production - Associates or Bachelors degree; design, paste-up & lay-out skills. 1986 openings will probably be the clerical positions.

BARKS PUBLICATIONS, INC.
400 N. Michigan Avenue, Suite 1016
Chicago, IL 60611   (312)321-9440

MAGAZINES: Electrical Apparatus, Electromechanical Bench Reference (annual)

EXECUTIVE: Horace B. Barks, President
CONTACT   : Elsie Dickson, Associate Publisher
BRANCHES : None   DEPARTMENTS: 1,2,3,4,6,8,11,13,14,15
EMPLOYEES: 10   EL1984: b2   EL1986: 1

OPPORTUNITIES: Assistant in Circulation Department and General Office ("gopher") - Preferably some college, but degree not required. History or geography major better than journalism, because this job will not lead to editorial work ("for which our requirements would be quite different"). A bright high school graduate motivated to learn publishing could qualify for this position. Other requirements: Attention to detail; enthusiasm; careful research habits; good spelling; neat handwriting and/or knowledge of geography a plus; data processing aptitude (if not experience).

COMMENTS: "We admire the students who comes in in person with portfolio and resume, not expecting to have an appointment on this `cold call' but hoping to be able to make one. We give extra points for this kind of initiative." - Ms. Dickson.

BAYARD PUBLICATIONS, INC.
500 Summer Street,
Stamford, CT 06901   (203)327-0800

MAGAZINES: Convention World, Health Care Conference Planner, Insurance Conference Planner

EXECUTIVE: George Lowden, President
CONTACT   : President
1984 REVENUES: $850,000   1985 REVENUES: $1,000,000
BRANCHES : US:1   DEPARTMENTS: 1,2,4,6,11
EMPLOYEES: a8, b1, d9   EL1984: 0   EL1986: 1

OPPORTUNITIES: Editorial Assistant - College degree; Journalism and English skills.

A. M. BEST COMPANY, INC.
Ambest Road,
Oldwick, NJ 08858   (201)439-2200

MAGAZINES: Best's Insurance Convention Guide, Best's Review (Life/Health Edition), Best's Review (Property/Casualty Insurance Edition), Best's Safety Directory.

EXECUTIVE: Arthur Snyder, Publisher
CONTACT   : E.L. Valentien (personnel)
BRANCHES : US:12. INTL:1 DEPARTMENTS: 1,2,3,5-13,27
EMPLOYEES: a275, b15, d290   EL1984: b2   EL1986: 2

OPPORTUNITIES: Assistant Editor - College degree (Journalism/ Communications major with Economics minor preferred); fully competent writer/editor; exposure to the business community.
COMMENTS: "Study potential employers' publications before interviews; submit relevant samples."

BEST-MET PUBLISHING COMPANY, INC.
5537 Twin Knolls Road, Suite 438
Columbia, MD 21045   (301)730-5013

MAGAZINES: Food Trade News, Food World.

EXECUTIVE: Richard J. Bestany, President
CONTACT   : President

BRANCHES : None   DEPARTMENTS: 2,4,6,14
EMPLOYEES: 10   EL1984: c2   EL1986: O

OPPORTUNITIES: Editorial - College degree; writing/editing
skills. Advertising Sales - College degree; knowledge of
and/or sales experience.

BILL COMMUNICATIONS, INC.
633 Third Avenue,
New York, NY 10017   (212)986-4800

MAGAZINES: Incentive Marketing/Incorporating Incentive Travel,
Industrial Chemical News, Institutional Distribution, Jobber
Retailer, Sales & Marketing Management, Modern Tire Dealer,
Restaurant Business, Successful Meetings, Plastics Technology,
Restaurant and Hotel Design

EXECUTIVE: John W. Hartman, Chairman
CONTACT : Irene Ricalde, Personnel Manager
1984 REVENUES: $49,477,000   1985 REVENUES: $55,000,000
BRANCHES : US:3   DEPARTMENTS: 1,2,3,4,6,7,8,9,10,11,12,13.
EMPLOYEES: a238, b62, d300   EL1984: 10(b+c)   EL1986: ?

OPPORTUNITIES: Editorial Assistant - College degree; typing;
writing/proofreading skills; experience or internships.
Production Assistant - High School or college; typing; some
experience with layouts and paste-ups. Marketing Assistant -
College degree (Marketing major preferred). Art Assistant -
College degree (Art major); experience on school newspaper and/or
yearbook. Accounting Clerk: High School and/or college.

BILLBOARD PUBLICATIONS, INC.
1515 Broadway,
New York, NY 10036   (212)764-7300

MAGAZINES: American Artist, Amusement Business, Billboard,
Interiors, Musician, Photo Weekly,

EXECUTIVE: Gerald S. Hobbs, President
CONTACT : Mary Boyle, Personnel Director
BRANCHES : US:6, INTL:4 DEPARTMENTS: 1-7, 9,10,11,13,14,15
EMPLOYEES: a175, b125, c10, d310   EL1984: b14   EL1986: 4-8

OPPORTUNITIES: Editorial Assistant, Sales Assistant, Production
Assistant, Circulation Assistant, Classified Ad Trainee -
College degree required for all thes3e entry-level positions.
"We look for candidates who are organized, detail-minded, able to
work accurately and quickly under pressure. Good summer employment records are looked upon favorably. Extra-curricular
activities are taken into consideration."

BROADCASTING PUBLICATIONS, INC.
1735 DeSales St., N.W.
Washington, DC 20036   (202)638-1022

MAGAZINES: Broadcasting Magazine, Broadcasting/Cablecasting
Yearbook (annual).

EXECUTIVE: Lawrence B. Taishoff, President
CONTACT   : Department heads
BRANCHES : US:3   DEPARTMENTS: 1,2,3,4,5,6,7,8,9,11,12,13,14
EMPLOYEES: 50   EL1984: 0   EL1986: 1

OPPORTUNITIES: Accounting/Secretarial Trainee -- 2 yrs. of
 college; some accounting and business courses; typing. Will be
 doing general administrative work, switchboard relief.

CBS MAGAZINES, A DIVISION OF CBS INC.
1515 Broadway,
New York, NY 10036   (212)719-6000

MAGAZINES: American Photographer, Audio, Backpacker, Boating, Car
and Driver, Cycle, Cycle World, Field and Stream, Flying, Home
Mechanix, Modern Bride, Pop ular Magazines (100-odd crossword,
word game and astrology titles), Popular Photography, Road &
Track, Skiing, Skiing Trade News, Stereo Review, The Runner,
Woman's Day, Woman's Day Specials (20-odd single-subject
magazines, Yachting plus various annuals and special issues.

EXECUTIVE: Peter G. Diamandis, President
CONTACT   : Kim Bedle, Mgr - Training & Development, CBS Magazines
BRANCHES : Editorial offices in NY (2), CA (2), MI & CT. Ad sales
offices in New York, Chicago, Detroit, Los Angeles, San Francis-
co. Administrative offices in NY (2), CT (2), CA (3) and MI.
DEPARTMENTS: 1,2,3,4,5,6,7,8,9,10,11,12,13,14,15,33
EMPLOYEES : NA   EL1984: 32(a2,b25,c5)   EL1986: 32

OPPORTUNITIES: District Representative, CMM-CBS Magazine
Marketing - College degree; analytical ability and sales aptitude
required; work out of home -- this is a sales position, selling
CBS titles at retailer outlets. Positions available throughout
the US. Floater (filling in for administrative assts. in various
departments in New York offices) - College degree; some office
experience; typing (50 wpm required); Editorial Assistant -
College degree (English or Journalism major preferred); typing
(60 wpm required); location: New York. Financial Analyst -
Bachelor of Accounting degree; knowledge of computer science and
applications preferred; Location: Greenwich, CT. Renewal/Billing
Analyst (Circulation Dept. of New York offices) - College degree,
statistical ability, typing.

CANON COMMUNICATIONS, INC.
2416 Wilshire Blvd.,
Santa Monica, CA 90403   (213)829-0315

MAGAZINES: Medical Device & Diagnostic Industry, Medical Product
Manufacturing News, Pharmaceutical Manufacturing, Microcontam-
ination.

EXECUTIVE: Evangeline Shears, Publisher
CONTACT : Department heads
1984 REVENUES: $2,500,000   1985 REVENUES: $3,500,000
BRANCHES : None   DEPARTMENTS: 1,2,3,4,6,7,8,9,11,12,13,15
EMPLOYEES: 28   EL1984: b2   EL1986: 0

CARSTENS PUBLICATIONS, INC.
PO Box 700,
Newton, NJ 07860   (201)383-3355

MAGAZINES: Flying Models, Railfan & Railroad, Railroad Model
Craftsman, Creative Crafts and Miniatures

EXECUTIVE: Harold H. Carstens, President/Publisher
CONTACT   : President
BRANCHES : None   DEPARTMENTS: 1,2,4,5,6,7,9,11,14
EMPLOYEES: 25   EL1984: 4(b2,c2)   EL1986: 4

OPPORTUNITIES: Editorial - College degree desirable (English
or Liberal Arts); writing, photography, drafting, typing skills;
knowledge of the subjects of their hobby publications preferred.
Production - Art school or college degree; art layout, English,
typing, drafting, pen & ink skills. Hobby knowledge helpful.
(Note: "Fine Arts background by itself is almost useless."
General office - Typing, mathematical, computer skills; business
sense; knowledge of magazine publishing -- advertising, sales,
circulation, etc. -- helpful.

CITY HOME PUBLISHING, INC.
5615 Kirby Dr., Suite 600
Houston, TX 77005   (713)524-3000

MAGAZINES: Dallas/Ft. Worth Home & Garden, Houston Home & Garden,
Houston Symphony Magazine

EXECUTIVE: Chris King, President
CONTACT   : Department heads
1984 REVENUES: $8,144,366   1985 REVENUES: $8,700,000 (est.)
BRANCHES : US:4   DEPARTMENTS: 1,2,3,4,5,6,8,9,11,13
EMPLOYEES: a44, b32, d76   EL1984: 0   EL1986: 0

COMMERCE PUBLISHING COMPANY
408 Olive Street,
St. Louis, MO 63102   (314)421-5445

MAGAZINES: American Agent & Broker, Club Management, Decor, Life
Insurance Selling, Mid-Continent Banker

EXECUTIVE: W. H. Clark, Chairman
CONTACT   : James J. Poor, President
1984 REVENUES: $6,000,000   1985 REVENUES: $10,000,000
BRANCHES : None   DEPARTMENTS: 1,2,4,5,6,9,15
EMPLOYEES: 52   EL1984: b2   EL1986: ?

OPPORTUNITIES: Editorial - College degree (Journalism or
English); good spelling and grammar.

COMMUNICATIONS CHANNELS, INC.
6255 Barfield Road,
Atlanta, GA 30328   (404)256-9800

MAGAZINES: Adhesives Age, Air Cargo World, Airline Executive,
American City and County, Art Material Trade News, Atlanta
magazine, Better Nutrition, Buildings Design Journal, Business
Atlanta, Commuter Air, Container News, Design Graphics World,
Elastometrics, Fence Industry, Health Food Retailing, Midwest
Real Estate News, Modern Paint and Coatings, National Real
Estate Investor, Pension World, Robotics World, Selling Direct,
Shopping Center World, Southeast Real Estate News, Southwest
Real Estate News, Swimming Pool Age, Today's Living, Trusts and
Estates, World Wastes, California Real Estate Directory, New
England Real Estate Directory plus various annual directory
editions, postcard decks and convention dailies.

EXECUTIVE: B. J. Kotsher, President
CONTACT   : Lawrence Moores, Exec. VP
BRANCHES : US:6, INTL:1   DEPARTMENTS: 1,2,3,4,6-15,18,21
EMPLOYEES: a196, b82, c1, d279 EL1984: 20(b15,c5) EL1986: 10-15

OPPORTUNITIES: Sales Representative - College degree a plus but
not required; some sales experience (part-time or full-time)
preferred in a related business field or communications company;
person must be aggressive, organized and personable. Editorial
Assistant - College degree (Journalism, Communications or Liberal
Arts); School-related publication editing experience a plus;
writing and writing/editing skills must be top-notch. Ability to
learn quickly the field the publication represents is most
important. Promotion Writer - College degree (Marketing, Communications or Advertising); sales-oriented writing skills a must; a
good eye for graphic design necessary. Art Assistant - Two-year
degree in art or college degree (BFA or BA in Art, Graphic Arts
or the like); Some knowledge of type helpful; General design
skills required. Ability to illustrate not necessary but a plus.
Production or Circulation Assistant - College degree not re-

quired; detail oriented, organized and efficient; careful record
keeping involved.
COMMENTS: "Write to me and I'll channel your resume and cover
letter to the appropriate department heads." -- Mr. Moores.

CUMMINS PUBLISHING COMPANY, INC.
1495 Maple Way,
Troy, MI 48084   (313)643-8655

MAGAZINES: Excavating Contractor, Hildy's Ford Blue Book,
Industrial Education, Gourmet Today/Telefood

EXECUTIVE: Andrew J. Cummins, Publisher
CONTACT : Publisher
1984 REVENUES: $1,000,000   1985 REVENUES: $1,500,000
BRANCHES : US:1   DEPARTMENTS: 1,2,3,4,5,6,9,11
EMPLOYEES: a11, b4, c15   EL1984: 3(b1,c2)   EL1986: 2

OPPORTUNITIES: Key Liner - Graphic skills requried; educational
requirements flexible. Editorial Assistant - College degree;
English and journalism skills. Sales - College degree; "sales"
personality.

DABORA,INC.
PO Box 1007, 1211 E. Lane Street,
Shelbyville, TN 37160   (615)684-8123

MAGAZINES: Aviation Buyers Guide, Horse World, Saddle Horse
Report, Walking Horse Report

EXECUTIVE: David L. Howard, President
CONTACT : President
1984 REVENUES: $3,500,000   1985 REVENUES: $4,000,000
BRANCHES : None   DEPARTMENTS: 1,2,3,4,5,6,8,9,11,12,13,15
EMPLOYEES: 40   EL1984: b1   EL1986: 2

DAVIS PUBLICATIONS, INC.
380 Lexington Avenue,
New York, NY 10017   (212)557-9100

MAGAZINES: Ellery Queen's Mystery Magazine, Alfred Hitchcock's
Mystery Magazine, Isaac Asimov's Science Fiction Magazine,
Analog, Income Opportunities, Architectural Designs, Woodworker,
Ellery Queen Anthology, Alfred Hitchcock Anthology.

EXECUTIVE: Joel Davis, President
CONTACT : President
1984 REVENUES: $11,000,000   1985 REVENUES: $11,500,000
BRANCHES : US:1   DEPARTMENTS: 1,2,3,4,5,6,7,10,11,14
EMPLOYEES: a63, b2, d65   EL1984: 6(b5,c1)   EL1986: 3-4

OPPORTUNITIES: Editorial and Sales - both entry-level positions
require someone with a college degree, writing skills and initiative.
SUGGESTIONS; "Use Literary Market Place and the Magazine Publishers Association."
COMMENTS: See separate listing for Sylvia's Porter's Personal
Finance Magazine (by same publisher).

DINAN COMMUNICATIONS, INC.
24 Locust Avenue,
New Canaan, CT 06840   (203)966-9377

MAGAZINES: Housewares Merchandising, Totally Housewares

EXECUTIVE: Ted Meredith, President
CONTACT   : President
1984 REVENUES: $3.000,000   1985 REVENUES: NA
BRANCHES : US:1   DEPARTMENTS: 1,2,3,4,6,9,11
EMPLOYEES: a12, b12, d24   EL1984: b3   EL1986: 3

OPPORTUNITIES: Advertising Sales - College degree. Editorial
Assistant - College degree; experience on a college newspaper or
magazine

EDITORIAL AMERICA, S.A.
6355 N. W. 36th Street,
Virginia Gardens, FL 33166   (305)871-6400

MAGAZINES: Twelve monthly Spanish-language publications plus
approximately 50 "one shot" publications and educational books.

EXECUTIVE: Armando de Armas, President
CONTACT : Luis Eljaiek, Personnel Director
1984 REVENUES: $55,000,000   1985 REVENUES: $58,000,000
BRANCHES : US:1, INTL:10   DEPARTMENTS: 1 - 14
EMPLOYEES: a350, b6, c150, d506   EL1984: a8   EL1986: ?

OPPORTUNITIES: Editorial America is in the process of consoli-
dating their markets in Latin America. Therefore, they are unable
to supply information as to how many people will be hired and
what positions they would fill. IF you are interested in the
company - especially if you're bi-lingual (Spanish/English) - we
suggest you apply to Mr. Eljaiek.

ESQUIRE ASSOCIATES
2 Park Avenue,
New York, NY 10016   (212)561-8100

MAGAZINES: Esquire

EXECUTIVE: Alan Greenberg, Publisher

CONTACT   : Department heads
BRANCHES : US:5 DEPARTMENTS: 1-4,6,7,11,13,14,17,18,23,24,26,33
EMPLOYEES: a120, b10, d130   EL1984: b10   EL1986: 5

OPPORTUNITIES: Secretary (Ad Sales Department) - College degree;
typing; interest in ad sales. Secretaries (other departments) -
College degree; typing; interest in particular department.
Editorial Staff - College degree (English, Journalism, Literature majors preferred); typing; related extra-curricular and/or
job experience (part-time okay);good writing skills. Junior
Accountant - College degree (Accounting); strong accounting
skills. Data Entry (in Finance Department) - High school graduate; typing and math skills. Art Assistant - Art school degree;
creative design skills and a good portfolio.
SUGGESTIONS: "If applying for editorial position, include writing
samples with your resume and cover letter. If applying for an art
position, drop off your portfolio for the Art Director to review.
(Call to find out when the portfolio should be dropped off and
picked up)" -- Kristin Semmelmeyer, Personnel Supervisor
COMMENTS: Company is owned by 13-30 Corporation (Tennessee). See
separate listing in Chapter 30.

GPI PUBLICATIONS
20085 Stevens Creek,
Cupertino, CA 95014   (408)446-1105

MAGAZINES: Frets, Guitar Player, Keyboard
Acquired by Maclean Hunter Publishing (Chicago, Il)July, 1985.

EXECUTIVE: Jim Crockett, President/Publisher
CONTACT   : Laurie Walters (Personnel)
1984 REVENUES: $7,004,000   1985 REVENUES: $7,400,000
BRANCHES : None   DEPARTMENTS: 1-11,14,18,22,36
EMPLOYEES: 70   EL1984: 4(b2,c3)   EL1986: 3

OPPORTUNITIES: Phone Sales (to retailers) - experience with music
and the retail business needed. Production - experience with stat
cameras, paste-up and layout. Editorial - editing experuience
(freelance okay) and knowledge of music. No educational requirements specified for any of these positions.

GALLANT/CHARGER PUBLICATIONS, INC.
34249 Camino Capistrano,
Capistrano Beach, CA 92624   (714)493-2101

MAGAZINES: Bow & Arrow, Gun World, Horse and Horseman (plus 3
annuals).

EXECUTIVE: Jack Lewis, Publisher
CONTACT   : R. W. Avscherlt (Personnel)

BRANCHES : US:1   DEPARTMENTS: 1,2,3,4,5,6,7,8,9,10,11,15
EMPLOYEES: a20, b2, d22   EL1984: b2   EL1986: 1

OPPORTUNITIES: Layout Artist - High school graduate; prefer art
education, but may consider training on-the-job.

GORMAN PUBLISHING COMPANY
5725 E. River Road,
Chicago, IL 60631   (312)693-3200

MAGAZINES: Alimentos, Bakery, Dairy Record, Foodservice Bakery,
In Store Bakery, Prepared Foods.

EXECUTIVE: Peggy Stath, Director of Magazine Operations
CONTACT   : Department heads or Vivian Gorman, Personnel Director
1984 REVENUES: $12,500,000   1985 REVENUES: $15,000,000
BRANCHES : US:1   DEPARTMENTS: 1-16
EMPLOYEES: a110, b9, d119   EL1984: 11(b8,c3)   EL1986: 10-12

OPPORTUNITIES: Fulfillment Assistant, Sales Secretary, Promotion
Assistant, Research Assistant, Editorial Assistant - "We look for
bright articulate individ uals who are enthusiastic and ambitious." No other educational or skill requirements specified.

GRUNER + JAHR USA PUBLISHING
685 Third Avenue,
New York, NY 10017   (212)878-8700

MAGAZINES: Expecting, Parents, Young Miss

EXECUTIVE: John J. Beni, President
CONTACT   : Department heads or Susan Levy, Personnel Director
BRANCHES : US:2   DEPARTMENTS: 1,2,3,4,6,9,10,11,13
EMPLOYEES: a150, b12, d162   EL1984: 5(b3,c2)   EL1986: 3

OPPORTUNITIES: Secretaries - High school graduates; good typing,
stenography and communication skills.

HAL PUBLICATIONS, INC.
342 Madison Avenue,
New York, NY 10173   (212)309-9800

MAGAZINES: Working Woman, Success!
CONTACT   : Department heads
BRANCHES : US:2   DEPARTMENTS: 1,2,3,4,6,7,8,9,10,11,12,13
EMPLOYEES: 120   EL1984: Some out of college EL1986: 2

OPPORTUNITIES: Receptionist/Editorial Assistant - BA; some
related experience on college newspaper, magazine or yearbook;
summer internships.

HALSEY PUBLISHING COMPANY
12955 Biscayne Blvd.,
North Miami, FL 33181   (305)893-1520

MAGAZINES: Aircal, Butler's "Skylite", Delta "Sky", Expressions, USAir.

EXECUTIVE: Seymour Gerber, President
CONTACT : Department heads
BRANCHES : US:1   DEPARTMENTS: 1,2,3,6,7,8,9,11,12,13
EMPLOYEES: a52, b5, d57   EL1984: NA   EL1986: ?

OPPORTUNITIES: Art Apprentice - Two-year college degree
(minimum); art skills. Editorial Assistant - Two-year college
degree (minimum) - English or Journalism major preferred.

HARCOURT BRACE JOVANOVICH PUBLICATIONS
7500 Old Oak Boulevard,
Cleveland, OH 44130   (216)826-2820

MAGAZINES: Communications News, Telco Craftsman, Telephone Engineer and Management, Instructor, Instructor Computer Directory
for Schools, Instructor Books, Brown's Directory of North American and International Gas Companies, Drilling, LP/Gas, Petroleum
Engineer International, Pipeline and Gas Journal, SGA Directory,
Colorado Rancher & Farmer, Kansas Farmer, Michigan Farmer, Mis-
souri Farmer, Nebraska Farmer, The Ohio Farmer, Pennsylvania
Farmer, Dental Laboratory Review, Dental Management, Dermatology
Times, DVM, The Newsmagazine of Veterinary Medicine, Geriatrics,
Hearing Instruments, Hospital Formulary, Modern Medicine, Neuro-
logy, Ophthalmology Times, Optometry Times, Physician's Manage-
ment, Urology Times, American Automatic Merchandiser, Concrete,
CP100, Food Management, Food Sanitation, Lawn Care Industry, Pest
Control, Pit & Quarry, Roof Design, RSI (Roofing/Siding/Insula-
tion), Weeds, Trees and Turf, Body Fashions/Intimate Apparel,
Flooring, Home & Auto, Hosiery and Underwear, Housewares, Pets/
Supplies/Marketing, Paperboard Packaging, Paper Sales, Plastics
Compounding, Plastics Design Forum, Plastics Machinery & Equip-
ment, Beverage Industry, Candy Industry, Candy Marketer, Dairy
Field, Drug & Cosmetic Industry, Food & Drug Packaging, Meat
Processing, Quick Frozen Foods, Snack Food, Bicycle Dealer Show-
case, Flotation Sleep Industry, Motorcycle Dealernews, Spa and
Sauna, Video Store, Corporate Meetings & Incentives, Corporate
Travel Agent, Hotel & Motel Management plus a variety of newslet-
ters, convention dailies, directory issues, "Buyer's Guide"
issues and post card decks.

EXECUTIVE: Richard J. Moeller, President
CONTACT : Department heads
BRANCHES : US:21, INTL:1   DEPARTMENTS: 1 - 15
EMPLOYEES: a250, b1000, c6, d1256   EL1984: 125(b25,c100)
EL1986: 20-30

OPPORTUNITIES: Editorial - College degree; writing/journalism skills. Circulation, Production, Key Punching, Accounting Depts. - High school graduates who are accurate and detail-oriented.

HARRIS PUBLISHING, INC.
520 Park Avenue, PO Box 981,
Idaho Falls, ID 83401   (208)522-5187

MAGAZINES: Potato Grower of Idaho, Snowmobile West, The Sugar Producer.

EXECUTIVE: Darryl W. Harris, President/Publisher
CONTACT : President
1984 REVENUES: $1,200,000   1985 REVENUES: $1,300,000
BRANCHES : None   DEPARTMENTS: 2,3,4,6,12
EMPLOYEES: 12   EL1984: 0   EL1986: 0

HART PUBLICATIONS, INC.
PO Box 1917, 1900 Grand Street, Suite 400,
Denver, CO 80201   (303)837-1917

MAGAZINES: Gulf Coast Oil World, Midcontinent Oil World, Northeast Oil World, Oil and Gas Investor, Southwest Oil World

EXECUTIVE: David R. Webster, VP/Magazine Operations
CONTACT : Department heads
1984 REVENUES: $4,800,000   1985 REVENUES: $5,300,000
BRANCHES : US:4   DEPARTMENTS: 1,2,3,4,5,6,7,8,9,11,21
EMPLOYEES: a50, b13, d63   EL1984: b4   EL1986: 5

OPPORTUNITIES: Proofreader/Copy Editor, Editorial Assistant, Advertising Assistant - College degree (Journalism); Layout Artist/Production Assistant - College degree (Art or Journalism). No other requirements specified.

HATTON-BROWN PUBLISHERS, INC.
PO Box 2268,
Montgomery, AL 36197   (205)834-1170

MAGAZINES: Paper Industry Equipment, Plywood & Panel World, Southern Loggin' Times, Timber Harvesting, Timber Processing.

EXECUTIVE: David H. Ramsey, President
CONTACT : Dianne Sullivan, Operations Manager
1984 REVENUES: $1,500,000   1985 REVENUES: $1,750,000
BRANCHES : None   DEPARTMENTS: 1,2,3,4,5,6,7,8,9,11,12,13,15
EMPLOYEES: 19   EL1984: 3(a2,c1)   EL1986: 0

HAYDEN PUBLISHING COMPANY, INC.
10 Mulholland Dr.,
Hasbrouck Heights, NJ 07604   (201)393-6000

MAGAZINES: Computer Decisions, Electronic Design, Microwaves &
RF, Personal Computing, Systems & Software

EXECUTIVE: James S. Mulholland, Jr., President
CONTACT : Sheila O`Niell, Employee Relations Administrator
BRANCHES : US:5   DEPARTMENTS: 1,2,3,4,5,6,7,9,10,11,12,13,14
EMPLOYEES: a370, b190, d560   EL1984: b3,c2   EL1986: 3-5

OPPORTUNITIES: Editorial - College degree (<u>Bachelor of Science
in Electrical Engineering</u>); an interest in writing. Sales - MBA
(Marketing); strong desire to be in sales. Artist - College
degree in art and design. Promotion Copywriter - College degree
(Marketing or English).

HEARST CORPORATION - MAGAZINE DIVISION
959 Eighth Avenue,
New York, NY 10019   (212)262-5700

MAGAZINES: Colonial Homes, Connoisseur, Cosmopolitan, Country
Living, Good Housekeeping, Harper's Bazaar, House Beautiful,
Motor Boating & Sailing, Popular Mechanics, Redbook, Science
Digest, Sports Afield, Town and Country.

EXECUTIVE: Gilbert C. Mauer, President (Magazine Division)
CONTACT : Recruiting Department (Ruth A. Diem, Director of
           Personnel)
BRANCHES : None   DEPARTMENTS: 1,2,3,4,5,6,7,8,9,10,11,12,13,14.
EMPLOYEES: 1600   EL1984: 200(b60,c140)   EL1986: ?

OPPORTUNITIES: Editorial Assistant - High School + some college;
typing, proofing & grammer skills. Sales Trainee - College degree
preferred; good verbal ability. Art Assistant - High school +
some college; typing and graphic arts skills. Production Assistant - High school. Circulation Analyst - College preferred;
numerical and verbal abilities; Secretary - High School (minimum); typing, steno & dictaphone skills. Secretary/Assistant -
High School (minimum); typing skills; Clerk Typist - high school,
typing skills.

HELDREF PUBLICATIONS
4000 Albemarle Street, NW
Washington, DC 20016 (202)362-6445

MAGAZINES: 43 journals in the fields of the Arts and Humanities,
Education, Health Care, Sciences and Social Sciences.

EXECUTIVE: Stuart F. Degnuff, Ad Director
CONTACT : Department heads
1984 REVENUES: Non-profit

BRANCHES : None   DEPARTMENTS: 1 - 15
EMPLOYEES: 90   EL1984: b15 EL1986: 5-10

OPPORTUNITIES: Subscriber Service Representative - Requirements
unspecified.
COMMENTS: The publication arm of the Helen Dwight Reid Educational Foundation.

INTERNATIONAL THOMPSON TRANSPORT PRESS
A division of International Thompson Holdings
424 West 33rd Street,
New York, NY 10001   (212)714-3100

MAGAZINES: Twelve transportation related (mainly regarding
railway shipping) trade journals.

EXECUTIVE: Paul M. Moore, President/ceo
CONTACT   : D. R. Demauro, Personnel Manager
1984 REVENUES: $10,000,000   1985 REVENUES: NA
BRANCHES : US:1   DEPARTMENTS: 1,2,3,4,5,6,7,8,9,10,11,13,14,15
EMPLOYEES: a60, b30, d90   EL1984: b1   EL1986: 1

OPPORTUNITIES: Data Management position - College degree. No
other requirements specified.

INTERTEC PUBLISHING CORPORATION
9221 Quivira Rd., P.O. Box 12901
Overland Park, KS 66212   (913)888-4664

MAGAZINES: Agricultura de las Americas, Broadcast Engineering,
Cellular Business, Electronic Servicing & Technology, Grounds
Maintenance, Implement & Tractor, Land Mobile, Lawn & Garden
Marketing, Lawn Servicing, Microservice Management, Radio y
Television, Sound & Video Contractor, Video Systems (plus Book
Publishing Division)

EXECUTIVE: R. J. Hancock, President
CONTACT   : Nancy Diebel, Personnel Director
BRANCHES : US:7, INTL:1 DEPARTMENTS: 1 - 14
EMPLOYEES: a200, b15, c1, d216 EL1984: 30(b20,c10)   EL1986: 20

OPPORTUNITIES: Associate Editor -College degree; knowledge of
magazine journalism and English. Editorial Assistant - High
school; English skills and oriented to detail. Advertising Sales
- College degree; sales ability and communication skills. Telemarketing - High School; persistence and good communication
skills. Copywriter - College degree; good business judgement;
writing skills. Graphic Designer - College degree; publication
design skills.

KANE COMMUNICATIONS, INC.
401 N. Broad Street,
Philadelphia, PA 19108   (212)925-9744

MAGAZINES: Podiatry Management, Souvenirs and Novelties, Tourist
Attractions and Parks

EXECUTIVE: Scott C. Borowsky, President
CONTACT : President
BRANCHES : US:1   DEPARTMENTS: 1,2,3,4,6,11
EMPLOYEES: a12, b4, d16   EL1984: b2   EL1986: 2

OPPORTUNITIES: Sales - College degree (BS or BA); previous sales
experience (can be in retail store).

THE KIPLINGER WASHINGTON EDITORS, INC.
1729 H Street, NW
Washington, DC 20006   (202)887-6400

MAGAZINES: Changing Times

EXECUTIVE: Nicholas Niles, Publisher
CONTACT : Nancy Fisher (personnel)
1984 REVENUES: $27,000,000   1985 REVENUES: $30,000,000
BRANCHES : US:3   DEPARTMENTS: 1,2,3,4,5,6,7,9,10,11,12,13,14
EMPLOYEES: a50, b18, d68   EL1984: NA   EL1986: 0

KIWANIS INTERNATIONAL
3636 Woodview Trace,
Indianapolis, IN 46268   (317)875-8755

MAGAZINES: Circle K, Keynoter, Kiwanis

EXECUTIVE: N. G. Geannopulos, Publisher
CONTACT : Department heads and/or Chuck Jonak, Executive Editor
BRANCHES : US:1, INTL:1   DEPARTMENTS: 1,2,3,4,5,6,7,9,10,11,13
EMPLOYEES: a133, c4, d137   EL1984: b2   EL1986: 0

KNAPP COMMUNICATIONS CORPORATION
5900 Wilshire Blvd.,
Los Angeles, CA 90036   (213)937-5496

MAGAZINES: Architectural Digest, Bon Appetit, Home

EXECUTIVE: Bud Knapp, Chairman
CONTACT : In Los Angeles, Rich West or Nancy Van Ness
           In New York, Dotty Robinson or Susan Selby (all in
           Personnel Dept.) or the appropriate department heads
1984 REVENUES: $101,500,000   1985 REVENUES: $110,700,000
BRANCHES : US:3   DEPARTMENTS: 1-6,10,11,12,13,19,20,30,32,34
EMPLOYEES: a250, b150, d400   EL1984: b28   EL1986: ?

OPPORTUNITIES: Editorial Assistant - College degree; typing 45
wpm; detail oriented; telephone skills; interest in photography.
Production Assistant - Bachelor of Fine Arts (from an accredited
institution); 2-3 yrs. paste-up/mechanical experience (make neat
mechanical boards); knowledge of typography; impeccable ruling
skills. Circulation Assistant - College degree (preferred);
general office/clerical experience; heavy detail orientation;
light typing; math abilities; computer experience (on a PC) a
plus. Research Assistant - College degree (preferred); math
abilities; insatiable curiosity; computer experience (PC) a plus.
Marketing Services Assistant - College degree; writing skills;
detail oriented; math abilities; computer experience (PC)a plus.

LAKE PUBLISHING COMPANY
Box 159, 17730 West Peterson Road,
Libertyville, IL 60048   (312)362-8711

MAGAZINES: Electri.onics, Microelectric Manufacturing and
Testing, Hybrid Circuit Technology, Connection Technology

EXECUTIVE: Lincoln R. Samelson, President
CONTACT : Department heads
BRANCHES : US:7 DEPARTMENTS: 1,2,3,4,5,6,7,9,10,11,12,13,14,15
EMPLOYEES: a85, b7, d92   EL1984: NA   EL1986: 0

MACLEAN HUNTER MEDIA
1351 Washington Blvd.,
Stamford, CT 06902   (203)325-3500

MAGAZINES: Progressive Grocer, Progressive Grocer Executive
Report.

EXECUTIVE: John W. Skeels, President
CONTACT : Personnel Department
1984 REVENUES: $10,900,000   1985 REVENUES: $13,500,000
BRANCHES : US:1   DEPARTMENTS: 1,2,3,4,5,6,7,8,9,10,11,12,13,14
EMPLOYEES: a95, b5, d100   EL1984: 5(b2,c3)   EL1986: "a few"

OPPORTUNITIES: Editorial - College degree. Accounting Department - College degree. Data Services Department - High school
graduate. No other requirements specified.

THE MCCALL PUBLISHING COMPANY
230 Park Avenue,
New York, NY 10169   (212)551-9500

MAGAZINES: Beauty, Diet and Exercise Guide, Cooking School,
McCall's, Working Mother, Working Mother Digest

EXECUTIVE: Raymond Eyes, President

```
CONTACT  : Department heads
1984 REVENUES: $128,819,000   1985 REVENUES: $134,112,600
BRANCHES : US:3    DEPARTMENTS: 1,2,3,4,6,9,10,11,12,13,14
EMPLOYEES: a178, b42, d220    EL1984: 10(b7,c3)  EL1986: ?
```

MCFADDEN PUBLISHING COMPANY
2900A Bristol, Suite 204
Costa Mesa, CA 92626   (714)241-9221

MAGAZINES: California Homes and Lifestyles, Orange County
Magazine

```
EXECUTIVE: Michael McFadden, Publisher
CONTACT  : Publisher
1984 REVENUES: $300,000       1985 REVENUES: $500,000
BRANCHES : None               DEPARTMENTS: 1,2,3,6,8,9,11
EMPLOYEES: 5                  EL1984: b1     EL1986: ?
```

OPPORTUNITIES: "We are a good example of an increasing number of
small publishing companies who can make a living independently of
the majors by using current technology, outside suppliers
(stripping, type, print, circulation, some ad reps) and by having
inside employees wear a number of hats. An understanding of
small business and an orientation toward sales is most important
regardless of the specific job function. People who just want to
be writers or editors and are not excited and challenged by an
entrepreneurials ituation are better off with large companies" -
Michael McFadden

MEDIATEX COMMUNICATIONS CORPORATION
PO Box 1569,
Austin, TX 78767   (512)476-7085

MAGAZINES: Texas Monthly

```
EXECUTIVE: Michael R. Levy, Publisher
CONTACT  : Deborah Giles, Office Manager
BRANCHES : US:5 DEPARTMENTS: 1,2,3,4,5,6,7,8,9,10,11,12,13,14,15
EMPLOYEES: a85, b35, d120  EL1984: 1    EL1986: 4-5
```

OPPORTUNITIES: All entry-level positions are Administrative
Assistants, who would function in a number of possible areas -
General Administration, Advertising, Editorial, Promotion,
Marketing or Circulation. A certain level of formal education is
not required. Applicants must possess an adequate level of
literacy in order to function well here. This level is quite
high, but no "formal" proof of achievement is needed. All these
clerical positions require good clerical skills (typing 50-60
wpm), some background in the area for which you're applying
(education, experience or a high level of interest) and good
organizational skills. All offer a high level of potential
responsibility.

COMMENTS: "We usually interview only for specific openings, but we will usually talk to someone if they want to discuss a career in publishing in general terms." - Ms. Leta Worthington, Administrative Services Manager.

MEREDITH CORPORATION
1716 Locust Street,
Des Moines, IA 50336   (515)284-3000

MAGAZINES: Better Homes and Gardens, Country Home, Successful Farming, Farm Computer News, WOOD and 15 Better Homes and Gardens special publications - All Time Favorite Recipies, Building Ideas, Christmas Ideas, Decorating, Do It Yourself Home Improvement and Repair, Garden Ideas and Outdoor Living, Holiday Cooking, Holiday Crafts, International Cooking, Home Plan Ideas, Kitchen and Bath Ideas, Low Calorie Recipes, Remodeling Ideas, Traditional Home and Window & Wall Ideas.

EXECUTIVE: Jack D. Rehm, Publishing Group President
CONTACT : Personnel
1984 REVENUES: $329,387,000   1985 REVENUES: $336,197,000
BRANCHES : US:14 DEPARTMENTS: 1,2,3,4,5,6,7,8,9,10,11,12,13,14,15
EMPLOYEES: a550, b5,450, c6,000 EL1984: 10(a1,b6,c3) EL1986: ?

OPPORTUNITIES: Entry-level jobs in the following three areas -- Accounting, Graphic Design, Data Processing -- require college degree in the applicable area. Advertising Sales Trainee - College degree (Marketing or Advertising major preferred). Management Trainee - Graduate degree preferred; some publishing experience required.

METROCORP
1500 Walnut Street,
Philadelphia, PA 19102   (215)545-3500

MAGAZINES: Philadelphia Magazine (Metrocorp also publishes Boston Magazine in its Boston office and Manhattan, Inc. in New York).

EXECUTIVE: D. Herbert Lipson, President
CONTACT : Department heads
BRANCHES : None   DEPARTMENTS: 1,3,4,6,8,9,11,13,14
EMPLOYEES: 50   EL1984: b1   EL1986: 0
COMMENTS : This entry is solely for Philadelphia operation and do not include employment statistics or possible entry-level opportunities at either its Boston or NYC offices.

MODERN HANDCRAFT, INC.
4251 Pennsylvania Avenue,
Kansas City, MO 64111   (816)531-5730

MAGAZINES: Flower and Garden, The Workbasket, Workbench

EXECUTIVE: John E. Tillotson III, President
CONTACT : Finley Tate (personnel)
BRANCHES : US:4   DEPARTMENTS: 1,2,3,4,5,6,7,10,11,12,13,14
EMPLOYEES: a120, b11, d131   EL1984: 0   EL1986: 0

NATIONAL REPORTER PUBLICATIONS, INC.
15115 S. 76 East Avenue,
Bixby, OK 74008   (918)386-4441

MAGAZINES: Bassin', Lost Treasure, Popular Lures, Total Fitness,
Treasure Industry Trade News, Winning!

EXECUTIVE: Gerald W. Pope, President
CONTACT : Department heads
1984 REVENUES: $6,500,000   1985 REVENUES: $8,000,000
BRANCHES : None   DEPARTMENTS: 1,2,3,5,6,7,9,11,13
EMPLOYEES: 45   EL1984: b3   EL1986: 2-3

OPPORTUNITIES: Art/Layout - College or vocational tech degree.
commercial art, layout & illustration skills. Accounting/Fi-
nance-Data Entry - Some college and experience or vocational
education. Computer and accounting skills. Assistant Editor -
College degree (in Journalism); writing, editing and organizational skills. Data Processing - Computer training; managerial
and organizational skills.

THE NATIONAL RIFLE ASSOCIATION OF AMERICA
1600 Rhode Island Avenue, N.W.
Washington, DC 20036   (202)828-6000

MAGAZINES: The American Hunter, The American Marksman, The
American Rifleman, Insights

EXECUTIVE: G. Ray Arnett, Executive VP
CONTACT : Frederick H. Smith III, Personnel Director
1984 REVENUES: $59,321,000   1985 REVENUES: $65,200,000
BRANCHES : NA   DEPARTMENTS: 1,2,3,4,5,6,7,9,10,11,15
EMPLOYEES: a320, b23, cNA, d343+ E1984: 58(b26,c32) EL1986: 48

OPPORTUNITIES: Design Assistant - Commercial art school degree
preferred; familiar with lay out/design; able to produce clean
art; Data Entry Operator - High School graduate; able to operate
alpha/numeric keyboard & key disc equipment; CRT Operator - High
School graduate; clerical experience; basic math skills; able to
operate CRT; Acctng Clerk - High School + two years of college;
experience in general accounting & reconciliations; able to
perform analytical tasks; Junior Accountant - Same requirements
as Accounting Clerk; Clerk Typist - High School; general clerical
& typing skills; good spelling & grammar; Receptionist/Secretary
- High School; typing; able to use standard office equipment;

excellent verbal/communication skills. Mail Clerk - High School,
some college preferred; 1-2 years clerical experience; word
processing skills; detail work; filing. General Clerk - High
School; general skills; Assistant Editor - College degree (Eng-
lish/Journalism); 6 months-1 year experience; knowledge of the
shooting sports; ability to write & edit; ability to prioritize,
organize and work within strict deadlines. Programmer Trainee -
Associates degree (or equivalent); knowledge of the types and
structures of DP systems. Developed skills in COBOL language.
Assistant Manager - College degree preferred; sp,e administra-
tive/supervisory experience preferred; budgeting skills; knowledge of general office management procedures.

THE NATIONAL UNDERWRITER COMPANY
The 420 E. 4th St.,
Cincinnati, OH 45202   (513)721-2140

MAGAZINES: National Underwriter (Property/Casualty Insurance and
Life/Health Insurance Editions), Florida Underwriter, Indiana
Underwriter, Ohio Underwriter.

EXECUTIVE: B.P. McMackin, Jr., President
CONTACT : Department heads
BRANCHES : US:2   DEPARTMENTS: 1,2,4,5,6,7,8,9,10,11,12,13,14
EMPLOYEES: a99, b37, d136   EL1984: 4(a2,b2)   EL1986: 0

NETWORK PUBLISHING CORPORATION
254 West 31st Street,
New York, NY 10001   (212)947-6300

MAGAZINES: Soap Opera Digest

EXECUTIVE: Marc Liu, President
CONTACT : President
1984 REVENUES: $12,000,000   1985 REVENUES: $15,000,000
BRANCHES : None   DEPARTMENTS: 1,2,3,6,11
EMPLOYEES: 24   EL1984: 5(b3,c2)   EL1986: 0

THE NEW YORK TIMES MAGAZINE GROUP
488 Madison Avenue,
New York, NY 10022   (212)593-8000

MAGAZINES: Cruising World, Family Circle, Golf Digest, Tennis.

EXECUTIVE: William Kerr, President/Magazine Group
CONTACT : Department heads
1984 REVENUES: $210,000,000   1985 REVENUES: NA
BRANCHES : US:9   DEPARTMENTS: 1,2,3,4,5,6,7,9,10,11,12,13,14
EMPLOYEES: a595, b150, d745 EL1984: 24(a2,b8,c14)   EL1986: 15

OPPORTUNITIES: Researcher/Junior Analyst - BA, strong quantitative skills, computer literacy. Promotion Copywriter - BA (English or Journalism); ability to write well. Editorial Assistant - BA (English or Journalism); ability to write well & assimilate information quickly. Typing required. Secretary - Educational requirements vary, but all demand strong command of grammar, good typing and telephone skills. Circulation Sales Representative - Educational requirements vary, but individual should be self-motivated and have aggressive personality.

NEWSWEEK, INC.
444 Madison Avenue,
New York, NY 10022   (212)350-4000

MAGAZINES: Bulletin, Newsweek, Newsweek On Campus, Newsweek International.

EXECUTIVE: Mark M. Edmiston, President
CONTACT : Michele Daly or Sue Patterson (personnel)
1984 REVENUES: $282,679,000   1985 REVENUES: $291,114,000
BRANCHES : US:11, INTL:Unspecified DEPARTMENTS: 1-13,19,20,28
EMPLOYEES: a959, b163, c19, d1141 EL1984: 0   EL1986: 0

OFFICIAL AIRLINE GUIDES, INC.
2000 Clearwater Drive,
Oak Brook, IL 60521   (312)654-6000

MAGAZINES: AirCargo Magazine, Official Airline Guide (North American, Worldwide & Electronic editions), Pocket Flight Guide (North American, European & Pacific area editions), Worldwide Ship and Cruise Guide, Travel Planner (North American, European, Pacific and Electronic editions).

EXECUTIVE: James W. Woodward, President
CONTACT : Robert B. Eberhardt, Mgr. Compensation & Benefits
1984 REVENUES: $125,000,000   1985 REVENUES: $125,000,000
BRANCHES : US:4, INTL:1   DEPARTMENTS: 1 - 14
EMPLOYEES: a1000, b55, c5, d1060   EL1984: b5   EL1986: 5

OPPORTUNITIES: Account Supervisor - BA (Marketing); some prior sales experience.

OILDOM PUBLISHING COMPANY OF TEXAS, INC.
PO Box 22267, 3314 Mercer Street
Houston, TX 77027   (713)622-0676

MAGAZINES: Pipeline, Pipeline and Underground Utilities Construction.
EXECUTIVE: Oliver C. Klinger, Jr., President

CONTACT   : President
BRANCHES : US:2, INTL:2   DEPARTMENTS: 2,3,4,6,11
EMPLOYEES: a8, b4, c4, d16   EL1984: b1   EL1986: 2

OPPORTUNITIES: Editorial Assistant - College degree (Journalism
preferred); good appearance, writing ability and knowledge of
word processing. Circulation/Promotion (position involves
upgrading and maintaining lists) - College degree; some knowledge
of computers.
COMMENTS: "As a small organizaton we provide the finest opportunity to gain experience in all phases of magazine publishing
plus outstanding training and experience in special departments." - Mr. Klinger

SYLVIA PORTER'S PERSONAL FINANCE MAGAZINE COMPANY
380 Lexington Ave.,
New York, NY 10017   (212)557-9100

MAGAZINES: Sylvia Porter's Personal Finance Magazine

EXECUTIVE: Joel Davis, President
CONTACT   : President
1984 REVENUES: $2,750,000   1985 REVENUES: $6,000,000
BRANCHES : None   DEPARTMENTS: 2,3,4,6,14
EMPLOYEES: 26   EL1984: 10(a2,b8)   EL1986: 3

OPPORTUNITIES: Editorial - College degree (minimum) Journalism
degree and/or advanced coursework helpful; writing skills a must.
COMMENTS: See additional listing for Davis Publications, Inc.
(same ownership).

PRIME NATIONAL PUBLISHING CORPORATION
470 Boston Post Rd.,
Weston, MA 02193   (617)899-2702

MAGAZINES: New England Senior Citizen, Senior American News,
American Journal of Hospital Care, Nursingworld Journal,
Healthcare Recruiter, PT Job News.

EXECUTIVE: Richard A. DeVito, Publisher
CONTACT   : Personnel Department
BRANCHES : None   DEPARTMENTS: 1,2,4,6,11,15

EMPLOYEES: 20   EL1984: b2   EL1986: 2-6

OPPORTUNITIES: Advertising Sales or Marketing entry-level positions: While educational requirements vary, key is the ability to
learn how to sell and stick with it until successful.

REESE COMMUNICATIONS, INC.
460 West 34th Street,
New York, NY 10001   (212)947-6500

MAGAZINES: Computer Entertainment, Front Page Detective, Inside
Detective, Master Detective, Official Detective, True Detective,
Video.

EXECUTIVE: Jay Rosenfield, Publisher
CONTACT   : Department heads
1984 REVENUES: $14,500,000   1985 REVENUES: $16,500,000
BRANCHES : US:1   DEPARTMENTS: 1,2,3,4,6,8,9,11,13,14
EMPLOYEES: a42, b2, d44   EL1984: b2   EL1986: 3

OPPORTUNITIES: Company indicates entry-level positions will be in
the Art and Editorial Departments, but has furnished us with no
further information about these openings.

RODALE PRESS, INC.
33 East Minor Street,
Emmaus, PA 18049   (215)967-5171

MAGAZINES: Prevention, Rodale's Organic Gardening, Bicycling,
Cross-Country Skier, Runner's World, The New Farm plus a variety
of newsletters.

EXECUTIVE: Robert Rodale, Chairman
CONTACT   : Ruth Carnevale (personnel)
1984 REVENUES: $117,000,000   1985 REVENUES: $125,000,000
BRANCHES : US:3   DEPARTMENTS: 1-15,31
EMPLOYEES: a850, b30, d880 EL1984: 25(a5,b5,c15)   EL1986: 10

OPPORTUNITIES: Clerk Typist - High School; business courses,
typing skills. Sales Trainee - College degree; strong communi-
tions and English background necessary. Circulation - College
degree; business and accounting skills. Marketing - College
degree; marketing and accounting. Research Assistant - College
degree; knowledge of the life sciences.

SCRANTON GILLETTE COMMUNICATIONS, INC.
380 Northwest Hwy.,
Des Plaines, IL 60016   (312)298-6622

MAGAZINES: Roads & Bridges, Seed World, Water/Engineering &
Management, Water & Wastes Digest

EXECUTIVE: H. S. Gillette, President
CONTACT   : Louise Draves, Personnel Manager
1984 REVENUES: $4,000,000   1985 REVENUES: $5,000,000
BRANCHES : US:1   DEPARTMENTS: 1,2,4,5,6,7,9,10,11,13,14
EMPLOYEES: a55, b7, d62   EL1984: c2   EL1986: ?
OPPORTUNITIES: Circulation Clerks - High School; typing 40wpm;
trainable.

SERVICE PUBLICATIONS, INC.
100 Park Avenue,
New York, NY 10017   (212)532-5588

MAGAZINES: American Salon, Salon Talk

EXECUTIVE: Donn Byrne, President
CONTACT   : Department heads or Diane Barkume, Personnel Manager
1984 REVENUES: $8,000,000   1985 REVENUES: $9,000,000
BRANCHES : US:2   DEPARTMENTS: 1,2,4,6,8,11,14,15
EMPLOYEES: a45, b5, d50   EL1984: 6(b4,c2)   EL1986: 5

OPPORTUNITIES: Production Assistant - detail and planning. Circulation Assistant - Analytical skills. Trade Show Coordinator -
Organization and detail skills. Editorial Writer - writing and
presentation skills. All above jobs require college degrees.

SPRINGER-VERLAG NEW YORK, INC.
175 Fifth Avenue,
New York, NY 10010   (212)460-1500

MAGAZINES: Abacus, Aesthetic Plastic Surgery, Structured Language
World, M.D. Computing, Math Intelligencer, APL.

EXECUTIVE: Jolanda von Hadgen, Chief Executive Officer
CONTACT   : Jo Ann Hallahan (personnel)
BRANCHES : US:1   DEPARTMENTS: 1,4,5,7,8,9,10,11,13,14,15
EMPLOYEES: NA   EL1984: 0   EL1986: 0

OPPORTUNITIES: Clerical - High School (college preferred); typing; good command of language (including technical vocabulary).

SPRINGHOUSE CORPORATION
1111 Bethlehem Pike,
Springhouse, PA 19477   (215)646-8700

MAGAZINES: Nursing '85, Learning, Office Systems 85, Nursing Life

EXECUTIVE: Daniel Cheney, President
CONTACT   : Jerry Locke (personnel)
BRANCHES : US:7   DEPARTMENTS: 1,2,3,4,5,6,8,9,10,11,12,13,14
EMPLOYEES: a266, b64, d330   EL1984: b12   EL1986: 6

OPPORTUNITIES: Copy Editors, Editorial Assistants, Assistant
Editors - College degree (English or Journalism); demonstrated
writing ability and motivation for a career in publishing. Junior
Market Analyst - College degree (Statistics/Marketing); interest
in marketing research and statistical analysis. Production
Artist/Paste-up Artist - College degree (Design/Art); demonstrated design skills.

TAUNTON PRESS, INC.
63 South Main Street,   PO Box 355,
Newtown, CT 06470   (203)426-8171

MAGAZINES: Fine Homebuilding, Fine Woodworking, Threads

EXECUTIVE: Paul Roman, Publisher
CONTACT   : Carol Marotti, Personnel Manager
1984 REVENUES: $8,000,000   1985 REVENUES: $10,000,000
BRANCHES : None   DEPARTMENTS: 1,2,3,4,5,6,7,8,9,10,11,13,14,15
EMPLOYEES: 82   EL1984: c1   EL1986: 1

OPPORTUNITIES: Production Assistant - Degree in graphic design
helpful. Graphic design/art and paste-up skills required.

THOMAS PUBLISHING COMPANY
One Penn Plaza,
New York, NY 10119   (212)695-0500

MAGAZINES: Industrial Equipment News, Thomas Register of American
Manufactuerers and numerous other American directories. Involved
in many international joint publishing ventures and partnerships.

EXECUTIVE: Jose E. Andrade, Chairman
CONTACT   : Ivy Molofsky, Personnel Manager
BRANCHES : None (400 ind. sales reps DEPARTMENTS: 1 - 14
EMPLOYEES: 325   EL1984: b2   EL1986: 0

OPPORTUNITIES: Sales/Marketing Assistants - BA (Marketing);
flexibility; excellent verbal/written communication skills.

TIME, INC.
1271 Avenue of the Americas,
New York, NY 10020   (212)586-1212

MAGAZINES: Creative Ideas for Living, Discover, Fortune, Life,
Money, People, Progressive Farmer, Southern Living, Sports
Illustrated, Time.

EXECUTIVE: J. Richard Munro, President
CONTACT   : Robert B. Mintz, Director/Management Resources
BRANCHES : US:27, INTL:34   DEPARTMENTS: NA
EMPLOYEES: a3887 b3661 c900 d8448 EL1984: 18(a12,b6)
EL1986: 6

OPPORTUNITIES: Source Manager Trainee - MBA or BA;quantitative &
analytical skills; interest/experience in magazine publishing;
consumer package goods experience. Copywriter Trainee - BA; interest in magazines; strong creative capability with the English
language; unde rstanding of promotion; exceptional interpersonal
skills.

U.S. CHAMBER OF COMMERCE
1615 H Street, NW,
Washington, DC 20062   (202)463-5650

MAGAZINES: Nation's Business

EXECUTIVE: David A. Roe, Director
CONTACT : Diane Large, Personnel Director
1984 REVENUES: $18,713,000   1985 REVENUES: $20,000,000
BRANCHES : 6   DEPARTMENTS: 1,2,3,4,5,6,7,10,11,12,13
EMPLOYEES: a44, b21, d65   EL1984: NA   EL1986: ?

OPPORTUNITIES: Editorial - BA in Journalism. Art - BA in Art.
Clerical - High School; strong clerical and communications
skills.

VERNON PUBLICATIONS, INC.
109 W. Mercer,
Seattle, WA 98119   (206)285-2050

MAGAZINES: Alaska Construction & Oil, The Nurse Practitioner,
Pacific Banker & Business, Pacific Builder & Engineer, Seattle
Business, Alaska from the Inside, Northwest Construction News,
Washington's Largest Companies (annual). Also produces two other
magazines, one newsletter and 6 annual directories for other
publishers.

EXECUTIVE: Bill R. Vernon, Chairman
CONTACT : Department heads
BRANCHES : US:1   DEPARTMENTS: 1,2,3,4,5,6,9,11,13,14,15
EMPLOYEES: a33, b3, d36   EL1984: b1   EL1986: 0

WALKER-DAVIS PUBLICATIONS, INC.
2500 Office Center,
Willow Grove, PA 19000   (215)657-3203

MAGAZINES: Energy Management Technology, Engineer's Digest

EXECUTIVE: Michael J. Gillespie, President
CONTACT : President or Frank McGill
1984 REVENUES: $3,000,000   1985 REVENUES: $3,750,000
BRANCHES : US: 7   DEPARTMENTS: 1,2,4,5,6,7,8,9,11,12
EMPLOYEES: a23, b8, d31   EL1984: b1   EL1986: ?

OPPORTUNITIES: Editorial - College degree (English or Journalism). Sales - College degree; some prior experience needed.

WEIGHT WATCHERS 21ST CORPORATION
360 Lexington Avenue,
New York, NY 10017   (212)370-0644

MAGAZINES: Weight Watchers Magazine & Special Edition. . . Weight
Watcher's Magazine - Fast & Easy Recipes.

EXECUTIVE: Kent Q. Kreh, Executive VP/Publisher
CONTACT   : Department heads
BRANCHES : US:2   DEPARTMENTS: 1,2,3,4,6,7,9,11,13,14
EMPLOYEES : a30, b2, d32   EL1984: 7(b5,c2)   EL1986: 3

OPPORTUNITIES: Publishing "generalist" and entry-level Editorial
positions. Both require college degrees. No other requirements
specified.

MY IDEAL PUBLISHER PROFILE

MUSTS	PREFERENCES	NEVERS

CHAPTER 29

1986 Internships And Training Programs

Those publishers listed in the previous chapter also provided us with information about availability of internships and whether or not they have organized, formal training programs.

In the first section of this chapter, we have listed all publishers who offer internships. Each listing includes the company name, the person in charge of their internship program and, preceding the listing, one of three letters - **N**, **S** or **B**:

> **N** = Publisher offers <u>non-salaried</u> internships <u>only</u>.
> **S** = Publisher offers <u>salaried</u> internships <u>only</u>.
> **B** = Publisher offers <u>some of each</u>.

In the second section, those offering formal training programs are listed. Each entry includes the name of the publisher and their own explanatory notes. Realize that any publisher must train new people, whatever their position. We have here attempted to identify those publishers offering <u>more</u> than such required "on-the-job" training.

Some publishers may have confused "formal training program" with their internship program. Rather than omit these companies altogether, we chose to include them in the training section. As you target publishers during your job search, be sure to ask them for more details on whatever programs we've listed.

PUBLISHING INTERNSHIPS AVAILABLE IN 1986

S A/S/M Communications, Inc.
Helen Gamm, Office Manager

S Allstate Enterprises Holdings, Inc.
Mary Selover, Associate Publisher

B American Association for the Advancement of Science
Department heads

S American Baby, Inc.
Judith Nolte, Editor

S American Broadcasting Companies - Publishing Division
Marion Hyman, Director of Personnel

S American Express Publishing Company
Program with the American Society of Magazine Editors

S American Journal of Nursing Co.
Mary Mallison, Editor

S American West Publishing Company
Carol Ryan, Business Manager

S Associated Business Publications, Inc.
Patricia E. Neri, Vice President

S Barks Publications, Inc.
Elsie Dickson, Associate Publisher

S Best-Met Publishing Company, Inc.
Laura Lang, Office Manager

B Bill Communications, Inc.
Robert H. Albert, VP/Corporate Communications

S Billboard Publications, Inc.
Mary Boyle, Personnel Director

S CBS Magazines, A Division of CBS Inc.
Kim Bedle, Manager - Training & Development, CBS Magazines

S Carstens Publications, Inc.
Harold Carstens, President

B City Home Publishing, Inc.
Anne Goldstein, Office Manager

S Commerce Publishing Company
James J. Poor, President

S Communications Channels, Inc.
   Lawrence Moores, Executive Vice President

B Cummins Publishing Co., Inc.
   Andrew Cummings, Publisher

N Dabora Inc.
   David Howard, President

N Davis Publications, Inc.
   Personnel Office

S Dinan Communications, Inc.
   Ted Meredith, President

N Editorial America, S.A.
   Carlos Obregon - Executive Assistant

S Esquire Associates
   Lucy Handley, Art Dept.; Andrew Wildes, Editorial Manager

S Gallant/Charger Publications, Inc.
   Jack Lewis, Publisher

S Gorman Publishing Co.
   Vivien Gorman, Personnel Director

B Gruner + Jahr USA Publishing
   Susan Levy, Personnel Director

N HAL Publications, Inc.
   No contact specified.

B Halsey Publishing Co.
   Gordon Russell, Senior Vice Ppresident

S Harcourt Brace Jovanovich Publications
   George Glenn, Vice President - Editorial

S Hart Publications, Inc.
   Department head in area of interest

B Hatton-Brown Publishers, Inc.
   Dianne Sullivan, Operations Manager

S Hayden Publishing Co., Inc.
   Charles Asymkos, Personnel Manager or Sheila O'Niell

N Heldref Publications
   Stuart Funke-Degnuff, Advertising Director

B International Thompson Transport Press
   D. R. Demauro, Personnel Manager

S   Intertec Publishing Corp.
    Patty Goff, Employment Services Manager

B   Kane Communications, Inc.
    Scott Borowsky, President

S   The Kiplinger Washington Editors, Inc.
    Nicholas Niles, Publisher

S   Kiwanis International
    Chuck Jonak, Executive Editor

B   Knapp Communications Corp.
    Richard West, Personnel Director
    ("Internships are offered occasionally. It is really up to the
    student to actively seek these opportunities and do the neces-
    sary follow-up.)

B   The McCall Publishing Company
    Helen McGrath, Personnel Director

B   McFadden Publishing Company
    Susan McFadden, Co-Publisher

B   Mediatex Communications Corp.
    Leta Worthington, Administrative Services Manager

S   Meredith Corporation
    Personnel Department

N   Metrocorp
    Carol Saline, Senior Editor

S   National Reporter Publications, Inc.
    Richard Pope, Associate Publisher

N   The National Rifle Association of America
    Frederic Smith, Director

S   The National Underwriter Company
    No contact specified

B   Network Publishing Corporation
    Joe Flasch, Director of Finance and Administration

S   The New York Times Magazine Group
    Sheila Rickin or Eileen Miller, Personnel Managers

S   Newsweek, Inc.
    Michele Daly or Sue Patterson, Personnel Managers

B   Official Airline Guides, Inc.
    Michael Roberts, Employment Manager

N   Sylvia Porter's Personal Finance Magazine Co.
Personnel Office

B   Prime National Publishing Corp.
William Haslam, General Manager

N   Reese Communications, Inc.
Jay Rosenfield, President

B   Rodale Press, Inc.
Barrie Atkin, Director of Corporate Planning

S   Scranton Gillette Communications, Inc.
Louise Draves, Personnel Manager

S   Service Publications, Inc.
Diane Barkume, Personnel Manager

N   Springhouse Corporation
Jerry Locke, Personnel Manager

N   Taunton Press, Inc.
Carol Marotti, Personnel Manager

S   Thomas Publishing Company
Ivy Molofsky, Personnel Manager

B   Time, Inc.
(Ms.) K. Vinton Taylor, College Relations Manager

N   U.S. Chamber of Commerce
Diane Large, Personnel Director

N   Vernon Publications, Inc.
Christine Laing, Editorial Director

S   Walker-Davis Publications, Inc.
Michael Gillespie, Publisher

B   Weight Watchers 21st Coorporation
Kent Kreh, Executive VP/Publisher

PUBLISHERS OFFERING FORMAL TRAINING PROGRAMS

Allstate Enterprises Holdings, Inc.
Cooperative program with Northwestern University

American Baby, Inc.
Work with ASME Internship Program; Summer editorial internship
program.

American Broadcasting Companies - Publishing Division
Internship programs

Baker Publications Inc.
Primarily in Sales, but also in Circulation and Editorial

Barks Publications, Inc.
Printing Institute courses (tuition paid upon completion); American Business Press and BPA programs

CBS Magazines, A Division of CBS Inc.
While there are no specific entry-level programs, there are a
wide variety of courses, seminars and conferences available
through CBS Inc. (parent company).

Canon Communications, Inc.
Individualized by department, 90 day probationary periods

Cummins Publishing Company, Inc.
On-the-job training for applicants with potential

Editorial America, S.A.
In each editorial department

Gallant/Charger Publications, Inc.
On-the-job training

Gorman Publishing Company
Sales training and on-the-job training

Halsey Publishing Company
In the Editorial and Art Departments

Hearst Corporation - Magazine Division
In ad sales, geared to people with one to three years publishing
experience

Heldref Publications
On-the-job training

Intertec Publishing Corp.
Ad Sales has a formal program, others vary by department

Kane Communications, Inc.
Sales Training Program (only)

Mediatex Communications Corp.
Orientation session

Meredith Corporation
On-the-job

Prime National Publishing Corp.
In the advertising sales department

Reese Communications, Inc.
Not formal program, but training is done on-the-job

Rodale Press, Inc.
Internships and work experience programs

Scranton Gillette Communications, Inc.
First three months on the job

Springhouse Corporation
In the editorial department

CHAPTER 30

Other Consumer Magazine Publishers To Contact

1330 Corporation
505 Market Street
Knoxville, TN 37902   (615)521-0600
EXECUTIVE: Christopher Whittle, Chairman
MAGAZINES: a variety of "single sponsor" publications, "poster" publications and school and college magazines. (They are also the parent company of Esquire.)

American Association of Retired Persons
215 Long Beach Blvd.,
Long Beach, CA 90801   (213)432-5781
EXECUTIVE: Robert E. Wood, Publications Director
MAGAZINES: Modern Maturity

American Museum of Natural History
Central Park West at 79th Street,
New York, NY 10024   (212)873-1498
EXECUTIVE: L. Thomas Kelly, Publisher
MAGAZINES: Natural History

Argus Publishing Corp.
12301 Wilshire Blvd.,
Los Angeles, CA 90025   (213)820-3601
EXECUTIVE: Gorden Behn, President
MAGAZINES: Fabulous Mustangs & Exotic Fords, Off-Road, Popular Hot Rodding Magazine, Super Chevy, VW & Porsche.

Army Times Publishing Co.
Springfield, VA 22159   (703)750-2000
EXECUTIVE: William F. Donnely, President
MAGAZINES: Air Force Times, Army Times, Army Times Military
Group, Federal Times, Navy Times.

The Atlantic Monthly Co.
8 Arlington Street,
Boston, MA 02116   (617)536-9500
EXECUTIVE: David Achincloss, Publisher
MAGAZINES: The Atlantic

B.A.S.S. Publications
PO Box 17900, 1 Bell Road,
Montgomery, AL 36117   (205)272-9530
EXECUTIVE: Ray Scott, Publisher
MAGAZINES: Bassmaster Magazine, Southern Outdoors.

Benjamin Franklin Literary & Medical Society
Box 567, 1100 Waterway Boulevard,
Indianapolis, IN 46206   (317)634-8881
EXECUTIVE: Dr. Cori serVass, President
MAGAZINES: Child Life, Children's Digest, Children's Playmate
magazine, Humpty Dumpty magazine, Jack & Jill, Turtle magazine
for Preschool Kids. (Also, as Curtis Publishing, publishes
the Saturday Evening Post and Country Gentleman magazines.)

Boy Scouts of America, Inc.
1325 Walnut Hill Lane,
Irving, TX 75062   (214)659-2000
EXECUTIVE: J. Warren Young, Publisher
MAGAZINES: Boy's Life, Scouting.

Charlton Publications, Inc.
Charlton Building,
Derby, CT 06418   (203)735-3381
EXECUTIVE: John Santanglo, Jr., President
MAGAZINES: Charlton Comics Group, Charlton Muscle Group, Country
Song Roundup, Gung-Ho, Hit Parader, New Sounds, Official Karate,
Real West, Rock & Soul, Song Hits Combination

Conde Nast Publications, Inc.
350 Madison Avenue,
New York, NY 10017   (212)880-8800
EXECUTIVE: Robert J. Lapham, President
MAGAZINES: Bride's, Gentlemen's Quarterly, Glamour, Gourmet,
House & Garden, Mademoiselle, Self, Street & Smith's Yearbooks
(Baseball, College Football, Pro Football, College & Pro Basket-
ball editions), Vanity Fair, Vogue.

Diner's Club, Inc.
641 Lexington Avenue, 2nd Floor,
New York, NY 10022   (212)888-9450
EXECUTIVE: Horace Sutton, Editor
MAGAZINES: Signature

East/West Network, Inc.
34 East 51st Street,
New York, NY 10022   (212)888-5900
EXECUTIVE: James A. Kennedy, President
MAGAZINES: Amtrak Express, Eastern Review, East/West Network,
Inc., Northwest Orient, Ozark, Pan Am Clipper, PSA Magazine,
Repubic Scene, Southwest, United, Western's World.

Fairchild Publications Inc.
7 East 12th Street
New York, NY 10003   (212)741-4000
EXECUTIVE: Daniel Newman, President
MAGAZINES: Consumer titles - M, W, Entree. Trade titles - Amer-
ican Metal Market, Clinical Psychiatry News, Daily News Record,
Electronic News, Electronics Retailing, Energy User News, Family
Practice News, Footwear News, Heat Treating, HFD, Home Fashion
Textiles, Internal Medicine News & Cardiology News, Managing
Pain, Metal Center News, Metal Statistics, Metalworking News,
MIS Week, Ob Gyn News, Pediatrics News, Skin & Allergy News,
SportStyle, Supermarket News, Women's Wear Daily, Interline
Reporter, Travel Agent. (They are the parent company of American
Traveler, Inc. and Professional Press, Inc. The latter's addi-
tional titles include International Contact Lens Clinic, Journal
of Learning Disabilities, Optical Index and Optometric Monthly.)

Family Media, Inc.
Three Park Avenue,
New York, NY 10016   (212)340-9200
EXECUTIVE: Robert E. Riordan, President
MAGAZINES: Grayzel, Health, The Homeowner, Ladies' Home Journal,
1,001 Home Ideas.

Forbes, Inc.
60 Fifth Avenue,
New York, NY 10011   (212)620-2200
EXECUTIVE: Malcolm S. Forbes, Chairman
MAGAZINES: Forbes

Harpers Foundation
2 Park Avenue,
New York, NY 10016   (212)481-5220
EXECUTIVE: Louisa D. Kearney, Publisher
MAGAZINES: Harpers

Harris Publications, Inc.
1115 Broadway,
New York, NY 10010 (212)807-7100
MAGAZINES: Country Almanac, Country Decorating Ideas, Guitar
World, Woman.

Historial Times Inc.
PO Box 8200, 2245 Kohn Road,
Harrisburg, PA 17105 (717)657-9555
EXECUTIVE: Warren L. Syer, President
MAGAZINES: American History Illustrated, British Heritage, Civil
War Times Illustrated, Country Journal, Early American Life, Fly
Fisherman, The New England Skiers Guide, The Original New England
Guide.

Honolulu Publishing Co., Ltd.
36 Merchant Street,
Honolulu, HI 96813 (808)524-7400
EXECUTIVE: David M. Pellegrin, President
MAGAZINES: Hawaii, Hawaii Drive Guides, Hawaii TV Digest, Honolulu magazine, Honolulu Publishing's Inflight Group, Spirit of Alo-
ha.

Johnson Publishing Co., Inc.
820 S. Michigan Ave.,
Chicago, IL 60605 (312)322-9220
EXECUTIVE: John H. Johnson, President
MAGAZINES: Ebony, Jet.

L.F.P., Inc.
2029 Century Park East, Suite 3800
Los Angeles, CA 90067 (213)556-9200
EXECUTIVE: Larry Flynt, Publisher
MAGAZINES: Chic, Hustler.

MacFadden Women's Group
215 Lexington Avenue,
New York, NY 10016 (212)340-7500
EXECUTIVE: Peter J. Callahan, President
MAGAZINES: Moriarty, Macfadden Women's Group, True Story.

McGraw-Hill, Inc.
1221 Avenue of the Americas,
New York, NY 10020 (212)997-1221
EXECUTIVE: John G. Wrede, President
MAGAZINES: Consumer titles: Business Week, International Week,
Business Week's Guide to Careers. Trade titles: Modern Plastics,
Textile World, Textile Products & Processes, Chemical Week,

Chemical Engineering, Electrical World, Power, American Machinist, 33 Metal Producing, Coal Age, Engineering and Mining Journal, Aviation Week and Space Technology, Fleet Owner, Platt's and other newsletters, Architectural Record, Communications/Systems Equipment Design, Data Communications, EC&M Electrical Construction and Maintenance, Electrical Wholesaling, ElectronicsWeek, Engineering News-Record, Engineering and Mining Journal, Graduating Engineer, International Management, International Power Systems, Military/Space Electronics Design, NC Shopowner, Physician and Sportsmedicine, Postgraduate Medicine.

Ms. Foundation for Education & Communication
119 West 40th Street,
New York, NY 10018   (212)719-9800
EXECUTIVE: Patricia Carbine, Publisher
MAGAZINES: Ms.

Murdoch Magazines
210 South Street,
New York, NY 10002   (212)815-)800
EXECUTIVE: John Evans, President
MAGAZINES: New Woman, New York Magazine, The Star, Elle; Travel Weekly, Hotel and Travel Index and other trade publications in the hotel, travel and aviation industries. (Parent company is News America Publishing Co., which also publishes major newspapers such as The New York Post, Boston Herald and Chicago Sun-Times. Both companies, and others involved in the communications field -- including 20th Century Fox -- are owned by Australian press baron Rupert Murdoch.)

National Geographic Society
17th and M Streets, NW
Washington, DC 20036   (202)775-6169
EXECUTIVE: Gilbert M. Grosvenor, President
MAGAZINES: National Geographic, National Geographic Traveller

Omni International Ltd.
1965 Broadway,
New York, NY 10023   (212)496-6100
EXECUTIVE: Bob Guccione, President
MAGAZINES: Omni (By same publisher, under different corporation, at same address -- Penthouse).

Parade Publications, Inc.
750 Third Avenue,
New York, NY 10017   (212)573-7000
EXECUTIVE: Carlo Vittorini, President
MAGAZINES: Parade

Peterson Publishing Co.
8490 Sunset Blvd.,
Los Angeles, CA 90069 (213)657-5100
EXECUTIVE: F. R. Waingrow, President
MAGAZINES: Car Craft, Circle Track, Dirt Rider Magazine, 4 Wheel
& Off-Road, Guns & Ammo, Hot Rod Magazine, Hunting, Motocyclist
Magazine, Motor Trend, Petersen's Photographic Magazine, Pickups
& Mini-Trucks, Sea Magazine, Skin Diver Magazine, Teen.

Playboy Enterprises, Inc.
919 N. Michigan Avenue,
Chicago, IL 60611 (312)751-8000
EXECUTIVE: Christie Hefner, Chairman
MAGAZINES: Games, Playboy

Reader's Digest Association, Inc.
Pleasantville NY 10570 (914)769-7000
EXECUTIVE: George V. Grune, Chairman
MAGAZINES: Reader's Digest (plus numerous international editions)

Scholastic Magazines, Inc.
730 Broadway,
New York, NY 10003 (212)505-3000
EXECUTIVE: Richard Robinson, Chairman
MAGAZINES: Electronic Learning, Forecast for Home Economics, Jun-
ior Scholastic, Scholastic Coach, Scholastic Magazines High
School Market, Teaching and Computers.

Smithsonian Institution National Associates
Arts & Industries Bldg., 900 Jefferson Drive,
Washington, DC 20560 (202)381-6311
EXECUTIVE: Joseph Bonsignore, Publisher
MAGAZINES: Smithsonian

Straight Arrow Publishers, Inc.
745 Fifth Avenue,
New York, NY 10151 (212)758-3800
EXECUTIVE: Jan Wenner, President
MAGAZINES: Record, Rolling Stone, US

Times Mirror Magazines, Inc.
380 Madison Avenue,
New York, NY 10017 (212)687-3000
EXECUTIVE: John A. Scott, President
MAGAZINES: Golf Magazine, Outdoor Life, Popular Science, Ski, The
Sporting News (1212 N. Lindbergh Blvd. St. Louis, MO 63132, a
division of Times Mirror Co).

Triangle Publications, Inc.
Radnor, PA   19088   (215)293-8500
EXECUTIVE: Walter Annenberg, President
MAGAZINES: TV Guide, Seventeen

U.S. News and World Report, Inc.
2400 N Street, NW
Washington, DC   20037   (202)955-2000
EXECUTIVE: Willian G. Dunn, Vice-President
MAGAZINES: U.S. News and World Report

The Webb Company
1999 Shepard Road,
St. Paul, MN   55116   (612)690-7200
EXECUTIVE: Robert Sallman, President
MAGAZINES: AAA World, Beef, Dairy, The Family Handyman, The Far-
mer, Farm Industry News, Friendly Exchange, Irrigation Age, KOA
Handbook and Directory for Campers, Motorcycle, National Hog
Farmer , Snow Goer, Snow Week

Whitney Communications Co. Publications Group
850 Third Avenue,
New York, NY   10022   (212)715-2600
EXECUTIVE: John Prescott, President
MAGAZINES: 50 Plus, The Hockey News, Waterway Guide

CHAPTER 31

Other Trade Magazine Publishers To Contact

BMT Publications, Inc.
254 West 31st Street,
New York, NY 10001   (212)594-4120
EXECUTIVE: Irwin Breitman, President
MAGAZINES: Convenience Store News, Gaming and Wagering Business Magazine, Smokeshop, United States Tobacco Journal.

Babcox Publications
11 S. Forge Street,
Akron, OH 44304   (216)535-6117
EXECUTIVE: Tom B. Babcox, President
MAGAZINES: Automotive Rebuilder, BodyShop Business, Brake and Front End, Counterman, Import Car, Specialty & Custom Dealer, Tire Review, WarehouseDistributor News

Bell Publications
2403 Champa Street,
Denver, CO 80205   (303)296-1600
EXECUTIVE: Allen Bell, Publisher
MAGAZINES: Alaska Beverage Analyst, Arizona Beverage Analyst, Colorado Beverage Analyst, Idaho Beverage Analyst, Montana Beverage Analyst, Nebraska Beverage Analyst, New Mexico Beverage Analyst, Oregon Beverage Analyst, Utah Beverage Analyst, Washington Beverage Analyst, Watch & Clock Review, Western & English Fashions, Wyoming Beverage Analyst.

R. R. Bowker Company
205 East 42nd Street,
New York, NY 10017 (212)916-1600
EXECUTIVE: Bruce W. Gray, President
MAGAZINES: Library Journal, Publishers Weekly, Small Press
School Library Journal. Also publishes numerous directories for
the publishing industry (both magazine and book).

Business Journals, Inc.
22 S. Smith Street,
East Norwalk, CT 06855 (203)853-6015
EXECUTIVE: G. Renfrew Brighton, Chairman
MAGAZINES: Diesel Equipment Superintendent, Turbomachinery Inter-
national, Accessories Magazine, Travelware Resources, Suppliers,
Modern Brewery Age (3 editions plus Blue Book).

Business News Publishing Co.
PO Box 2600, 755 W. Big Beaver Road,
Troy, MI 48007 (313)362-3700
EXECUTIVE: James E. Henderson, President
MAGAZINES: Air Conditioning, Heating & Refrigeration News, The
Cable Industry Master Product Catalog, The Master Catalog of
HVAC/R Products, Reeves Journal, Plumbing-Heating-Cooking, Solar
Engineering & Contracting.

Business Press International
205 East 42nd Street,
New York, NY 10017 (212)867-2080
MAGAZINES: ABC Air Cargo Guide, Asian Electricity, Computer Week-
ly, Cryogenics, Directory of Shipowners, Shipbuilders & Marine
Engineers, Electrical Review International, Electronics Weekly,
European Chemical News, European Plastics News, Far East Health,
Flight International, International Boat Industry, Middle East
Electricity, Middle East Electronics, Middle East Health, Middle
East Safety & Security, Motor Boat & Yachting, Motor Ship,
Nuclear Engineering International, Packaging Review, Petroleum
Times, Processing, Railway Gazette International, Textile Month,
TravelNews, Water Power and Dam Construction, Wireless World,
World Fishing, World Poultry Industry, Yachting World.

CES Publishing Corporation
345 Park Avenue South,
New York, NY 10010 (212)686-7744
EXECUTIVE: Stuart J. Horton, President
MAGAZINES: Audio Times, Autosound & Communications, Consumer
Electronics, Home Satellite Marketing, Video Business.

CMP Publications, Inc.
111 East Shore Road,
Manhasset, NY 11030   (516)365-4600
EXECUTIVE: Gerry G. Leeds, President
MAGAZINES: Business Travel News, Communications Week, Computer
Retail News, Computer Retailers' Guide, Computer Systems News,
Electronic Engineering Manager, Information Week, Electronic
Buyer's News, Electronic Engineering Times, VLSI Design.

Cahners Publishing Company
221 Columbus Avenue,
Boston, MA   02116   (617)536-7780
EXECUTIVE: Saul Goldweitz, President
MAGAZINES: Appliance Manufacturer, Brick and Clay Record, Build-
ing Design and Construction, Building Supply and Home Centers,
Business Computer Systems, Ceramic Industry, Construction Equip-
ment, Corporate Design and Realty, CPI Purchasing, Design News,
EDN, Electronic Business, Electronic Packaging and Production,
Emergency Medicine, Foodservice Equipment Specialist, Hotels and
Restaurants International, Journal of Cardiovascular Medicine,
Interior Design, Mini-Micro Systems, Modern Materials Handling,
Packaging, PC Products, Plastics World, Professional Builder &
Apartment Business, Purchasing, Restaurants & Institutions,
Security Distributing & Marketing, Semiconductor International,
Specifying Engineer, Traffic Management, U.S. Industrial Direc-
tory.

Chilton Company
Chilton Way,
Radnor, PA   19089   (215)964-4000
EXECUTIVE: Lawrence A. Fornasieri, President
MAGAZINES: Automotive Industries, Automotive Marketing, Commer-
cial Carrier Journal, Distribution, Electronic Component News,
Food Engineering Master, Hardware Age, I&CS, IMPO Distributor
News, Industrial Maintenance and Plant Operation, Industrial
Safety & Hygiene News, IAN, Iron Age, Jewelers' Circular Key-
stone, Motor/Age, Owner Operator Magazine, Product Design &
Development, Review of Optometry, Truck & Off-Highway Indus-
tries.

Crain Communications, Inc.
740 N. Rush,
Chicago, IL   60611   (312)649-5200
EXECUTIVE: Rance Crain, President
MAGAZINES: Advertising Age, Crain's Chicago Business, Crain's New
York Business, Business Insurance, Crain's City & State, Crain's
Cleveland Business, Electronic Media, Business Marketing, Rubber
and Plastics News, Automotive News, Illinois Business, Modern
Healthcare, Pensions & Investment Age. (Also inquire at subsidi-
ary company -- American Trade Magazines Co., 500 N. Dearborn St.,
Chicago, IL 60610   312-337-7700.)

Ebel-Doctorow Pubications, Inc.
PO Box 2147,
Clifton, NJ   07015   (201)779-1600
EXECUTIVE: Donald Doctorow, President
MAGAZINES: American Glass Review, Antiques Dealer, Home Lighting
and Accessories, China Glass and Tableware.

Fairchild Publications, Inc
(See listing in Chapter 30)

Geyer-McAllister Publications, Inc.
51 Madison Avenue,
New York, NY   10010   (212)689-4411
EXECUTIVE: Arthur M. Spence, President
MAGAZINES: Geyer's Office Dealer, Geyer's Who Makes It Directory,
Gifts and Decorative Accessories, Office Administration and Auto-
mation, Playthings, Shipping Digest.

Gordon Publications Inc.
13 Emery Avenue,
Randolph, NJ   07869   (201)361-9060
EXECUTIVE: Kennth M. Nelson, President
MAGAZINES: Chemical Equipment, Heating, Air Conditioning & Plumb-
ing Products, Industrial Product Bulletin, Material Handling Pro-
duct News, Metalworking Digest, Mining/Processing Equipment, Oil
& Gas Technology, Biomedical Products, Laboratory Equipment, Med-
ical Care Products, Scientific Computing & Automation, Surgical
Products, Computer Dealer, Mart Magazine, Computer Products,
Office Automation Systems & Technology, plus various show dailies
and specialty books and issues.

Gralla Publications
1515 Broadway,
New York, NY   10036   (212)869-1300
EXECUTIVE: Lawrence Gralla, President
MAGAZINES: Bank Systems & Equipment, Catalog Showroom Business,
Contract, Corporate Travel, Facilities Design & Management, Gift-
ware Business, Health Care Systems, Impressions, Kitchen & Bath
Business, Meeting News, Merchandising, Multi-Housing News,
National Jeweler, Premium/Incentive Business, Sew Business,
Sporting Goods Business, Travel Agents Marketplace.

Hanson Publishing Group
PO Box 697, 125 Elm Street,
New Canaan, CT   06840   (203)972-0761
EXECUTIVE: Joseph J. Hanson, President
MAGAZINES: FOLIO:, Catalog Age, Magazine Age, Career Educations,
Guidance and Testing, Early Childhood Materials, Elementary
School Materials, Gifted and Talented Materials, Mathematics

Materials, Microcomputers in the Classroom, Reading/Language Arts
and English, Science Materials and Supplies, Adult, Social Studies Materials, Special Education Materials, Advertising World,
International Media. (Titles are published by one of three subsidiary companies -- Folio Publishing Corp., Educat Publishers,
Inc., and Directories International, Inc.

The Irving-Cloud Publishing Company
7300 N. Cicero,
Lincolnwood, IL 60646   (312)588-7300
EXECUTIVE: Taylor L. Kennedy, President
MAGAZINES: Automotive Products Report, Aviation Equipment Main-
tenance, Equipment Management, Fleet Equipment, Hardware Mer-
chandiser, Home Center Products Report, Jobber Topics, Super
Service Station, Dental Lab Products, Dental Products Report.

Keller International Publishing Corp.
150 Great Neck Rd.,
Great Neck, NY 11021   (516)829-9210
EXECUTIVE: Gerald E. Keller, President
MAGAZINES: Beverage World (four editions) and numerous Spanish-
language trade magazines.

Lebhar-Friedman, Inc.
425 Park Ave.,
New York, NY 10022   (212)371-9400
EXECUTIVE: J. Roger Friedman, President
MAGAZINES: Apparel Merchandising, Cahin Store Age, Computer +
Software News, Discount Store News, Drug Store News, Pharmacy
Practice, National Home Center News, Nation's Restaurant News.

McGraw-Hill, Inc.
(See listing in Chapter 30)

Morgan Grampian Publishing Company
1050 Commonwealth Ave.,
Boston, MA 02215
MAGAZINES: Circuits Manufacturing, Computer and Electronics Mar-
keting, Digital Design, Electronic Imaging, Electronics Test,
Food Manufacture Int'l, Manufacturing Chemist.

North American Publishing
401 N. Broad Street,
Philadelphia, PA 19108   (215)238-5300
MAGAZINES: American Import/Export Management, American School &
University Magazine, Business Forms and Systems, Custom House
Guide, In-Plant Reproductions, Magazine & Bookseller, Official
Export Guide, Package Printing, Printing Impressions, World-Wide
Printer, Zip Target Marketing.

PTN Publishing Corporation
101 Crossways Park West,
Woodbury, NY   11797   (516)496-8000
EXECUTIVE: Rudolph Maschke , Publisher
MAGAZINES: Functional Photography, Information Management, Photo-
graphic Processing, Photographic Trade News PTN, PTN/Photokina
News, Security Systems Administration, Shooting Commercials, Stu-
dio Photography, Technical Photography.

Pennwell Publishing Company
1421 S. Sheridan,
Tulsa, OK   74112   (918)835-3161
EXECUTIVE: Philip C. Lauinger, Jr., President
MAGAZINES: Dental Economics, Guia Petrolera de Equipos y Servic-
ios, Laser Focus The Magazine of Electro-Optics Technology, Off-
shore, Offshore Petroleum, Oil & Gas Journal, Oil & Gas & Petro-
chem Equipment, Petroleo Internacional, Proofs, The Magazine of
Dental Sales; (A subsidiary company -- Advanced Technology
Group at 119 Russell St., Littleton, MA 01460 617-486-9501 --
publishes these additional titles - Business Computing, Computer
Design and Computer Graphics World.)

Penton/IPC
1111 Chester Avenue,
Cleveland, OH   44114   (216)696-7000
EXECUTIVE: Thomas L. Dempsey, Chairman
MAGAZINES: Computer-Aided Engineering, Contracting Business,
Fluid Power Handbook & Directory, Foundry Management & Techno-
logy, Government Product News, Handling & Shipping Management,
Heating/Piping/Air Conditioning, Hydraulics & Pneumatics, Lodging
Hospitality, Machine Design, Material Handling Engineering,
Materials Engineering, Materials Selector, Modern Office Techno-
logy, New Equipment Digest, Safety/Security, Power Transmission
Design, Precision Metal, Production Engineering, Restaurant
Hospitality, School Product News, Welding Design & Fabrication,
Welding Distributor. (Air Transport World and Progressive Archi-
tecture are published by the Reinhold Publishing Division of
Penton/IPC, 600 Summer St., Stamford, CT 06904. Phone 203-348-
7531.)

Simmons-Boardman Publishing Corp.
345 Hudson Street,
New York, NY   10014   (212)620-7200
EXECUTIVE: Robert G. Lewis, Chairman
MAGAZINES: ABA Banking Journal, International Railway Journal,
Marine Engineering, Plant Location, Railway Age.

Standard Rate & Data Service, Inc.
3004 Glenview Road,
Wilmette, IL 60091   (312)256-6067
EXECUTIVE: Dale R. Bauer, President
MAGAZINES: Numerous magazine and advertising directories, including the Advertising and Advertiser Red Books and SRDS magazine
and television listing books.

Technical Publishing Company
875 Third Avenue
New York, NY 10022   (212)605-9400
EXECUTIVE: John K. Abely, President
MAGAZINES: American Journal of Cardiology, American Journal of
Medicine, American Journal of Surgery, Cutis, Datamation, Dun's
Business Month, Fire Engineering Graphic Arts Monthly, Industrial
Distribution, World Construction, World Mining Equipment.
(See following two listings for magazines published at other
addresses.)

Technical Publishing Company
14 Vanderventer Avenue
Port Washington, NY 11050   (516)883-6200
MAGAZINES: Solid State Technology, Solid State Processing & Production Buyers Guide and Directory.

Technical Publishing Company
1301 S. Grove,
Barrington, IL 60010   (312)381-1840
MAGAZINES: Consulting Engineer, Contractor Magazine, Control
Engineering, Control Engineering Microcomputer Interface Group,
Electric Light and Power, Highway and Heavy Construction,
Mechanical Contractor Literature Showcase, Plant Engineering,
Power Engineering, Research & Development.

Titsch Communications, Inc.
600 Grant Street, Suite 600,
Denver,CO 80203   (303)860-0111
EXECUTIVE: Thomas J. Corcoran, President
MAGAZINES: CableVision, Communications Engineering & Design,
Mobile Radio Handbook, Radio Communications Report, Two-Way Radio
Dealer.

U.S. Business Press
11 West 19th Street,
New York, NY 10011   (212)741-7210
EXECUTIVE: Roland De Silva, President
MAGAZINES: Electronics for Kids, Food & Beverage Marketing, Lei-
sure Time Electronics, Licensing Today, Modern Floor Coverings,
Non-Foods Merchandising, Product Marketing, Toy & Hobby World,
Trim-a-Tree Merchandising.

United Technical Publications, Inc.
645 Stewart Avenue,
Garden City, NY 11530 (516)222-2500
EXECUTIVE: Robert J. Males, President
MAGAZINES: Electronic Engineers Master, Electronic Products Magazine, Floor Covering Weekly, IC Master, Industrial Machinery News
Integrated Circuits, Office World News, Today's Office. (Company
is a susidiary of Hearst Business Communications).

Vance Publishing Corporation
400 Knightsbridge Pkwy.
Lincolnshire, IL 60069 (312)634-2600
EXECUTIVE: John B. O'Neill , President
MAGAZINES: Morse, The Drovers Journal, Pork '85, Coon, The Grower
(The latter two titles are published by the Produce Division, PO
Box 2939, Shawnee Mission, KS 66201 913-451-2200.)

Warren, Gorman & Lamont, Inc.
210 South Street
Boston, MA 02111 (617)432-2020
EXECUTIVE: Joseph Palazzolo, President
MAGAZINES: Accounting News, Banker's Magazine, Corporate Accounting, Estate Planning, Journal of Business Strategy, The Journal
of Taxation, Real Estate Review, Taxation for Accountants, Tax
News, Real Estate Outlook.

Watt Publishing Co.
Mount Morris, IL 61054 (815)734-4171
EXECUTIVE: Leslie A. Watt, Publisher
MAGAZINES: Animal Nutrition & Health, Broiler Industry, Farm Supplier, Feed International, Industria Avicola, Industria Porcina,
Petfood Industry, Pig International, Poultry Digest, Poultry Tribune, Turkey World, Who's Who in the Egg and Poultry Industries,
Who's Who International in the Egg & Poultry Industries

CHAPTER 32

Other Professional/Scientific/Technical Publishers To Contact

```
American Heart Association, Inc.
7320 Greenville Avenue,
Dallas, TX  75231   (214)750-5300
EXECUTIVE: Dudley H. Hafner, Executive V.P.
MAGAZINES: 6 professional journals

American Institute of Aeronautics and Astronautics
1633 Broadway,
New York, NY  10019   (212)581-4300
EXECUTIVE: James J. Harford, Executive Director
MAGAZINES: 7 professional journals

American Medical Association
535 N. Dearborn St.,
Chicago, IL  60610   (312)751-6204
EXECUTIVE: John T. Baker, Vice President
MAGAZINES: American Journal of Diseases of Children, American
Medical News, Archives of Dermatology, Archives of General Psy-
chiatry, Archives of Internal Medicine, Archives of Neurology,
Archives of Ophthamology, Archives  of Otolaryngology, Archives
of Pathology and Laboratory Medicine, Archives of Surgery, Jour-
nal of the AMA.

American Personnel and Guidance Association, Inc.
2 Skyline Place, Suite 400, 5230 Leesburg Pike
Falls Church, VA  22041   (703)820-4700
EXECUTIVE: Patrick J. McDonough, Executive V.P.
MAGAZINES: 15 professional journals
```

American Society of Civil Engineers
345 East 47th Street,
New York, NY 10017 (212)705-7510
EXECUTIVE: David R. Dresia, Publications Department Head
MAGAZINES: 2 professional journals

American Sociological Association
1722 N Street, NW
Washington, DC 20036 (202)833-3410
EXECUTIVE: William V. D'Antonio, Executive Officer
MAGAZINES: 6 professional Journals

Brentwood Publishing Corp.
825 S. Barrington Avenue,
Los Angeles, CA 90049 (213)826-8388
EXECUTIVE: Martin H. Waldman, President
MAGAZINES: Al Mustashfa, Applied Cardiology, Applied Radiology,
Association & Society Manager, Corporate Fitness and Recreation,
El Hospital, Geriatric Opthamology, Incentive Travel Manager,
Medicenter Management, Perinatology-Neonatology, Respiratory
Therapy, Vascular Diagnosis and Therapy

Clinical Psychology Publishing Co.
4 Conant Square,
Brandon, VT 05733 (802)247-6871
EXECUTIVE: C. S. Jakiela, President
MAGAZINES: 4 professional journals

Elsevier Science Publishing Co., Inc.
52 Vanderbilt Avenue,
New York, NY 10017 (212)867-9040
EXECUTIVE: Charles Ellis, President
MAGAZINES: Numerous research-oriented journals in the fields of
life sciences, computer science, engineering and some social
science.

International Universities Press Inc.
315 Fifth Avenue,
New York, NY 10016 (212)684-7900
EXECUTIVE: Martin V. Azarian, President
MAGAZINES: 4 professional journals

John Hopkins University Press
Baltimore, MD 21218 (301)338-7809
EXECUTIVE: Marie R. Hansen, Director
MAGAZINES: 16 professional journals (primarily medical).

MIT Press
28 Carleton Street, Journals Department
Cambridge, MA 02142 (617)253-2889
EXECUTIVE: Ann Reinke, Journals Manager
MAGAZINES: 6 professional journals

The C.V. Mosby Company
11830 Westline Industrial Dr.,
St. Louis, MO 63146 (314)872-8370
EXECUTIVE: Patrick A. Clifford, President
MAGAZINES: Numerous medical journals

Pergamon Press Inc.
Maxwell House, Fairview Park,
Elmsford, NY 10523 (914)592-7700
EXECUTIVE: Richard C. Rowson, President
MAGAZINES: Annals of Biomedical Engineering, Biorheology, Compu-
terized Radiology, Energy, Health Physics, International Journal
of Hydrogen, International Journal of Nuclear Medicine and Bio-
logy , International Journal of Hydrogen, Oncology, Biology,
Physics, The Journal of Criminal Justice, Journal of Emergency
Medicine, Magnetic Resonance Imaging, Neuroscience, Nuclear and
Chemical Waste Management, Physiology & Behavior, Robotics and
Computer-Integrated Manufacturing, Solar Engergy, Sunworld,
Telematics and Information, Thrombosis Research, Ultrasound in
Medicine and Biology, Underground Space, Vacuum.

Romaine Pierson Publishers Inc.
80 Shore Road,
Port Washington, NY 11050 (516)883-6350
EXECUTIVE: William R. Morando, President
MAGAZINES: Medical Times, Pharmacy Times, Resident & Staff Physi-
cian, Surgical Rounds

Slack Incorporated
6900 Grove Road,
Thorofare, NJ 08086 (609)848-1000
EXECUTIVE: Charles B. Slack, President
MAGAZINES: 19 medical/nursing journals

University of Wisconsin Press-Journal Division
114 N Murray St.,
Madison, WI 53715 (608)262-5839
MAGAZINES: 11 professional journals

Veterinary Practice Publishing Co.
PO Box 4457,
Santa Barbara, CA 93103 (805)965-1028
EXECUTIVE: Nancy A. Bull, President
MAGAZINES: Agri-Practice, Caning Practice, Equine Practice, Fel-
ine Practice.

John Wiley & Sons, Inc.
605 Third Avenue,
New York, NY 10158 (212)692-6000
EXECUTIVE: Mary C. Curtis, Publisher
MAGAZINES: Over two dozen scientific and educational journals

Williams & Wilkins Co.
428 E. Preston Street,
Baltimore, MD 21202   (301)528-4000
MAGAZINES: Over two dozen medical and surgical journals.

XII
Appendices

Industry Trade Organizations

THE ADVERTISING CLUB OF NEW YORK
45 East 45th Street, Suite 310
New York, N.Y.   10017
(212)697-0877

ADVERTISING WOMEN OF NEW YORK, INC.
153 East 57th Street,
New York, N.Y.   10022
(212)593-1950

AMERICAN ADVERTISING FEDERATION
1400 K Street, Suite 1000,
Washington, D.C.   20005
(202)898-0089

AMERICAN ASSOCIATION OF ADVERTISING AGENCIES (4A's)
666 Third Avenue,
New York, N.Y.   10017
(212)682-2500

AMERICAN INSTITUTE OF GRAPHIC ARTS
1059 Third Ave., 3rd Floor,
New York, N.Y.   10021
(212)752-0813

AMERICAN SOCIETY OF JOURNALISTS AND AUTHORS
1501 Broadway,
New York, N.Y.   10036
(212)997-0947

AMERICAN SOCIETY OF MAGAZINE EDITORS
575 Lexington Ave.,
New York, N.Y.   10022
(212) 752-0055

ART DIRECTORS CLUB, INC.
488 Madison Avenue,
New York, N.Y.   10022
(212)838-8140

BUSINESS/PROFESSIONAL ADVERTISING ASSOCIATION (B/PAA)
205 East 42nd Street,
New York, N.Y.   10017
(212)661-0222

GRAPHIC ARTISTS GUILD
30 East 20th St., Room 405,
New York, N.Y. 10003
(212)982-9298

MAGAZINE PUBLISHERS ASSOCIATION
575 Lexington Ave.,
New York, N.Y. 10022
(212)752-0055

THE ONE CLUB
251 East 50th Street,
New York, N.Y.   10022
(212)935-0121

PUBLIC RELATIONS SOCIETY OF AMERICA
845 Third Ave.,
New York, N.Y. 10022
(212)826-1750

THE SOCIETY OF AMERICAN GRAPHIC ARTISTS
32 Union Square,
New York, N.Y.
(212)260-5706

THE SOCIETY OF ILLUSTRATORS
128 East 63rd Street,
New York, N.Y.   10021
(212)838-2560

THE SOCIETY OF MAGAZINE PHOTOGRAPHERS
205 Lexington Ave.,
New York, N.Y.   10017
(212)889-9144

THE SOCIETY OF PUBLICATION DESIGNERS
25 West 43rd St., Suite 711,
New York, N.Y.   10036
(212)697-1246

Industry Trade Publications

AD FORUM
A/S/M Communications, Inc.
820 Second Avenue,
New York, NY   10017
(212)661-8080

Published exclusively for national consumer-advertising clients,
Ad Forum covers issues and trends in the advertising and marketing of consumer products and services. Recently bought by A/S/M
(which also owns Adweek). Good background for aspiring sales,
marketing and promotion people.

ADVERTISING AGE
Crain Communications, Inc.
740 N. Rush Street,
Chicago, IL   60611
(312)649-5200

Ad Age is considered "the bible" of the advertising industry (or,
alternately, one of the two, along with Adweek). It's available
at most New York newsstands and should be available at your local
library.   It is now semi-weekly -- Monday is the main issue,
Thursday what used to be Monday's "Magazine Section." The magazine business is an important part of Ad Age's coverage (as it
is with all of the advertising industry publications).

ADWEEK
A/S/M Communications, Inc.
820 Second Avenue,
New York, NY 10017
(212)661-8080

Adweek actually consists of five, separate, regional editions --
Adweek/East, Adweek/Southeast, Adweek/Midwest, Adweek/West and
Adweek/Southwest -- which include the same general editorial, but
different local news, account news and advertising (including
classifieds). Along with Ad Age, it must be considered mandatory
reading for news about both the advertising and magazine industries.

AMERICAN PRINTER
MacLean Hunter Publishing Co.
300 W. Adams St.,
Chicago, IL 60606
(312)726-2802

For members of the publishing, printing and graphic arts industries. Especially helpful for aspiring Manufacturing & Distribution professionals.

ART DIRECTION
10 East 39th Street,
New York, NY 10016
(212)889-6500

For aspiring artists, art directors and graphic designers.

ART PRODUCT NEWS
In-Art Publishing Company
P.O. Box 117,
St. Petersburg, FL 33731
(813)821-6064

For professional artists and designers. Interviews with successful art directors and designers are regular features, but 75% of
the editorial is, as the title implies, product-oriented.

BUSINESS MARKETING
Crain Communications, Inc.
740 N. Rush Street,
Chicago, IL 60611
(312)649-5260

Articles on the news, strategy and tactics of business-to-business marketing. Emphasis is on techniques and methods. (Anyone
interested in this specialized area should contact the B/PAA (see
Appendix B.)

COLUMBIA JOURNALISM REVIEW
Columbia University
School of Journalism, Room 700,
New York, NY 10027
(212)280-2716

A national media "monitor," helpful in defining standards of journalism and calling attention to the profession's strengths and weaknesses.

CREATIVE
Magazines/Creative, Inc.
37 West 39th Street,
New York, NY 10018
(212)840-0160

Subtitled The Magazine of Promotion and Marketing, Creative is published mainly for corporate executives in marketing, promotion and merchandising. A good resource if you're thinking of working in this area of publishing.

FOLIO: THE MAGAZINE FOR MAGAZINE MANAGEMENT
Folio Publishing Corp.
125 Elm Street,
New Canaan, CT 06840
(203)972-0761

The absolute "must read" for anyone interested in a career in magazine publishing. Subscribe to it immediately. It covers every area of publishing, from editorial and ad sales to promotion and production.

GRAPHIC ARTS MONTHLY
Technical Publishing
875 Third Ave.,
New York, NY 10022
(212)605-9574

For both graphic artists and aspiring production professionals. Focuses primarily on methods and techniques to lower costs and enhance productivity.

GRAPHIC DESIGN:USA
Kaye Publishing Corp.
120 East 56th Street,
New York, NY 10022
(212)759-8813

Edited for the people who create, produce and purchase advertising and art products and services. Goes to a variety of art and production executives.

GRAPHIS

This magazine is published in Zurich, Switzerland, but is sold in most well-stocked art supply stores. It covers the best art & design work on an international level. Bi-monthly with an annual hard-cover edition.

MADISON AVENUE
Madison Avenue Publishing Corp.
369 Lexington Avenue,
New York, NY 10017
(212)972-0600

A monthly that focuses on the "how's and why's" of advertising and marketing campaigns, rather than up-to-the-minute news (as Ad Age and Adweek purport to do). Excellent in-depth studies of major ad campaigns and various media-related topics are featured in each issue.

MAGAZINE AGE
MPE, Inc.
125 Elm St.,
New Canaan, CT 06840
(203)972-0761

A companion to FOLIO: (which now owns it), covering the industry primarily from an advertising perspective.

MAGAZINE DESIGN AND PRODUCTION
Globecom Publishing, Ltd.,
4551 W. 107th St., Suite 210
Overland Park, KS 66207
(913)642-6611

Fairly technical treatment of design and production techniques and technologies, for art directors, designers and production specialists. Applications-oriented, however, to magazine production.

MARKETING AND MEDIA DECISIONS
Decisions Publications, Inc.
1140 Avenue of the Americas,
New York, NY 10036
(212)725-2300

Each issue, planned with the aid of a "Guest Editor" from the industry, examines, evaluates and chronicles the factors involved in deciding who gets what share of a client's advertising dollars. Covers all media, but primarily for those interested in ad sales.

MARKETING NEWS
American Marketing Association
250 S. Wacker Drive,
Chicago, IL 60606
(312)993-9504

This bi-weekly is the official publication of the AMA and is, therefore, of particular use to aspiring marketing pros or advertising salespeople. Also helpful coverage and articles on Research.

MEDIA PEOPLE
P.O. Box 3905,
Grand Central Station,
New York, NY 10163
(212)573-8582

A good hunting ground for aspiring media pros, this magazine covers the personalities in the various media.

PHOTO DESIGN
Lakewood Publications, Inc.
50 South Ninth St.,
Minneapolis, MN 55402
(612)333-0471

For creative professionals who commission and/or produce photo/illustrations for magazines and other media.

PRINT
R.C. Publications, Inc.
355 Lexington Avenue,
New York, NY 10017
(212)682-0830

For design and, especially, production specialists.

PUBLIC RELATIONS JOURNAL
Public Relations Society of America
845 Third Ave.,
New York, NY 10022
(212)826-1757

Official publication of the PRSA and, as such, must reading for anyone seeking to enter the very specialized world of magazine PR.

STANDARD RATE & DATA
Standard Rate & Data Service, Inc.
3004 Glenview Rd.,
Wilmette, IL 60091
(312)256-6067

In its various editions, lists virtually every trade, consumer
or professional publication produced in the United States, with
an editorial profile, ad rate and circulation information and key
personnel. An excellent reference tool available in most libraries.

UPPER AND LOWER CASE (U&lc)
International Typeface Corporation
2 Dag Hammarskjold Plaza
New York, NY
(212)371-0699

For aspiring art directors and designers. Deals primarily with
typeface selection, design and use.

THE WRITER
120 Boylston St.,
Boston, MA 02116
(617)423-3157

AND

WRITER'S DIGEST
9933 Alliance Rd.,
Cincinnati, OH 45242
(513)984-0717

These are the two key publications for anyone -- of whatever age
-- who wants to be a writer or editor (not all editors are top
professional writers, but all can write). Long on technical tips
and training, but also important information on where to sell
your short stories, etc.

ZIP/TARGET MARKETING
North American Publishing Co.
401 North Broad Street,
Philadelphia, PA 19108
(215)238-5300

For direct marketers only, this magazine focuses on the creation,
printing and mailing of promotional, sales and informational material.